Christmas Carvings from Commercial Turnings

Kelley Stadelman

Text written with and photography by Douglas Congdon-Martin

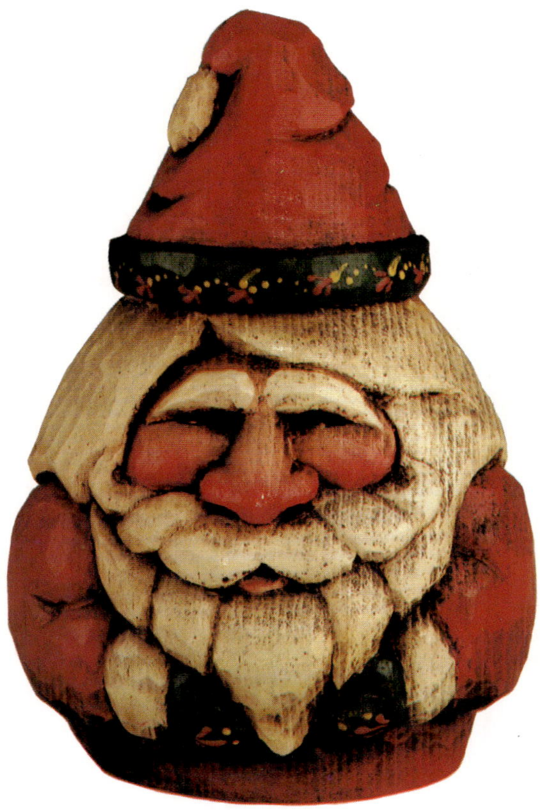

Schiffer Publishing Ltd

77 Lower Valley Road, Atglen, PA 19310

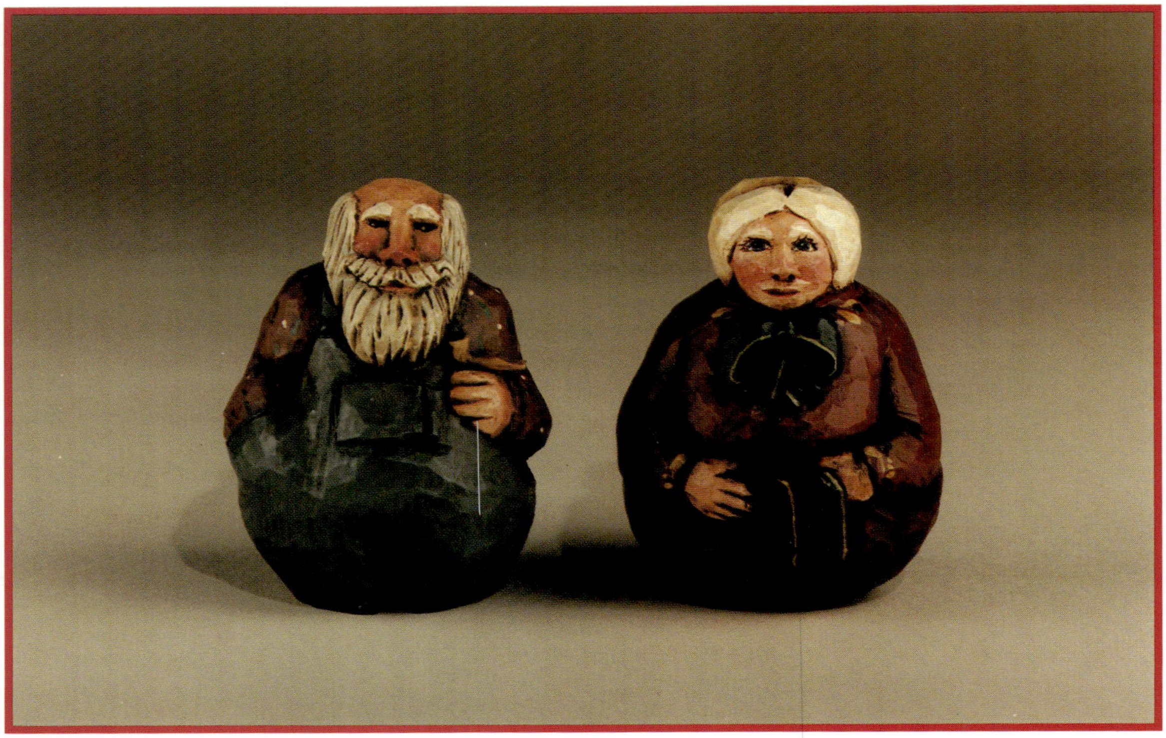

Contents

Library of Congress Number: 94-66375

Printed in China
ISBN: 0-88740-697-1

Published by Schiffer Publishing, Ltd.
77 Lower Valley Road
Atglen, PA 19310
Please write for a free catalog.
This book may be purchased from the publisher.
Please include $2.95 postage.
Try your bookstore first.

We are interested in hearing from authors with book ideas on related subjects.

The author would love to hear from you. You are welcome to call or write for information about wood or paint. Her address and phone number are:

P.O. Box 191
North Plains, OR 97133
(503) 647-0892

Introduction

Before I began carving my main creative outlet was tole painting. It is a great craft with limitless possibilities and a lot of satisfaction. One of the things that tole painters paint are these commercially prepared turnings of many varieties. They are often turned from a flawless sugar pine, which is a very nice wood to carve. Indeed, some of my earliest carving involved customizing these turnings for my painting.

My focus has shifted over the years, and now I carve and teach carving full-time. But these turned blanks still intrigue me and offer many challenges and opportunities for the carver. The challenge is seeing the possibilities in the form. Seen one way the turning can be one thing, and seen another it can be something totally different. The opportunities come because a lot of the tedious work of removing wood has been done on the lathe, leaving you with the enjoyable task of being creative.

The projects in this book use turnings that are readily available at most craft stores. They revolve around the theme of Christmas, with Santa Claus, Mrs. Claus, trees and ornaments found in these pages. In the gallery you will find a clown, but then, I suppose clowns have Christmas too!

I have tried to do in the book what I do in class, taking the carver from the laying out of the pattern to the final antiquing of the painted piece. While there is only room to show two projects, a Santa and a tree, you can apply these skills to the patterns and photographs in the gallery.

Painting is still a love of mine, and I apply some of the techniques of decorative tole painting to the details of these projects.

Carving Tools and Terms

Chisel: A tool with a flat cutting edge. It may have a single or double bevel.

Skew Chisel: This chisel has a double bevel and is slanted obliquely along the chisel edge.

Gouge: A tool with a single bevel and a cutting edge that is curved or shaped in a compound configuration.

Bench Knife: A carving tool with the cutting edge parallel to the handle.

Disposable blades: These blades fit into a special handle. They are made of thin metal and are extremely sharp. Generally they are not resharpened.

Care of Tools

After investing in quality tools, care should be taken to maintain their sharpness. Contact between your tools and surfaces other than wood may chip and dull them. Most towns have fine cutlery stores which provide sharpening services. However, I am of the opinion that the art of sharpening should be learned by carvers. There are several books that will give you instructions in the techniques of sharpening.

Carving Safety

Remember you are using a sharp tool. You may become comfortable with carving tools in your hand, but they are obviously more dangerous than a pen or a paint brush. I have held a paint brush in my mouth, scratched my head with one and even used one as a pointer. Doing these common gestures with a carving tool could cause harm to you or someone else. Protect yourself and your carving companions. Avoid pointing or talking with your hands while holding a carving tool. Avoid placing tools on the table top where they might roll off the table and onto (or into) someone's foot.

Whenever possible carve on the table top, not in your lap. Build up your chair with a pillow or two so you are well above your carving. Place your wood in a clamp or on some type of device to hold it in place. I like to use the non-skid grid that is used under throw rugs.

I have cut myself. I do not cut myself very often anymore. I have a good sense for what my tools and wood will do. Carving when you are tired or tense will increase the chance of being cut. Take many little breaks. Know your limits. Be careful and have a good time!

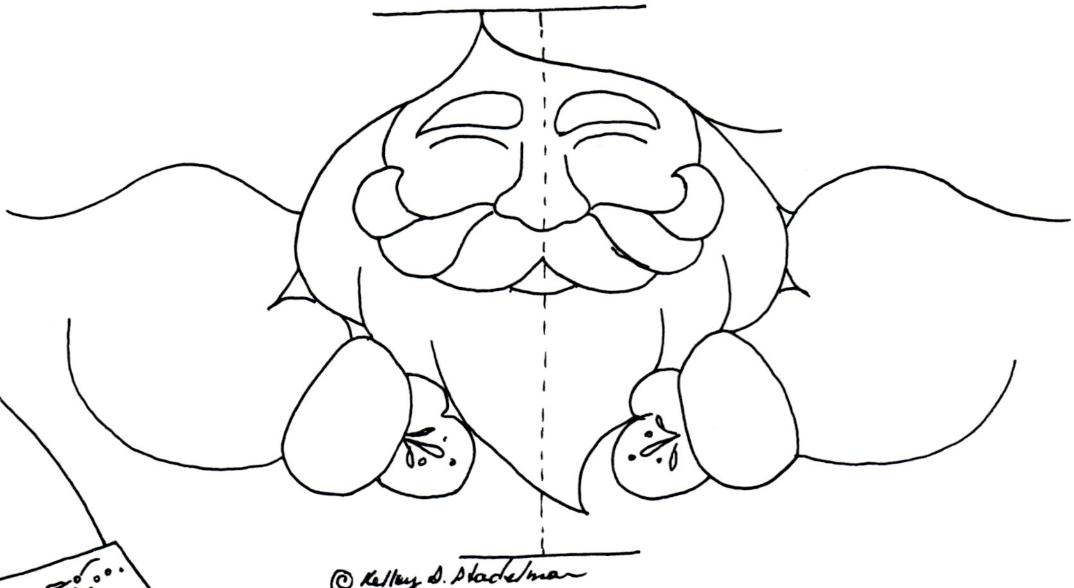

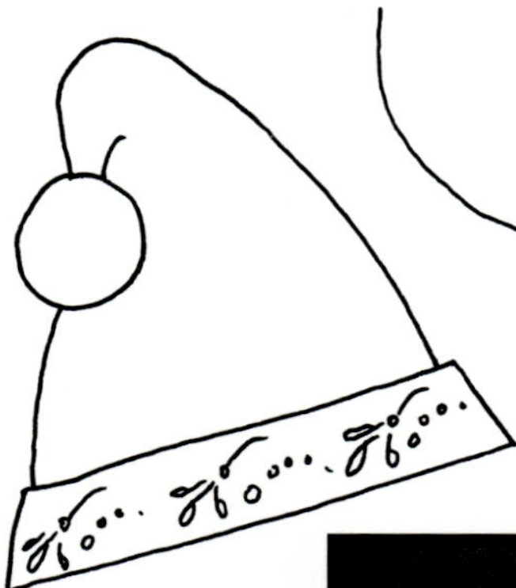

Patterns have been reduced to 75%.

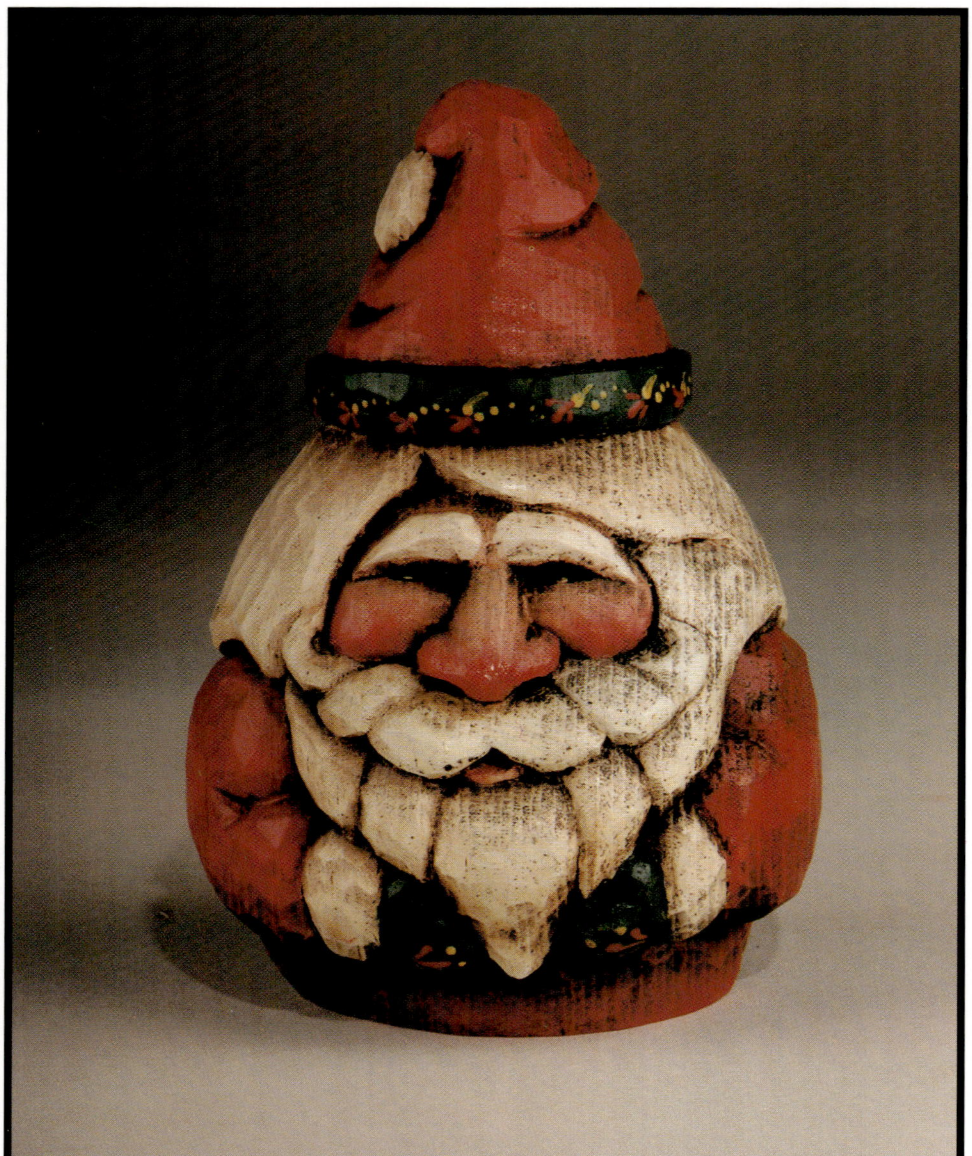

Carving the Santa

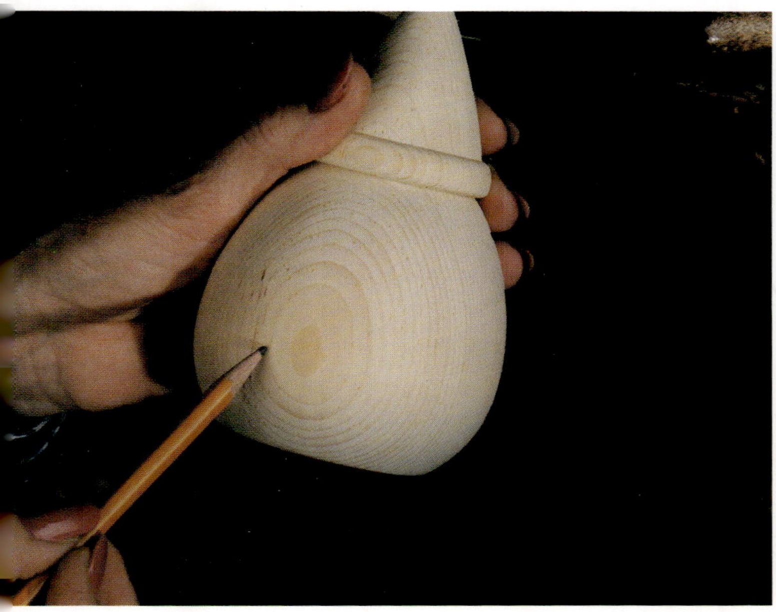

When working with turned wood it is more difficult to lay down the pattern than on a flat piece. Begin by looking at the wood. You will see that on two sides the grain is round like this.

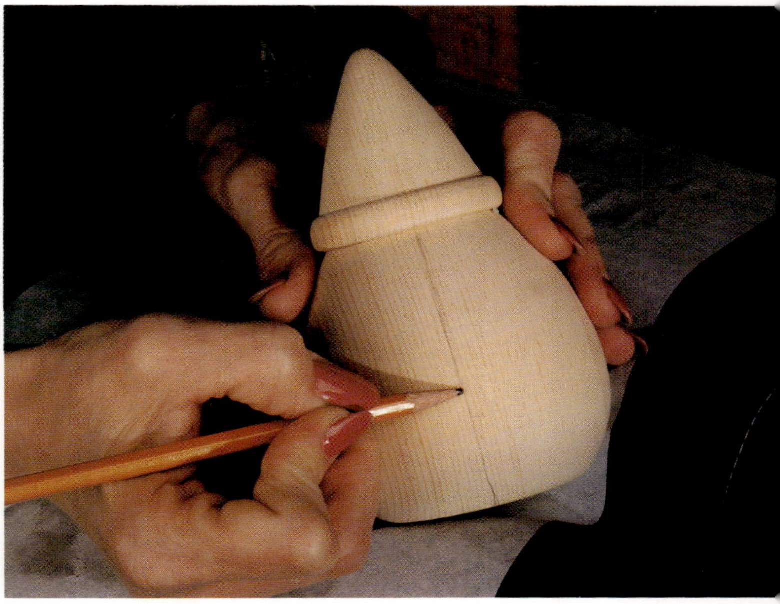

Draw a line down the face, perpendicular to the base.

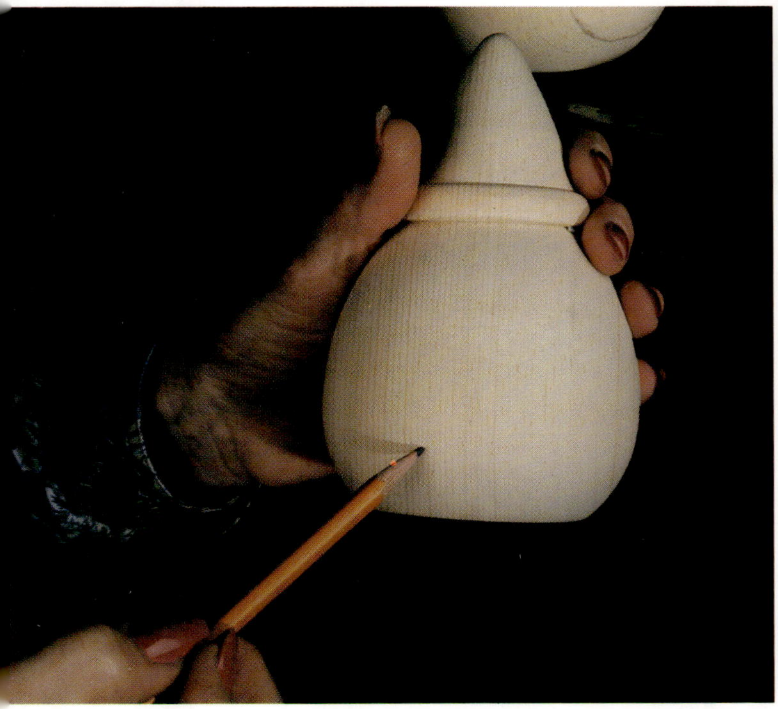

On the other two sides the grain is straight. This will be the face of the carving.

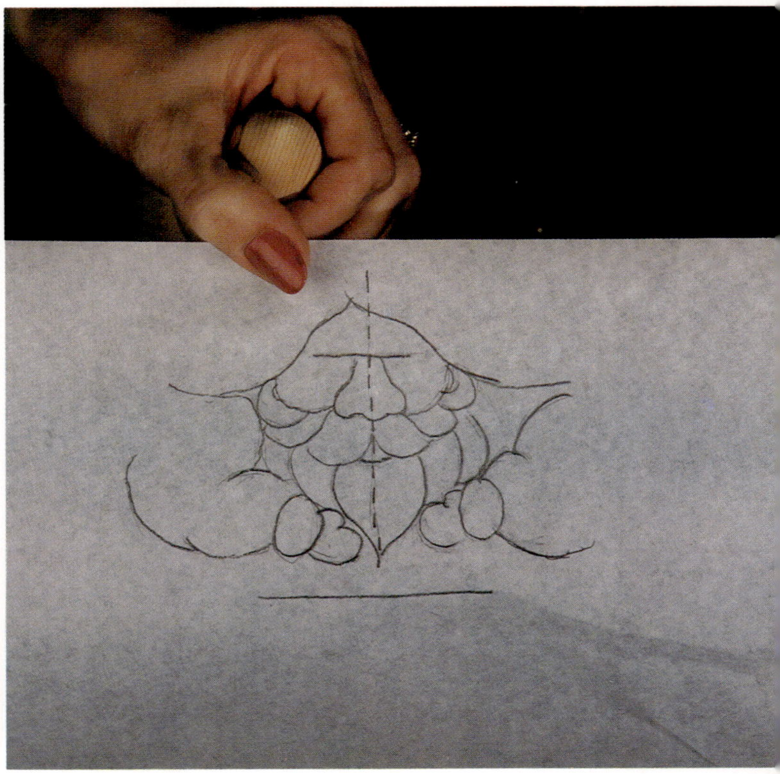

This corresponds to the dotted line in the pattern.

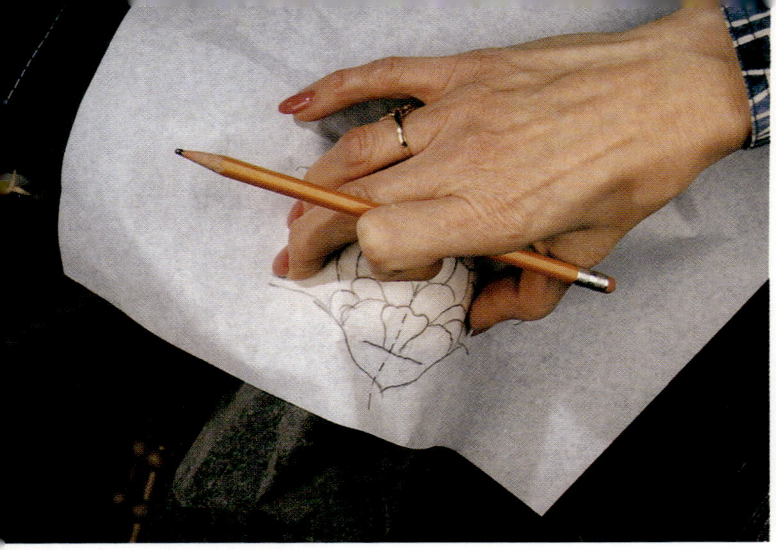

Align the pattern with the center line, and place a piece of graphite paper behind it.

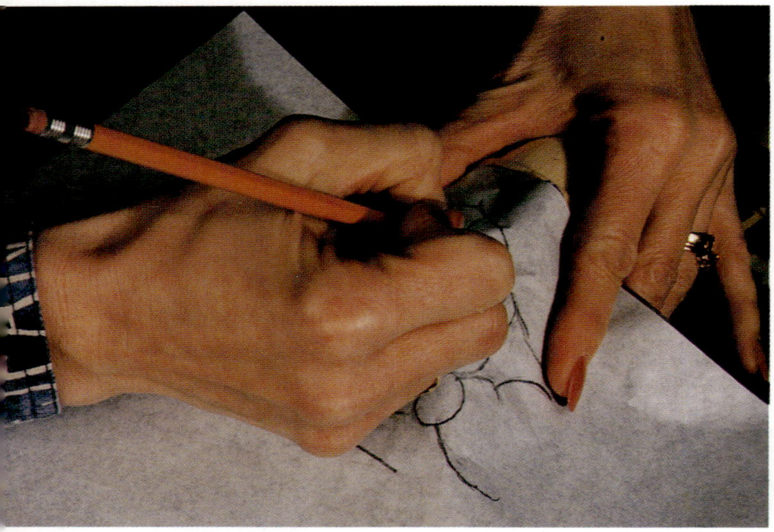

Trace the pattern onto the wood.

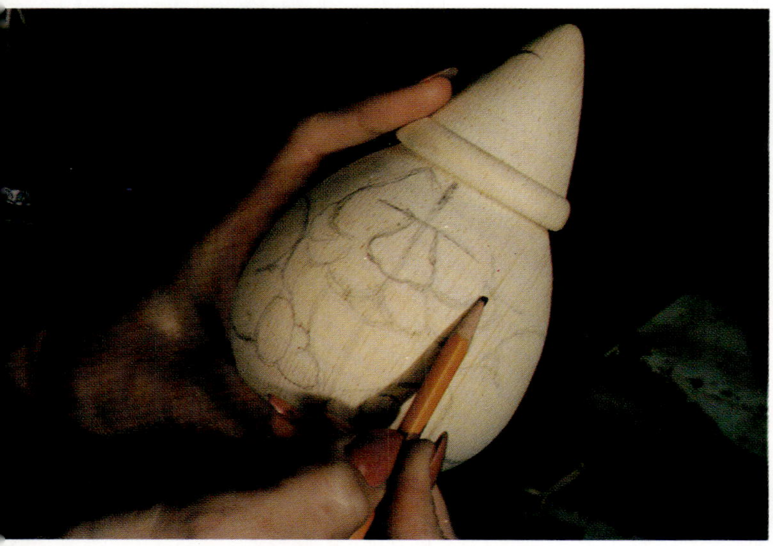

No matter how hard you try, transferring the pattern on to a round surface will not be perfect, so check to see that the cheeks and everything else are symmetrical.

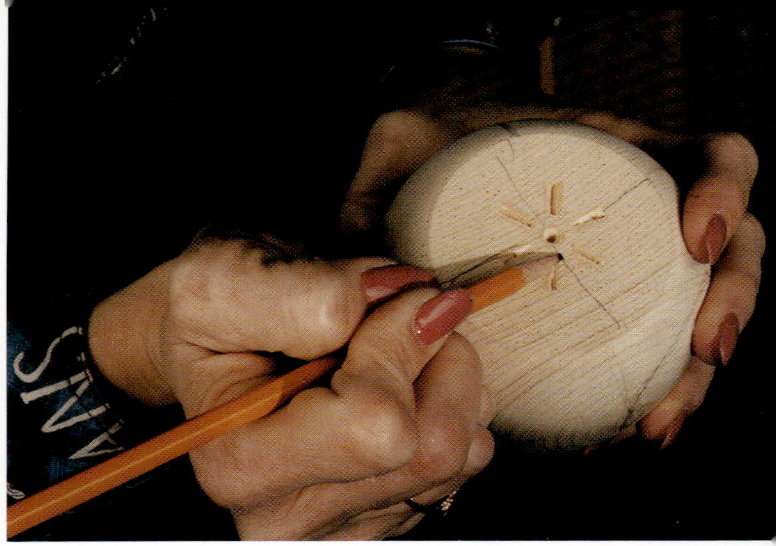

There are three basic rules I teach to all my students. 1. Begin by transferring the pattern. 2. Mark midlines, dividing the blank into quarters, 3. Round off edges. 4. Always work from the bottom up. All these rules are made to break, but serve as guidelines for successful carving.

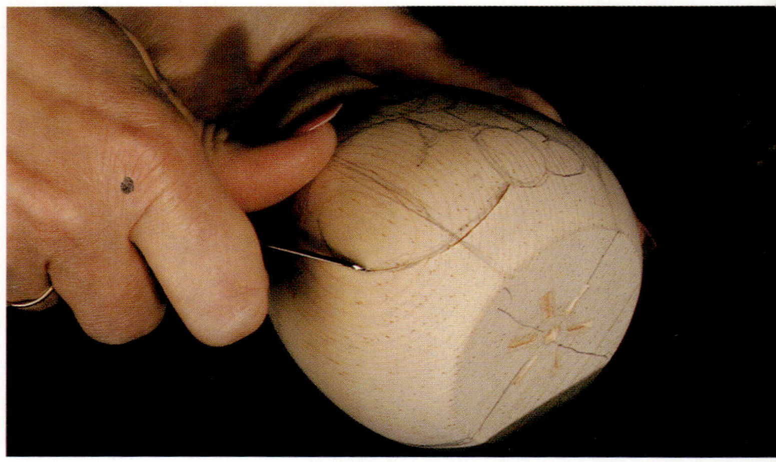

We'll begin by following rule 4 and starting at the bottom. Score the line at the bottom of the arm, creating a stop cut.

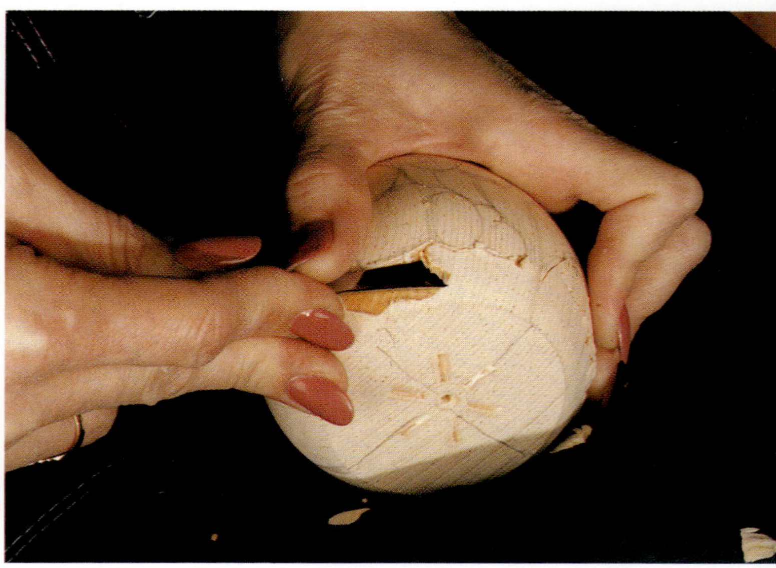

With a straight chisel take away the wood beneath the line.

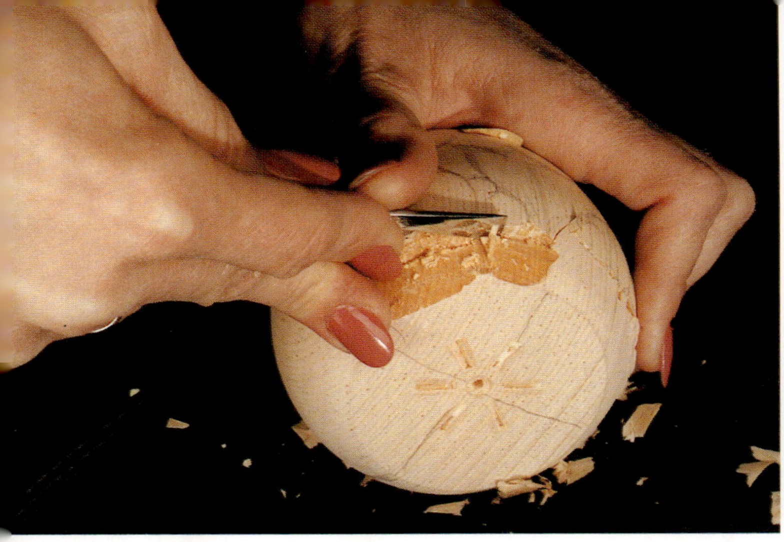

Repeat the process until you get deep enough to score the line with your chisel.

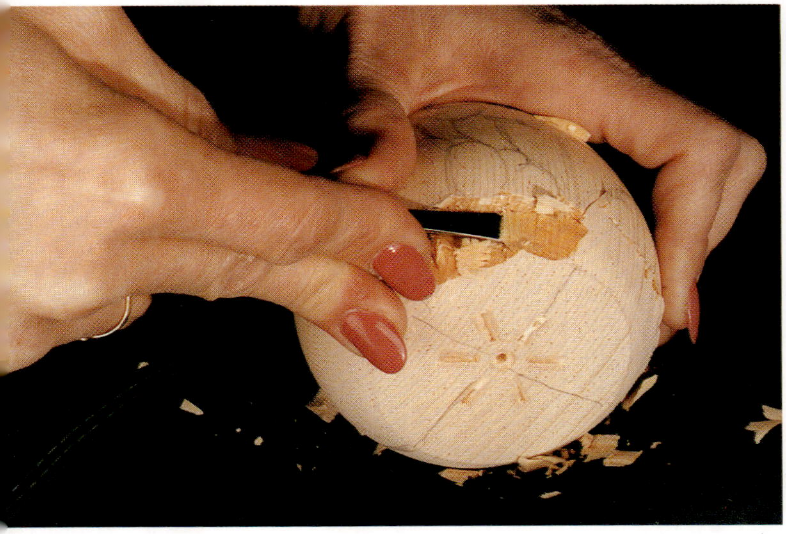

Continue removing wood at the base until you are 1/4" to 1/2" below the surface. You want this to look like a character, not a turning with a face on it, so you need to go deep enough.

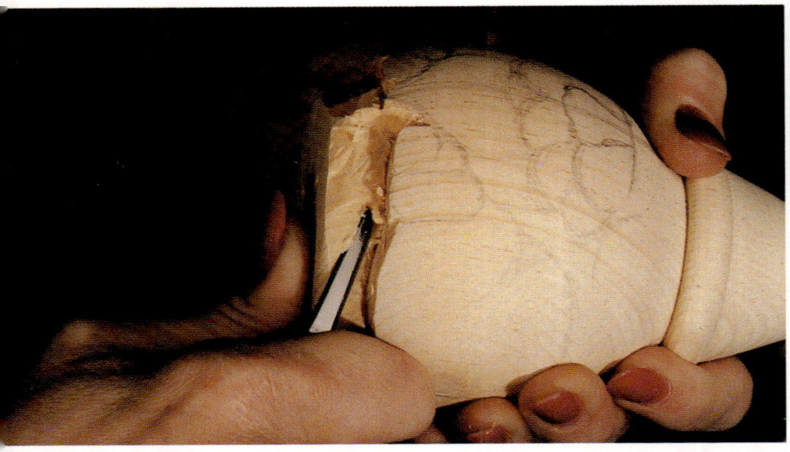

When carving a turning you want to cut away from the highest point. In this case the highest point is around Santa's belly, so here I need to carve toward the base. Otherwise the carving will chip because I am cutting into the grain.

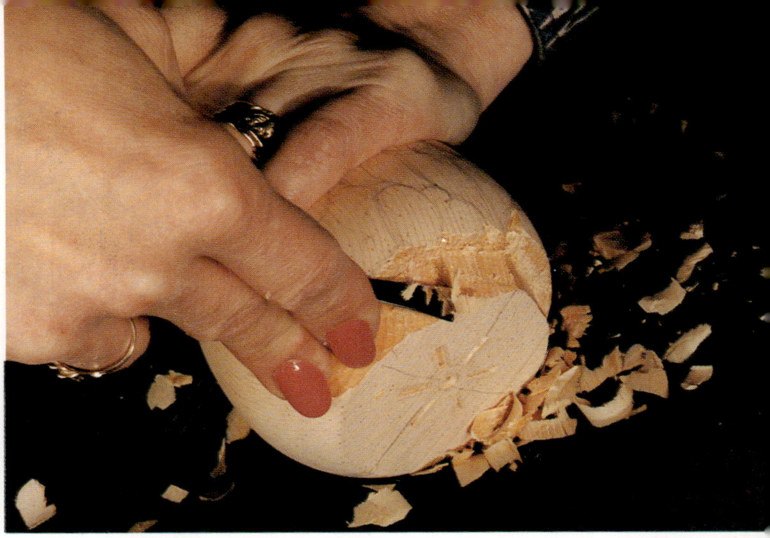

You can switch to the chisel when it is easier.

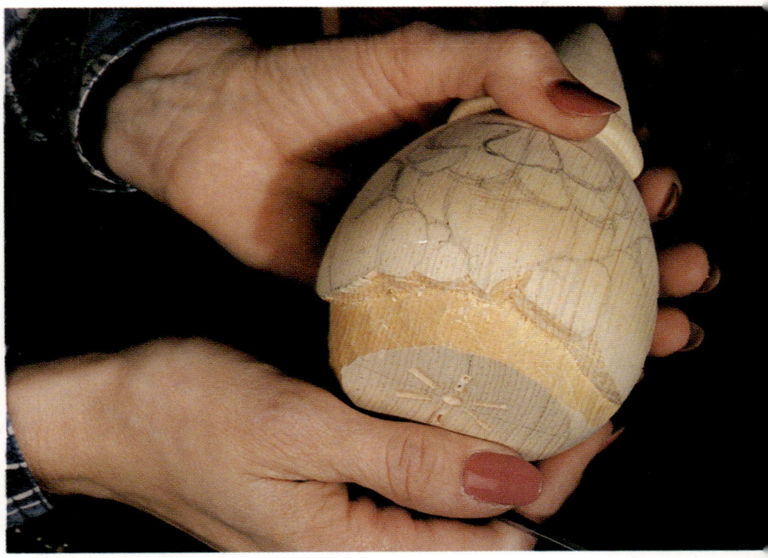

Progress.

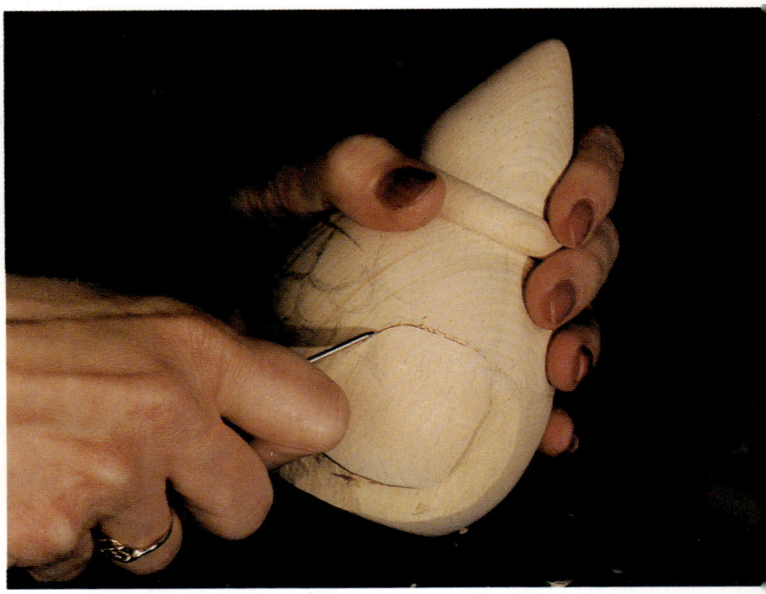

Score a line over the shoulder...

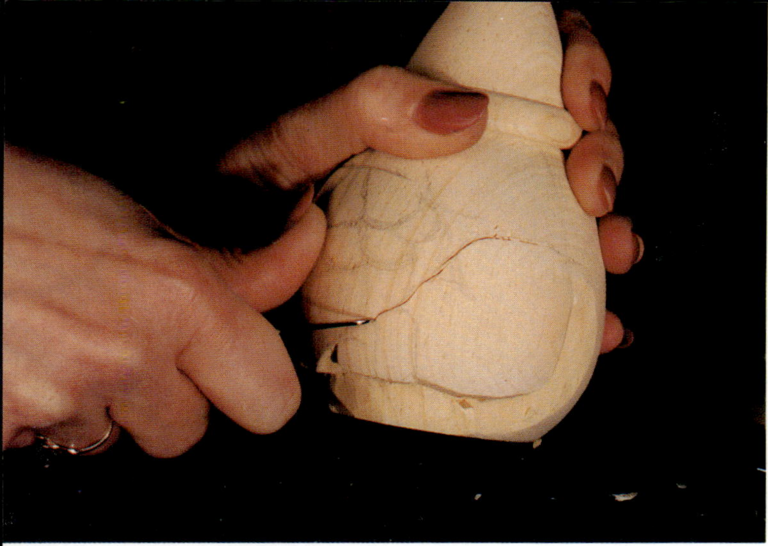

and between the beard and the arm.

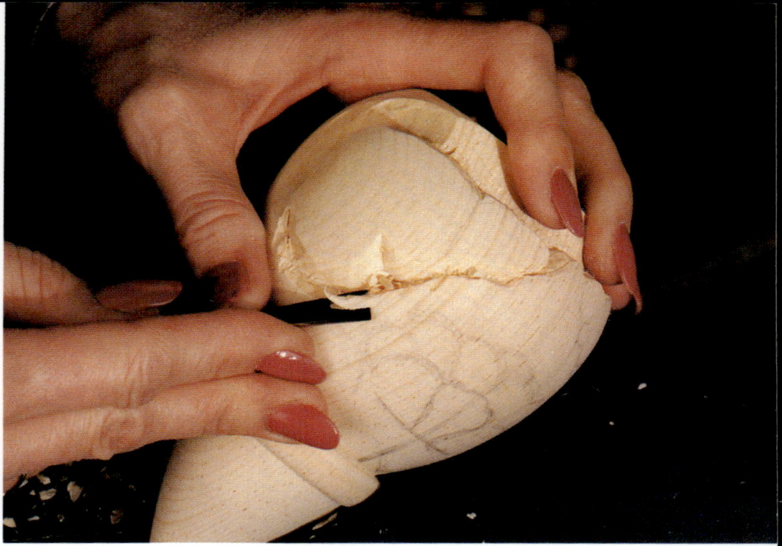

and the hair on the other.

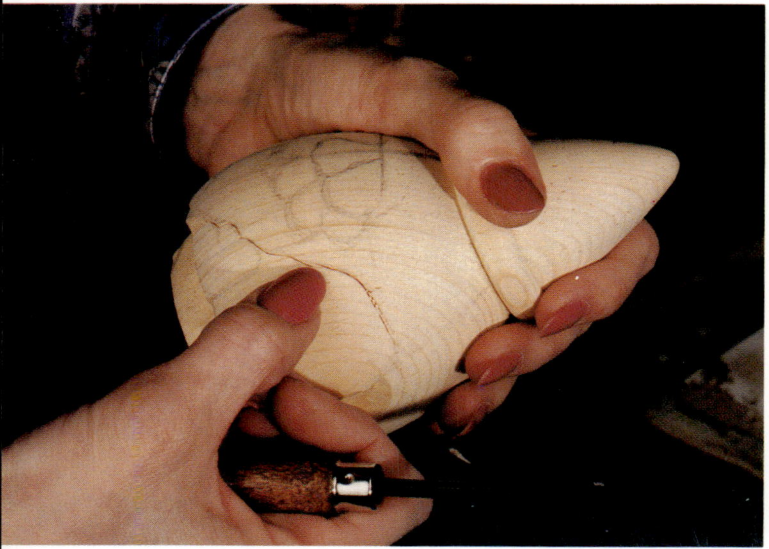

I'm going to round the arm and the beard back to this line.

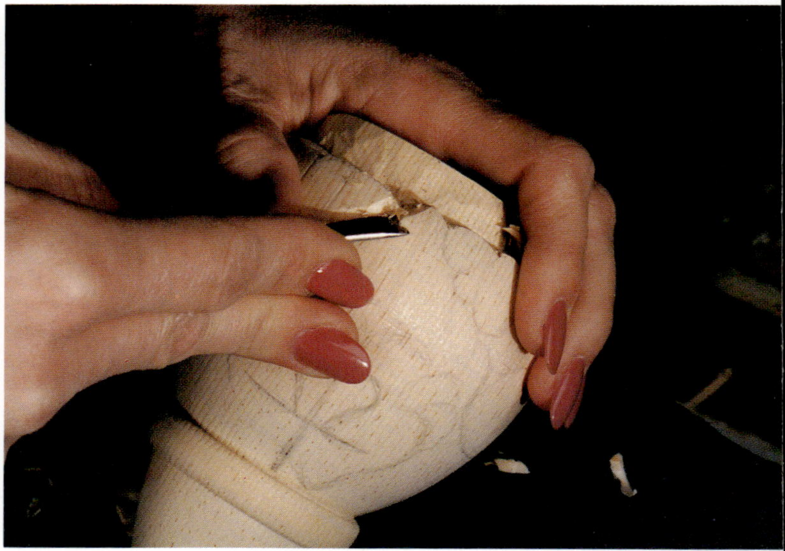

Again we are trying to get rid of the turned look. The advantage to using a turning is that it is rounded and has a unique shape, but we need a lot of depth to the features to get rid of the manufactured look.

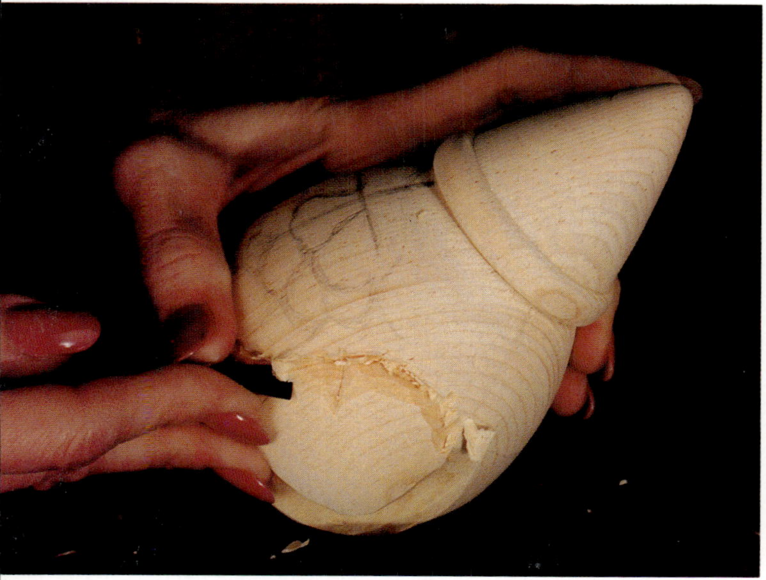

Round the arm and hand to the score line on one side...

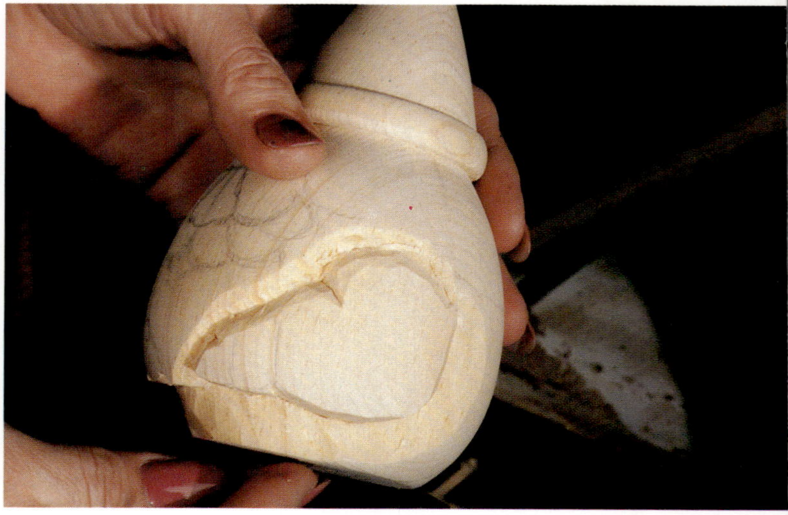

Progress.

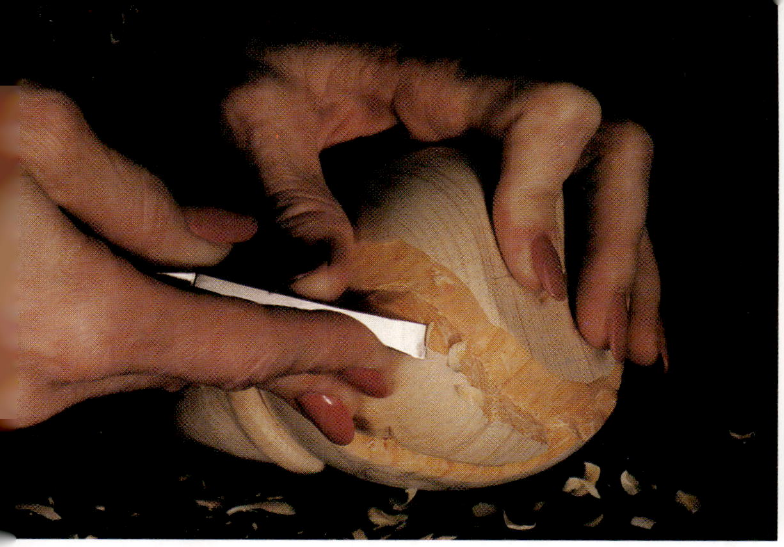

Shape the underside of the arm.

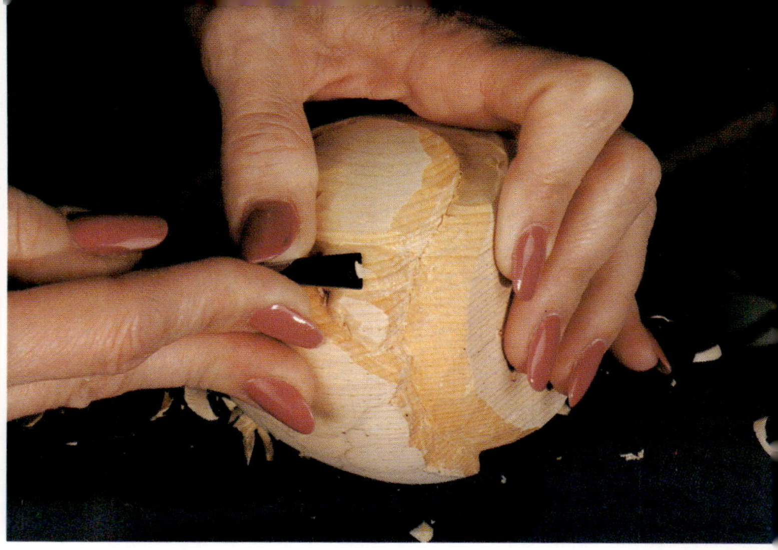

Round the fur area...

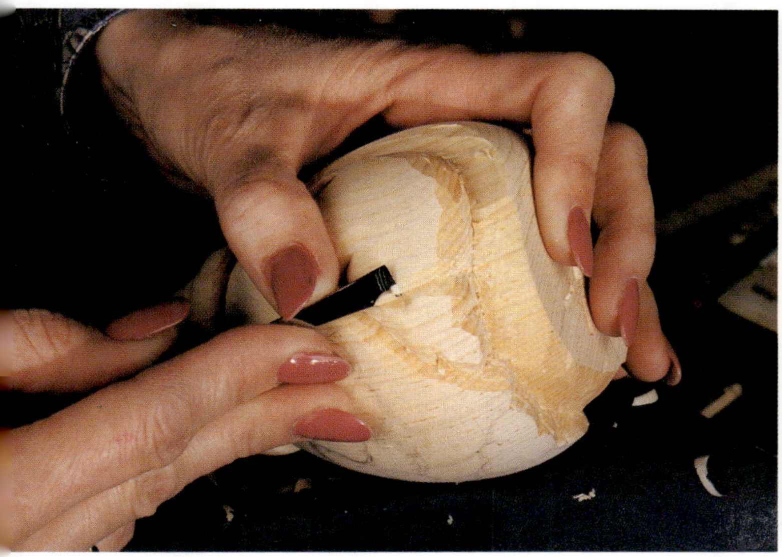

Cut a groove between the sleeve and the fur..

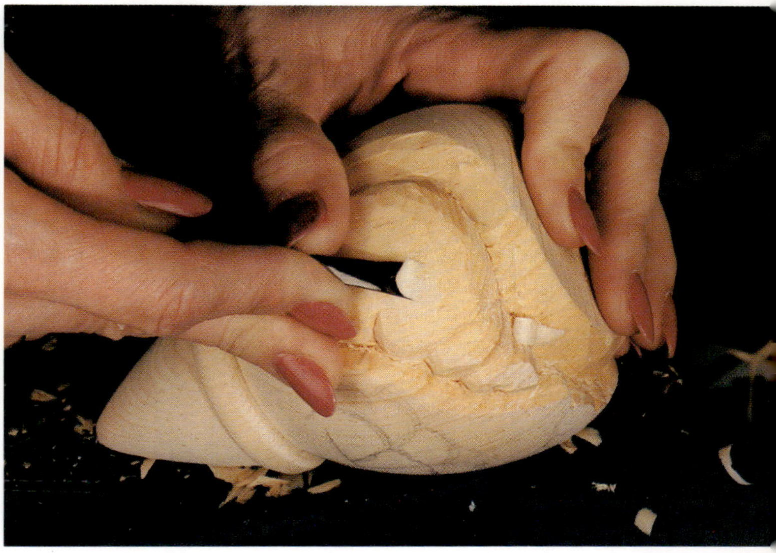

and the arm. You want to replace the smooth texture of the lathe with the marks of the tool over the whole piece.

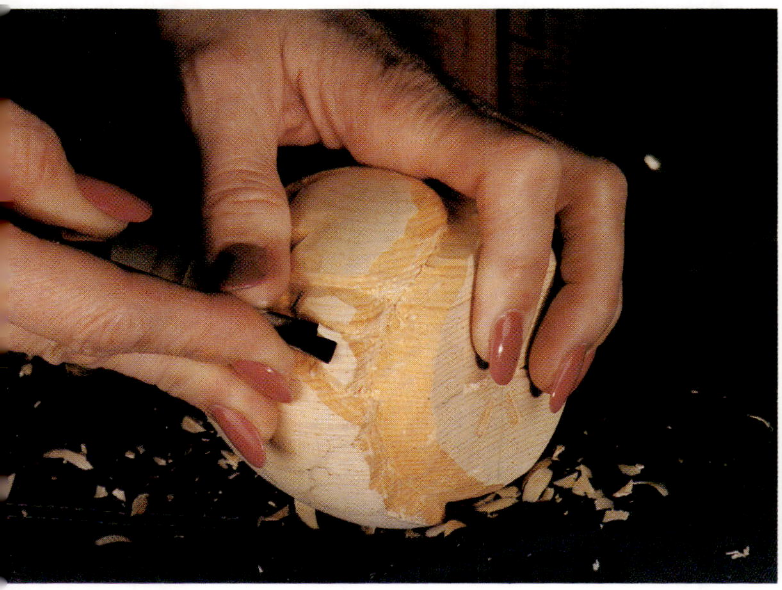

and between the fur and mitten.

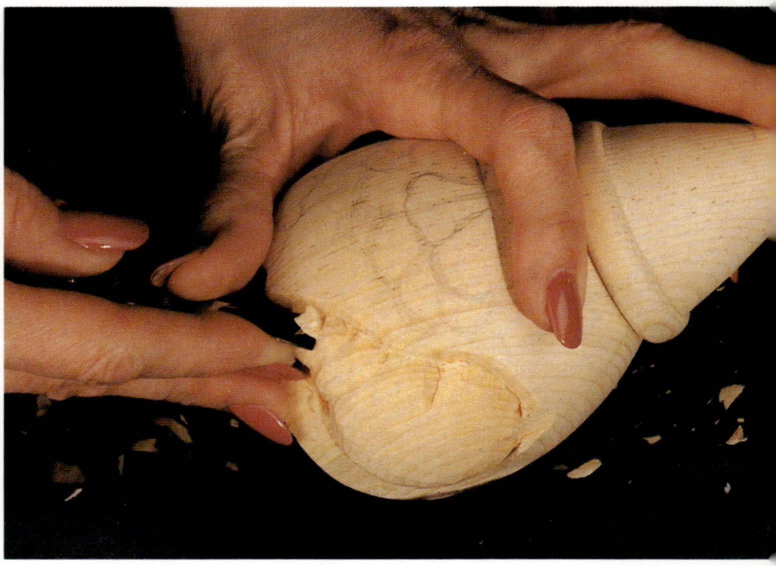

Round up the edge of the mitten to the thumb...

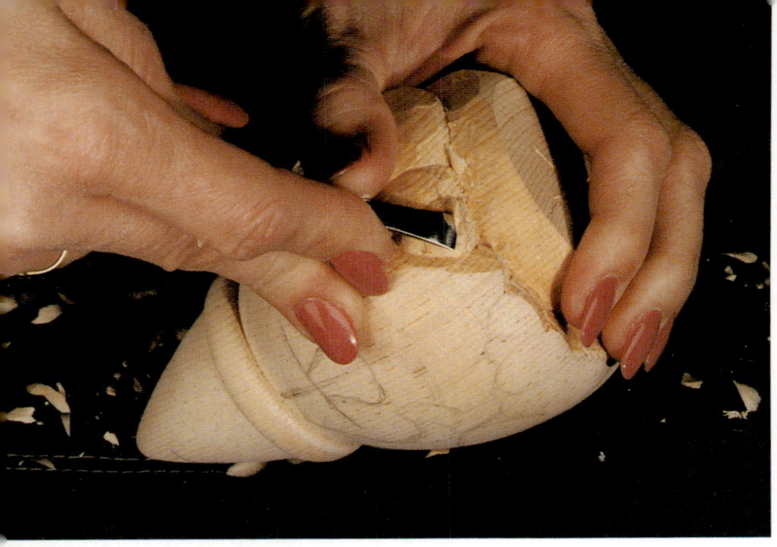

then round over the hand of the mitten.

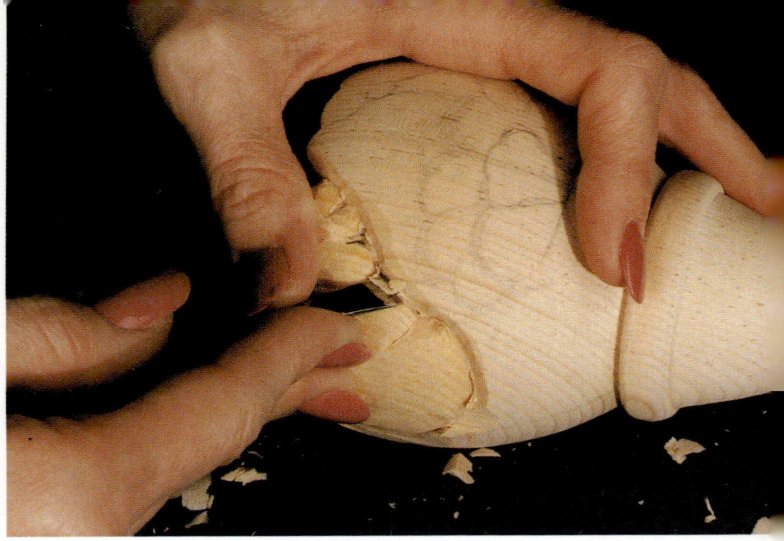

Continue to carve each V on the arm.

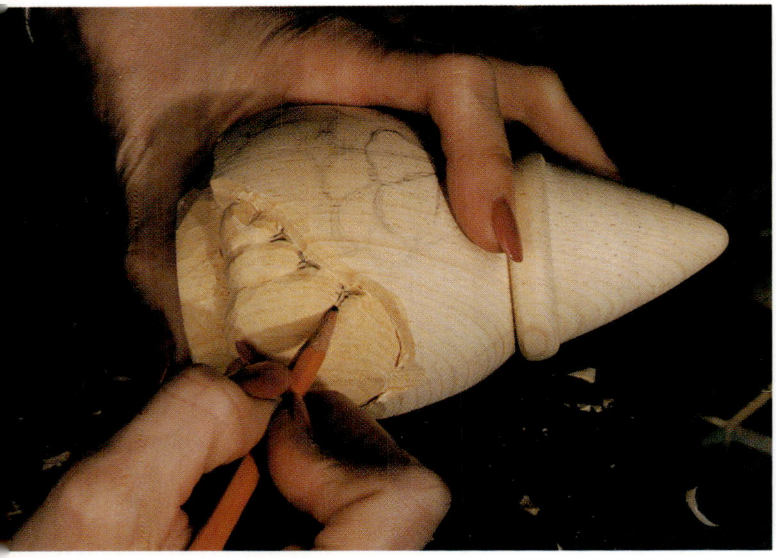

Wherever the surfaces come together to create a V, like here...

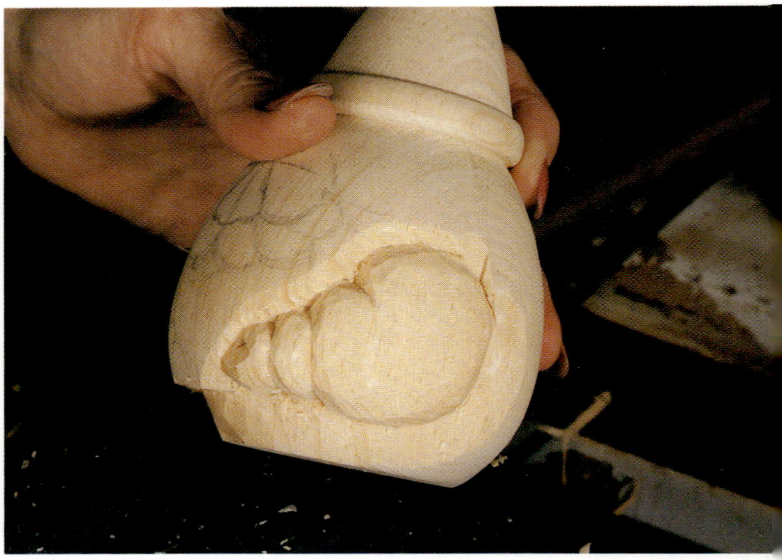

The first arm finished.

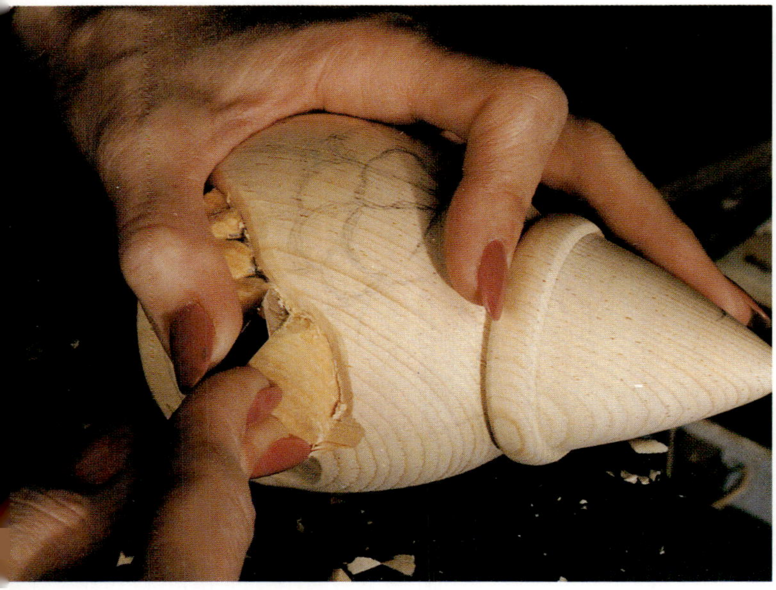

a little extra depth will add character to your carving.

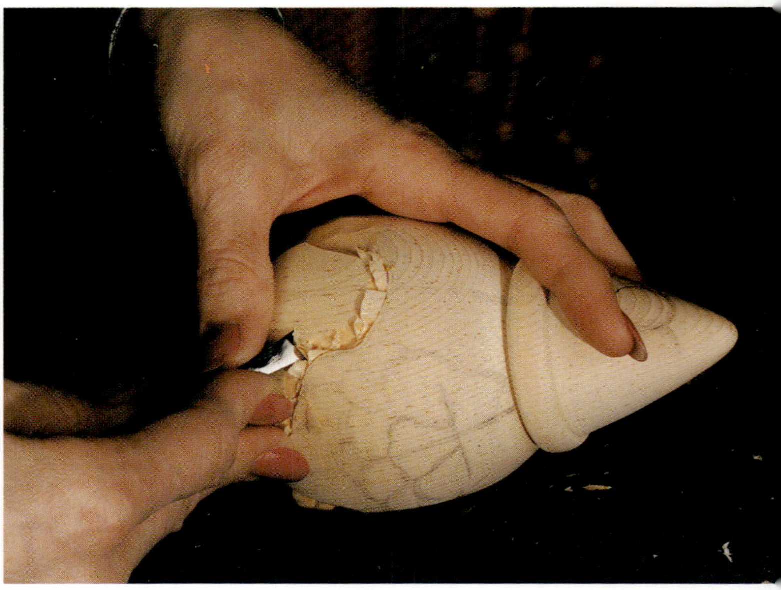

Repeat on the other side.

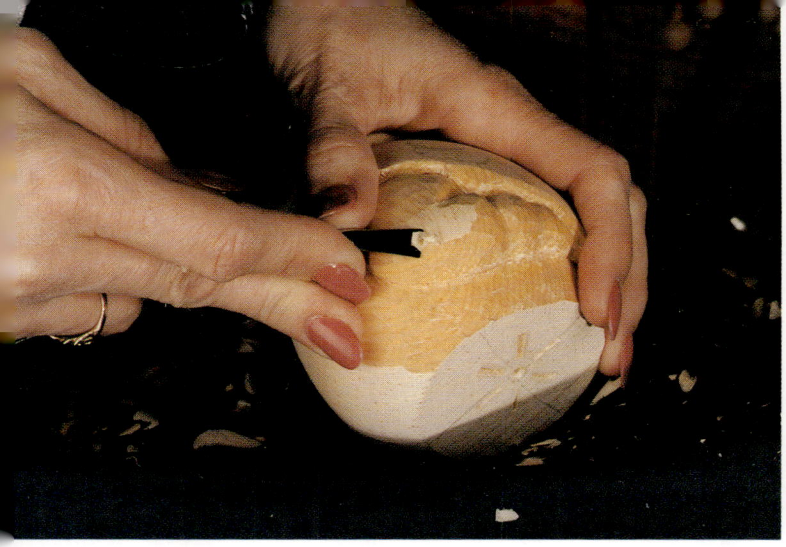

Continue to round the arms.

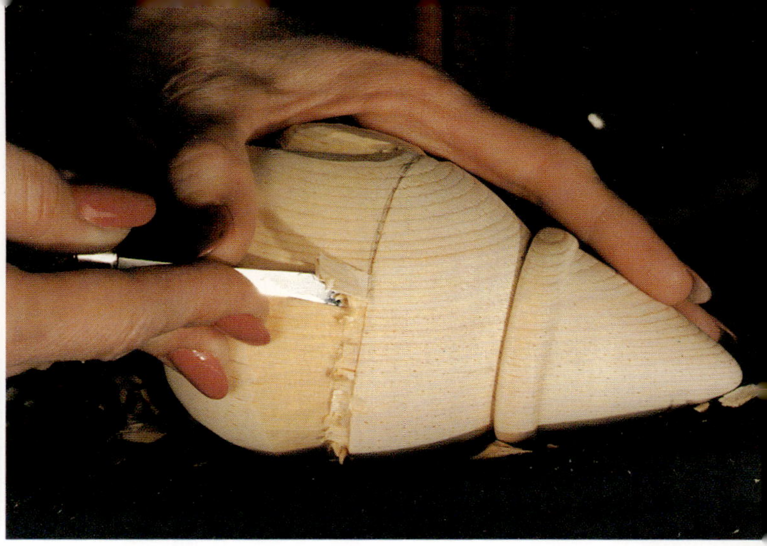

Trim back to it from below.

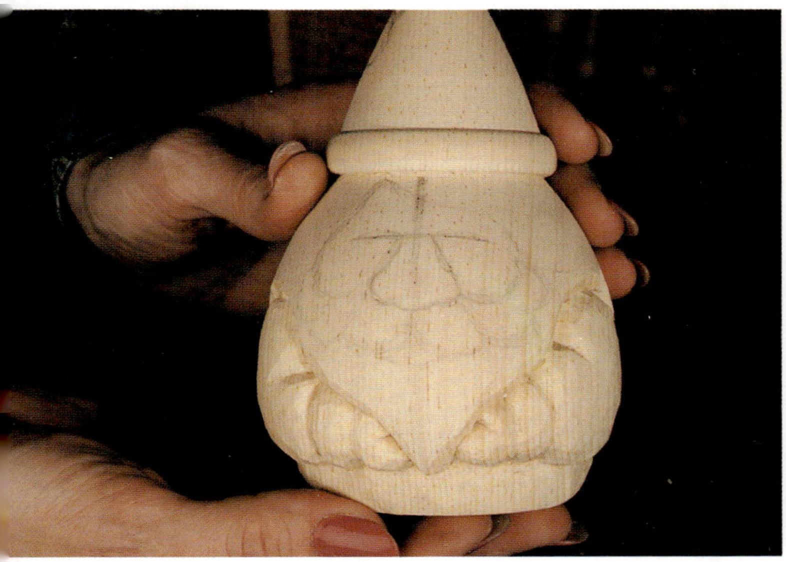

Progress.

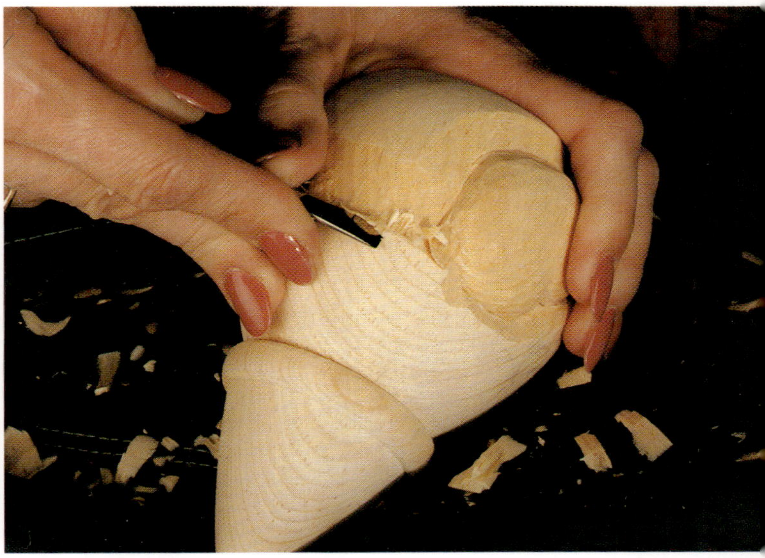

Round the hair off toward the score line.

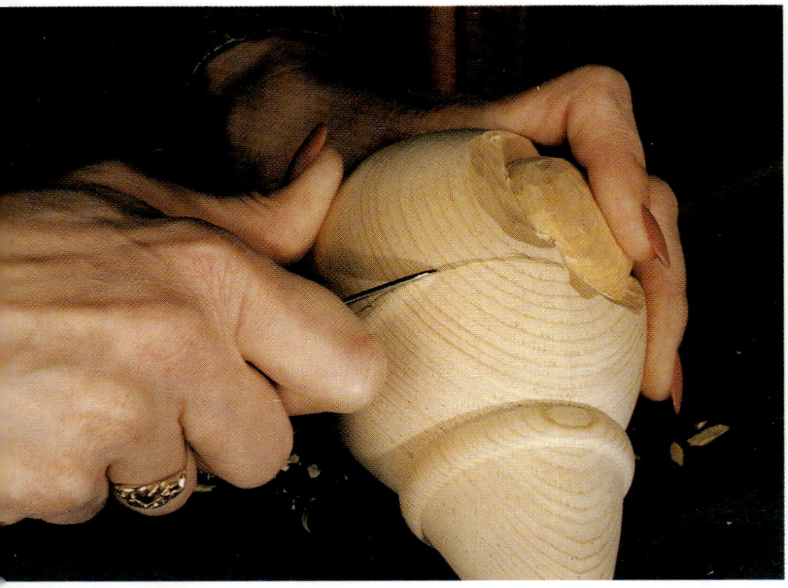

Score the hairline in the back...

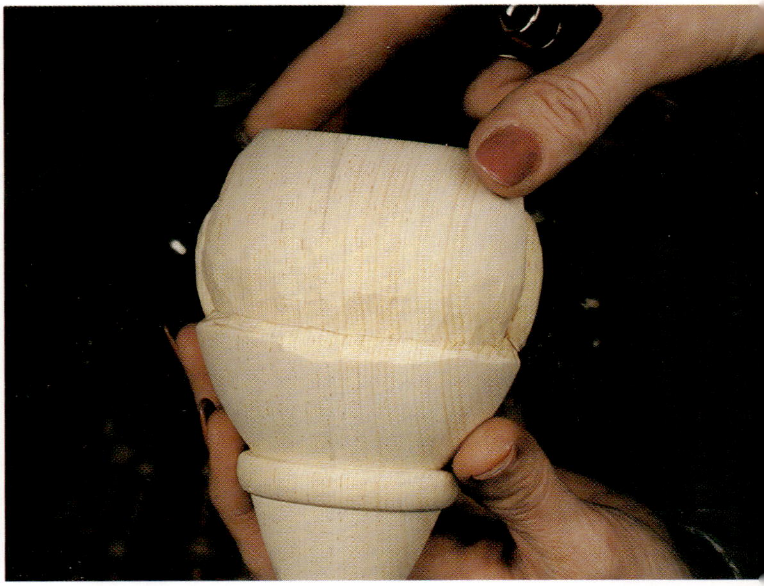

Deepen the shape to about this point.

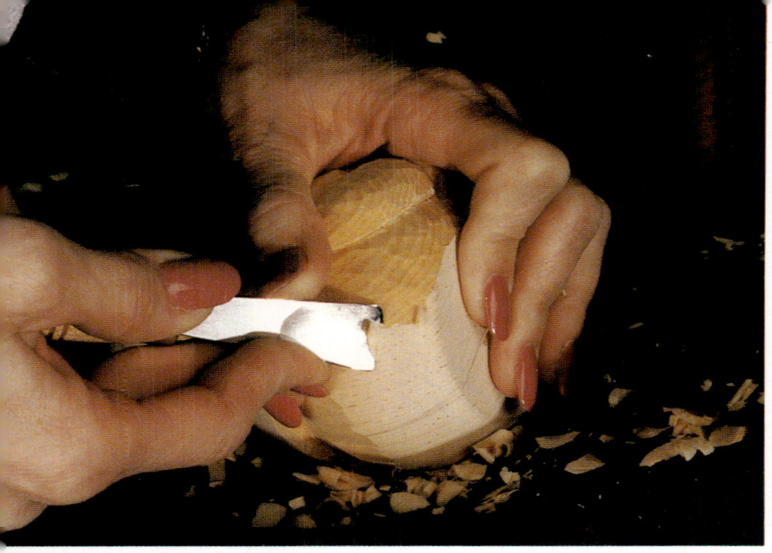

I switch to a broader gouge to clean up the back.

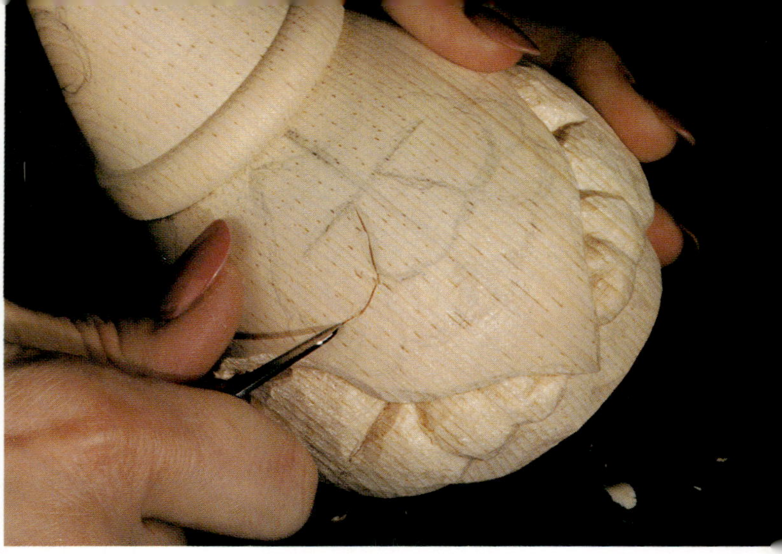

Continue around the underside of the cheek...

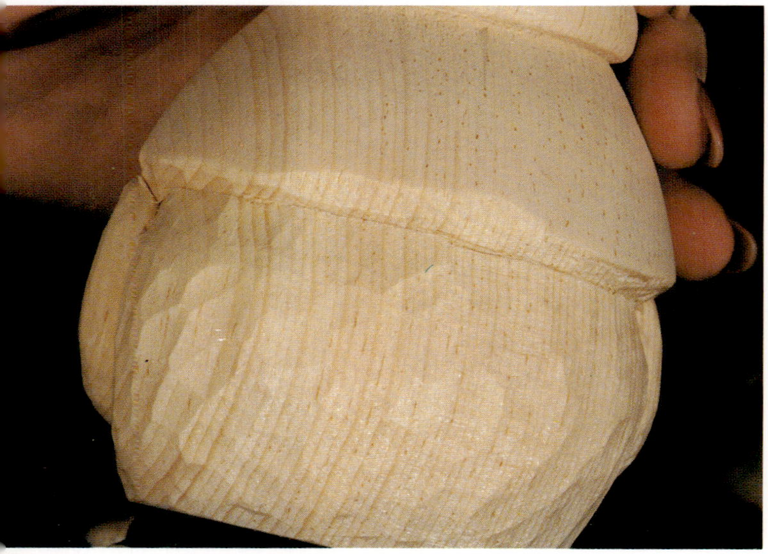

This gives me a more faceted surface than the smaller chisel.

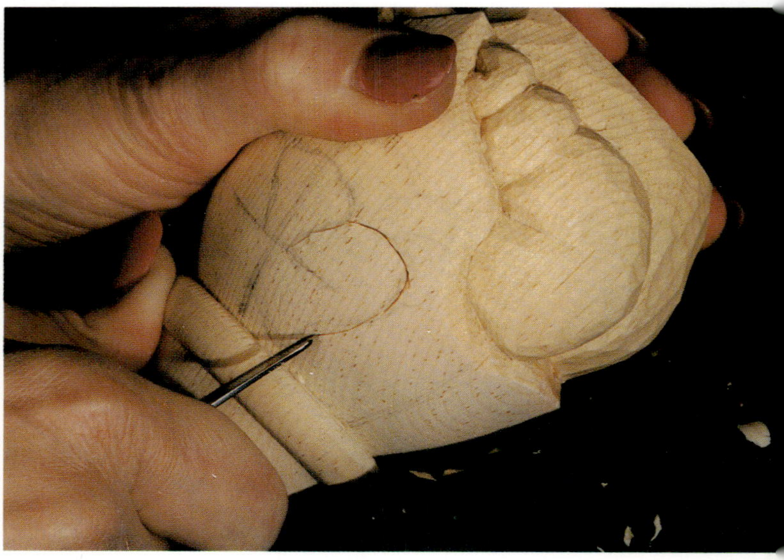

and up the side of the face.

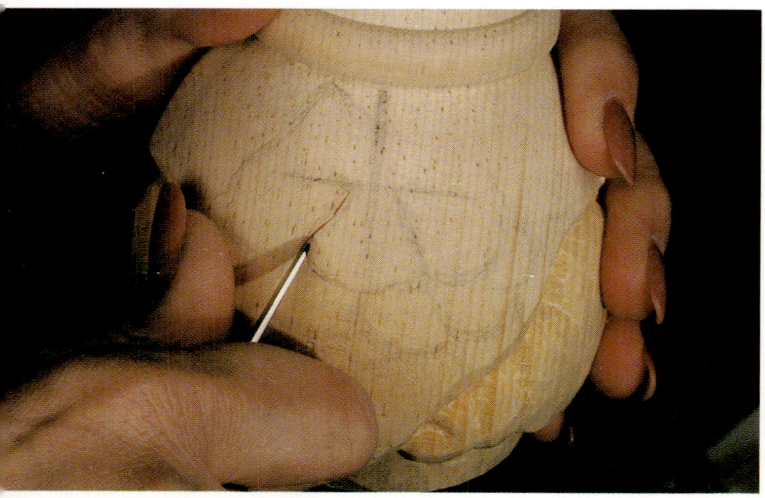

I break the bottom to top rule by doing the face before the beard. This allows me to get the proper depth. I also leave the nose extra wide for now so that, if there is a break or some other calamity, I have room to fix it. Come down the side of the nose with a score line.

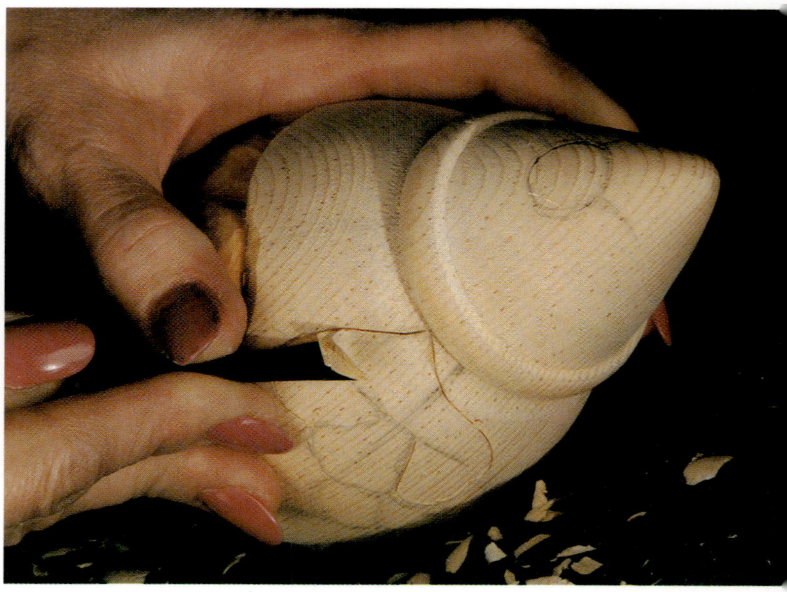

Cut back to the score line along the sides of the forehead...

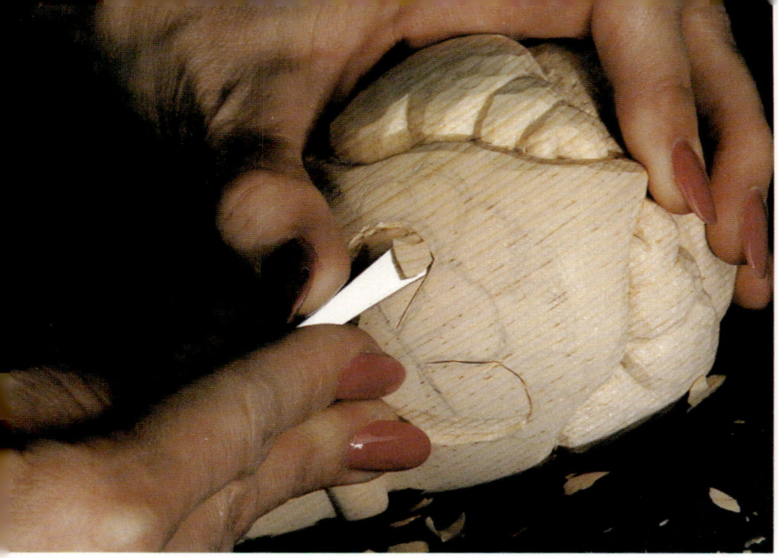

on the bottom surface of the cheek...

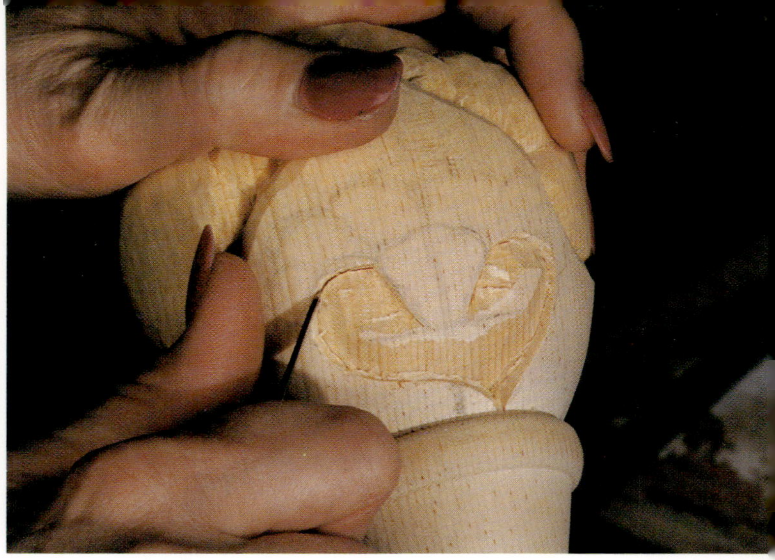

The nose needs to be brought out more. Do this by deepening the score around the bottom of the cheek...

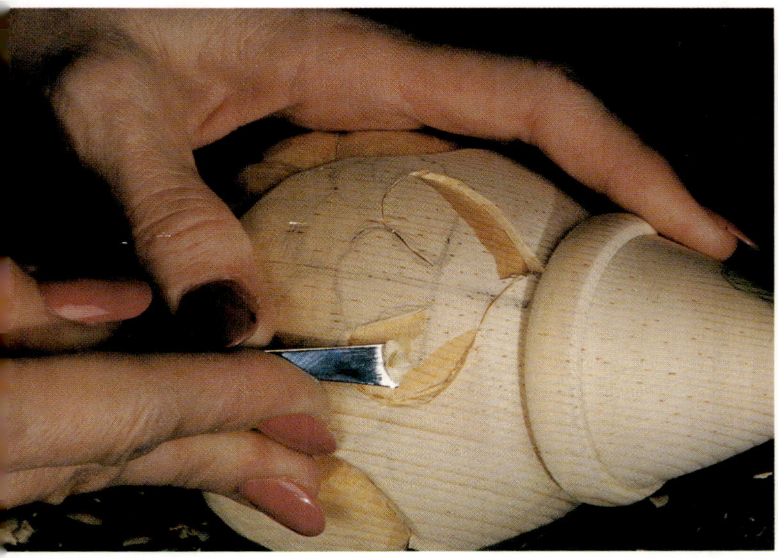

and along the side of the nose and over the top of the cheek.

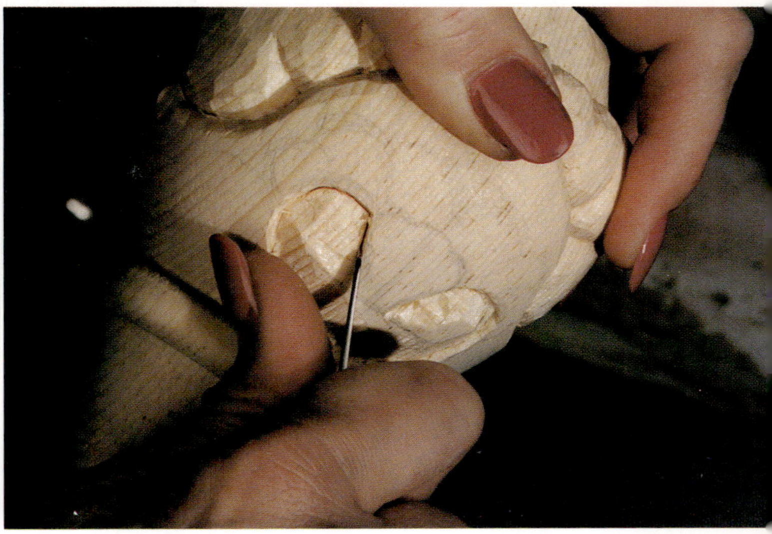

and along the side of the nose.

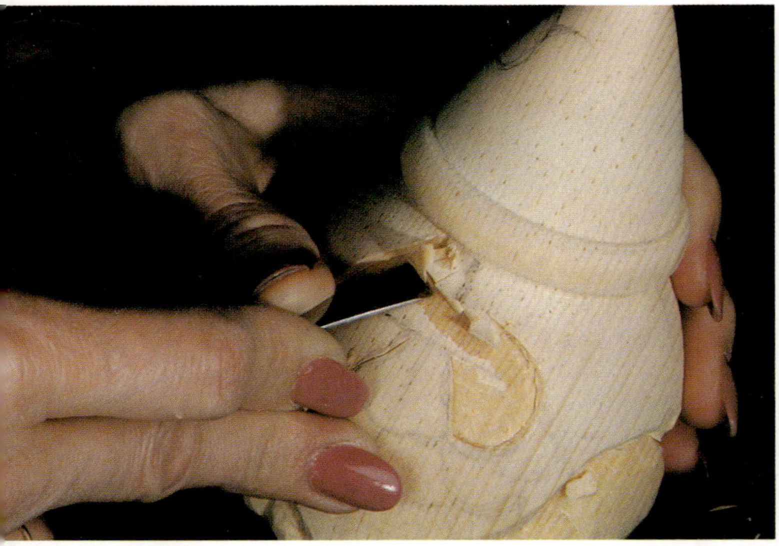

Cut from the browline up to the hairline. The face needs to be carved from the nose toward the top of the hat to get the correct grain direction.

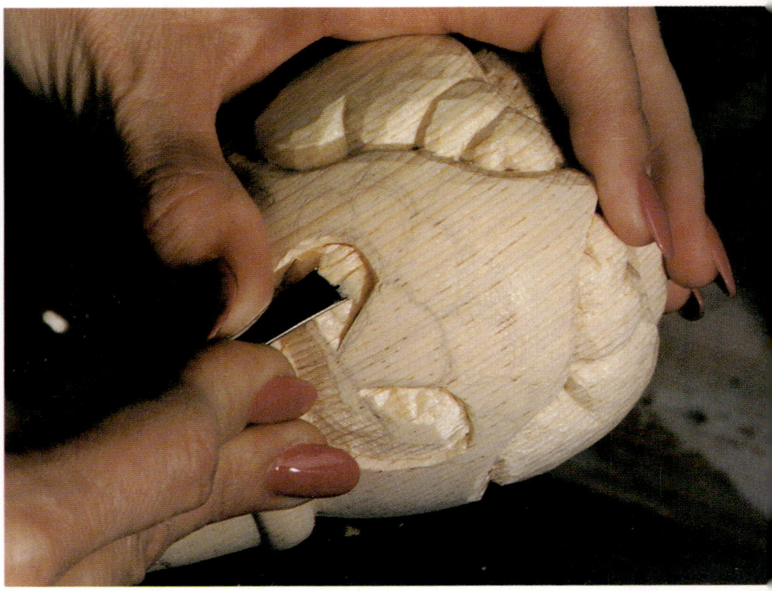

Shape and reduce the cheek by cutting back to the stop cuts.

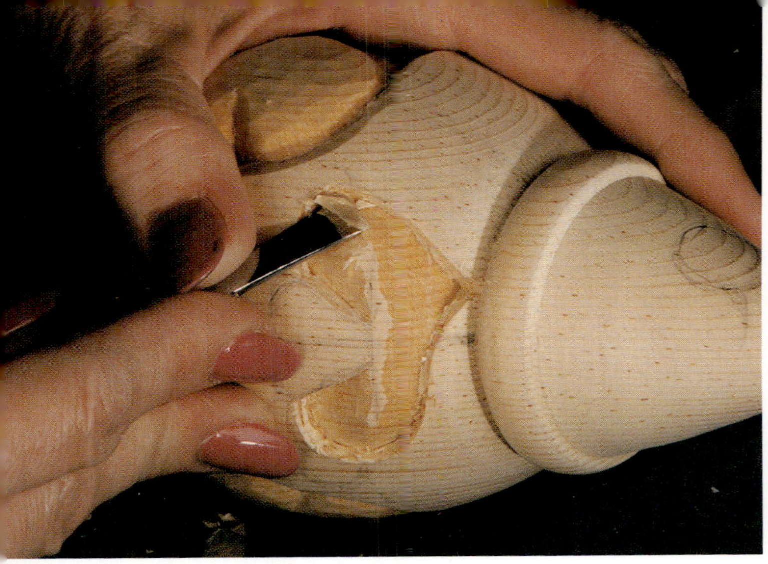

Repeat on the other side.

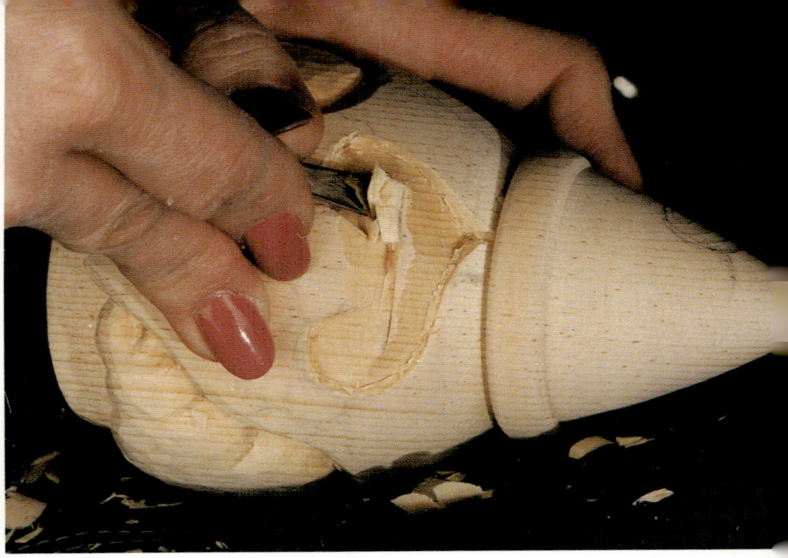

and from the cheek to form one eye socket...

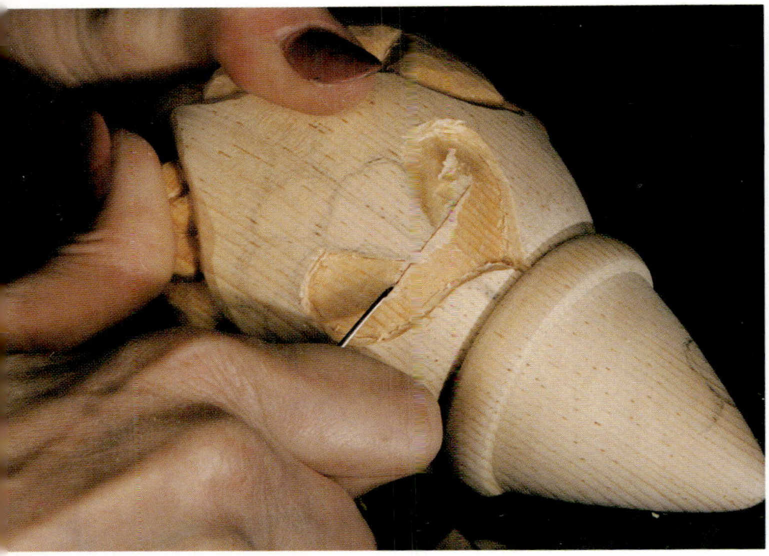

Cut a score line across the brow.

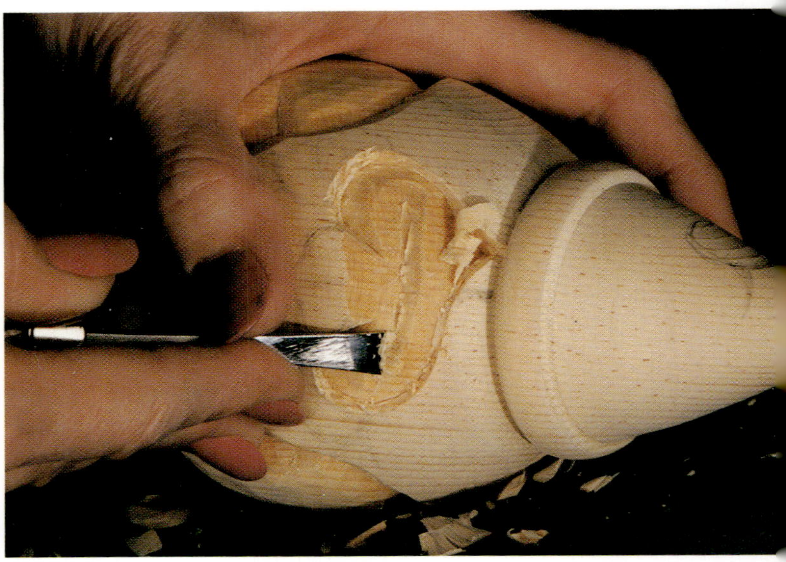

and the other.

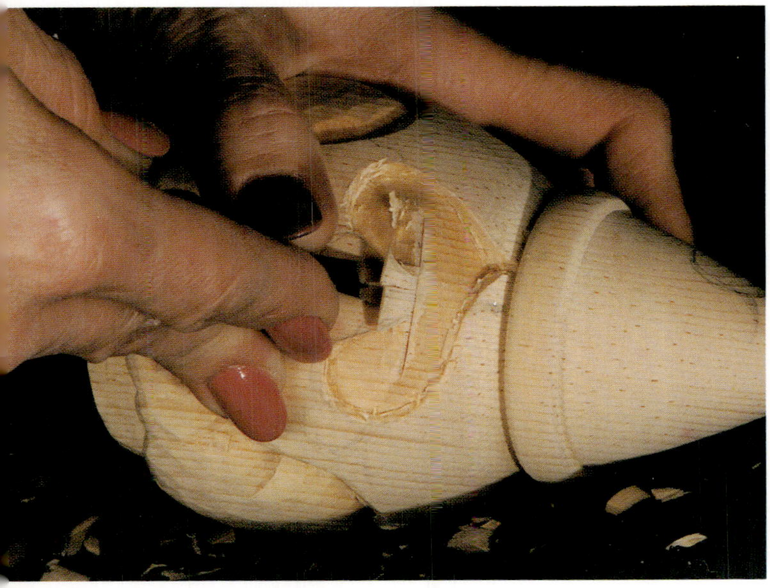

Cut back to it along the nose to form the bridge of the nose...

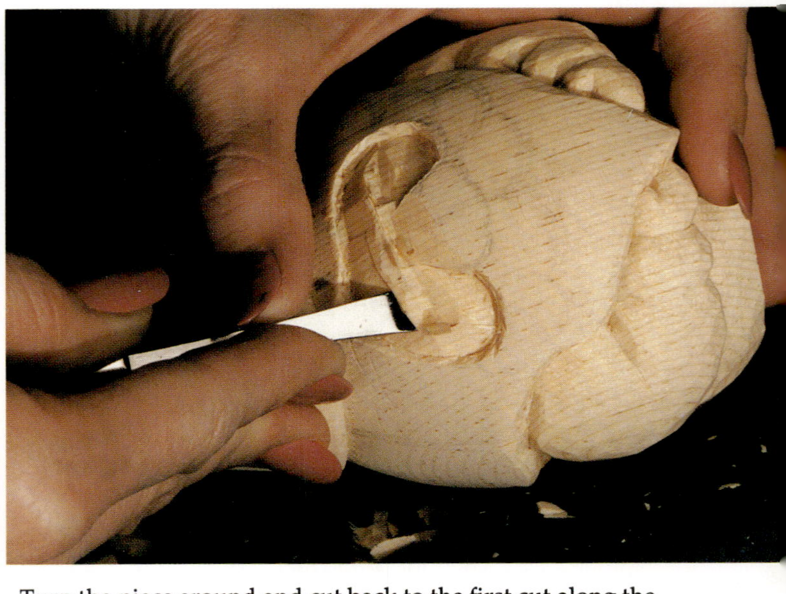

Turn the piece around and cut back to the first cut along the browline. This is against the grain and will be roughly cut.

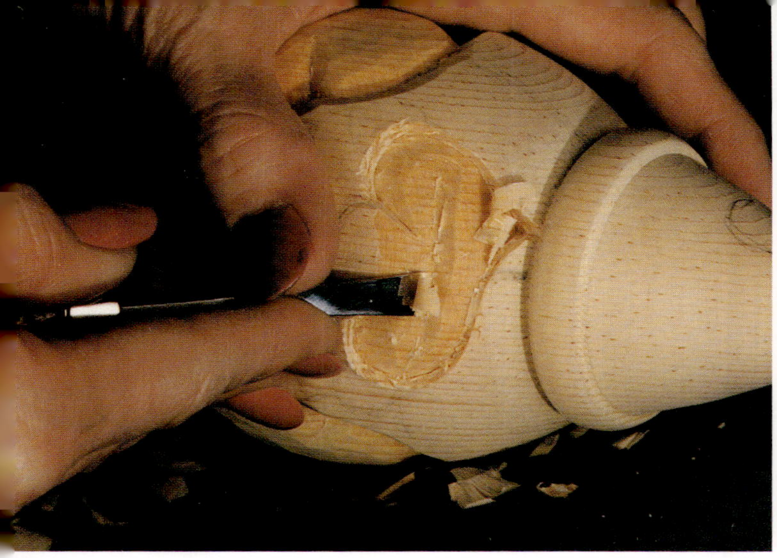

To clean it up turn the piece again remove the waste in the brow groove.

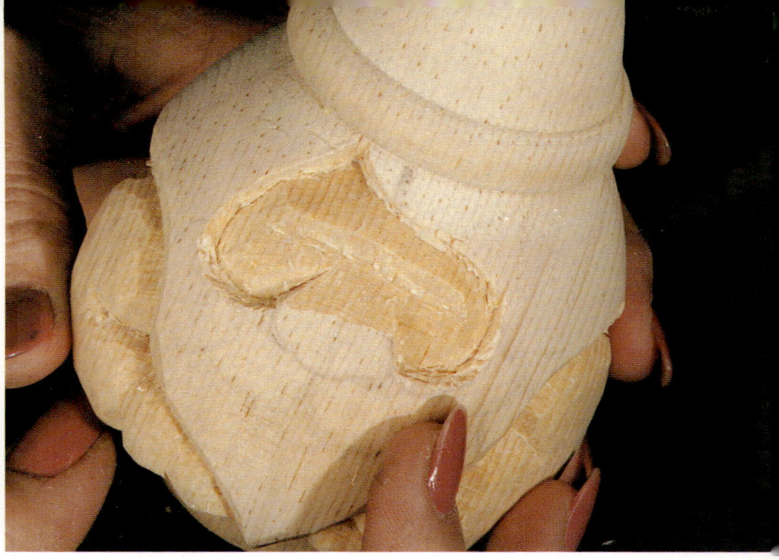

than his left.

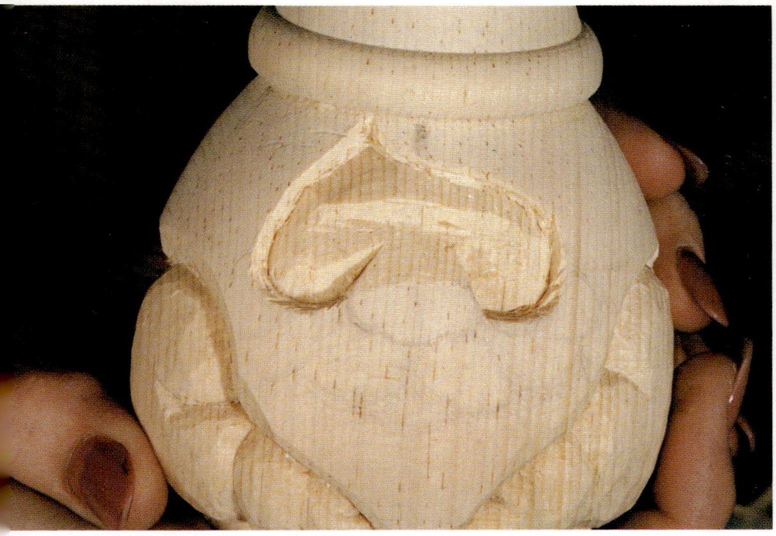

Progress. We need to look for symmetry at this point and fix any asymmetry.

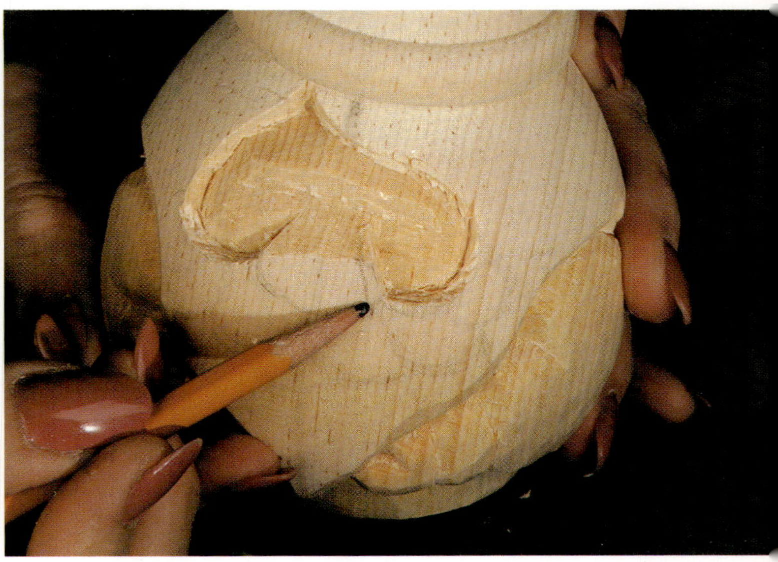

Because we left the nose wide we can fix this by narrowing one side of the nose...

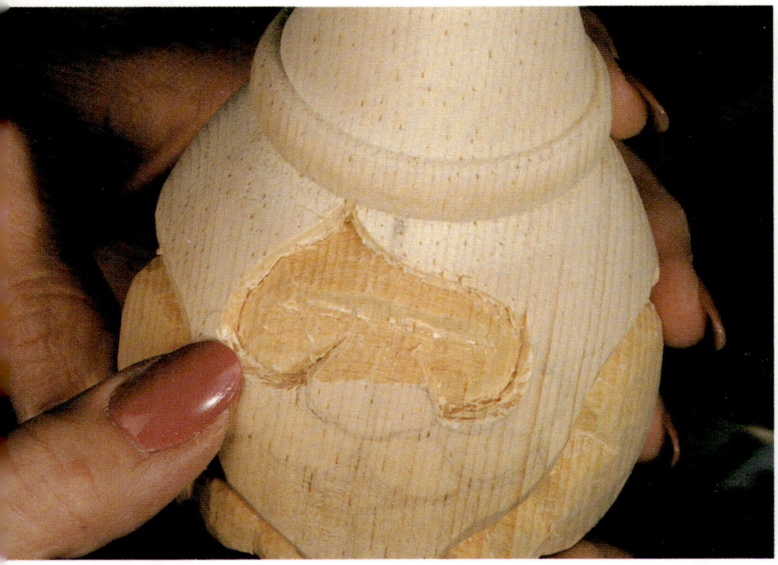

Santa's right cheek is wider...

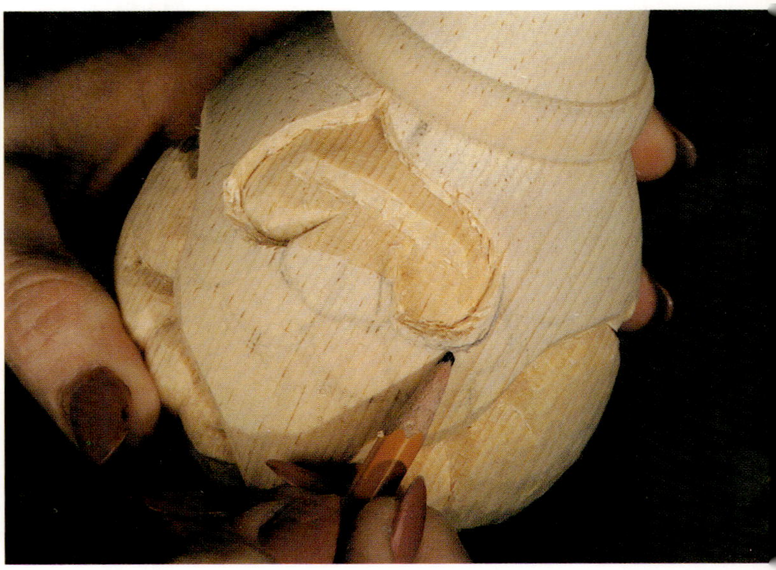

or we can fix it by widening the line of the cheek.

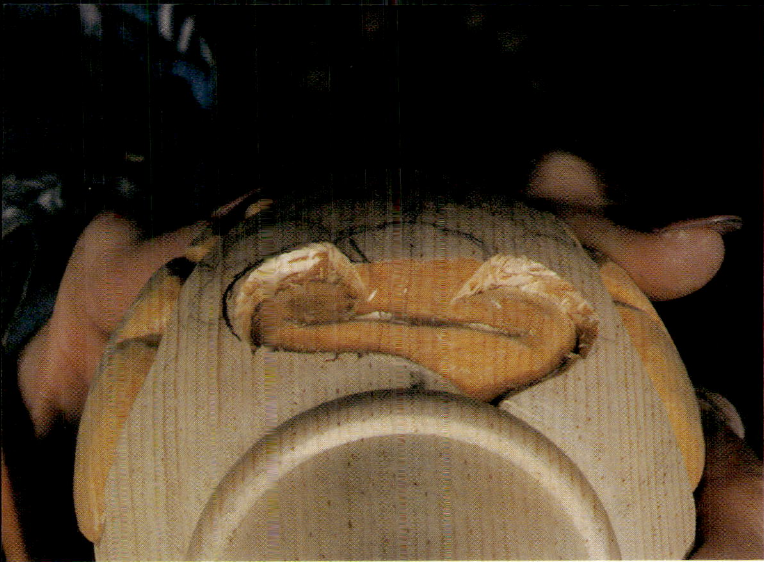

It is also important that the cheeks be the same depth, which can be seen by looking from the top. The right cheek is deeper than the left, so an adjustment is needed.

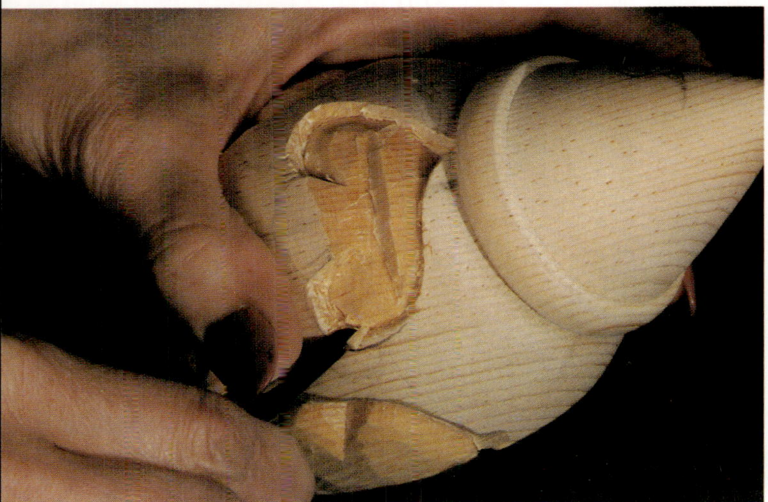

I've decided to widen the cheek to keep the width in the nose intact.

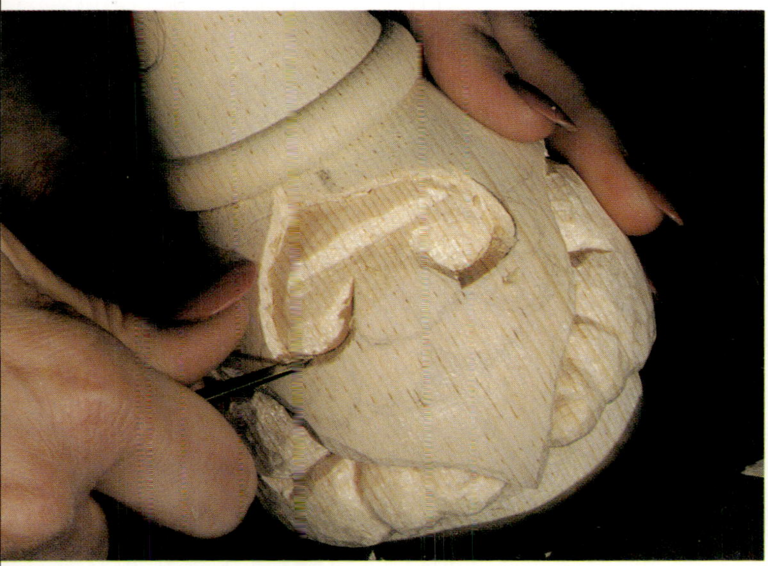

Deepen the shallow cheek if you have one.

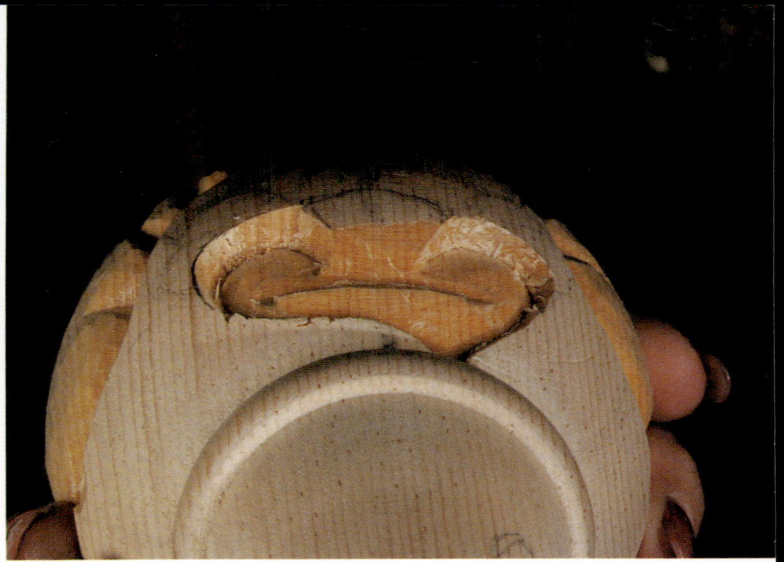

They look much better now.

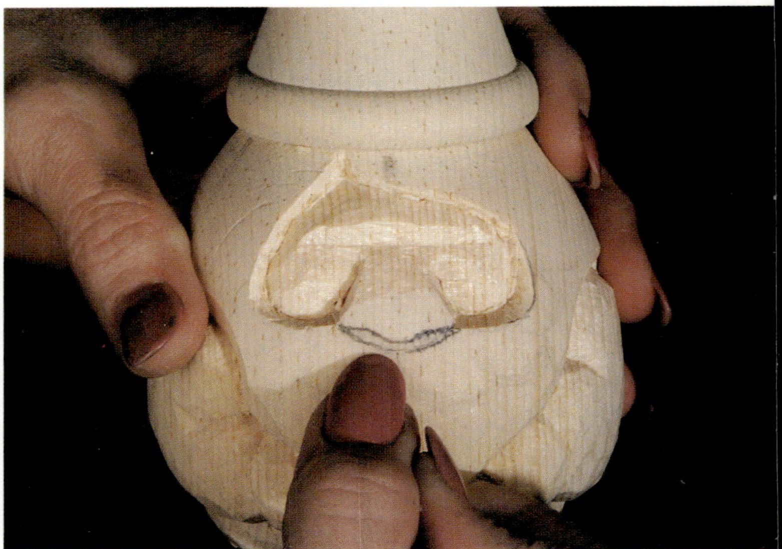

The pattern for underside of the nose has a shaped line, but we will begin by cutting an arc under it. This is because we want to bring the nose out before we shape it.

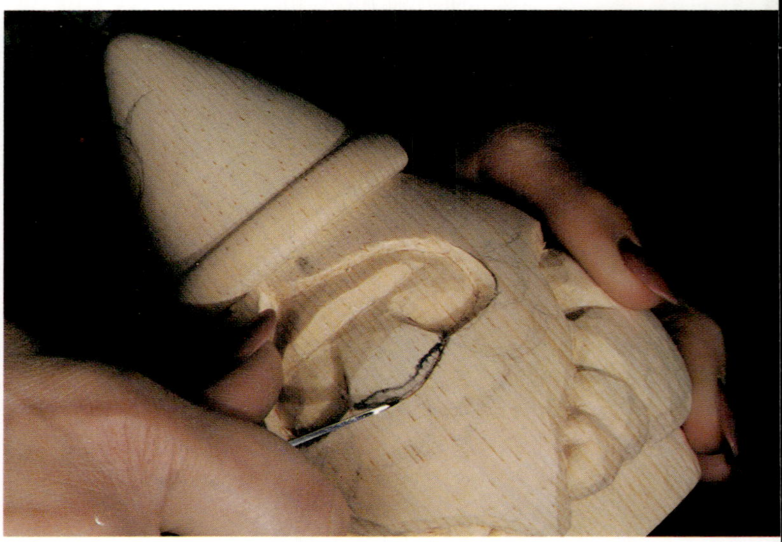

Score the line...

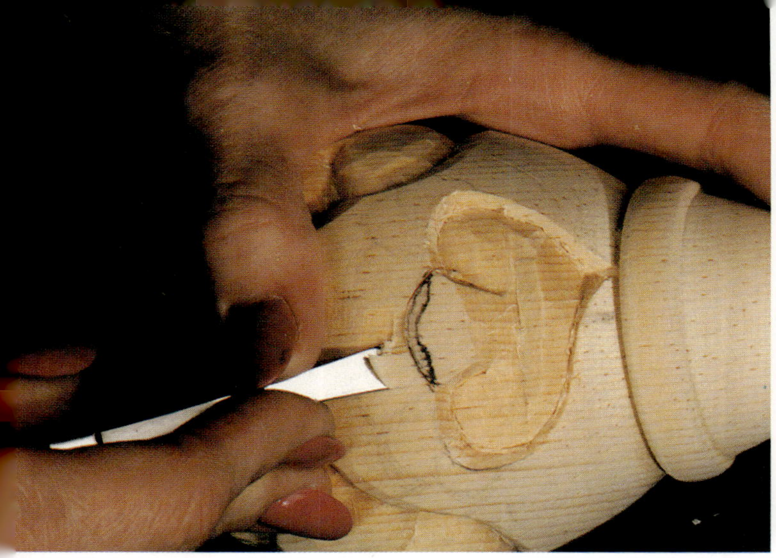

and come back to it from the moustache.

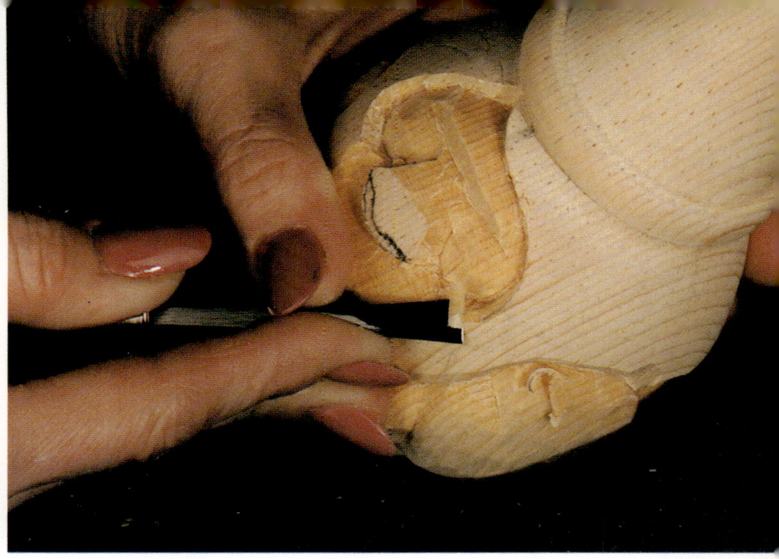

Round the sides of the moustache back to the cheek.

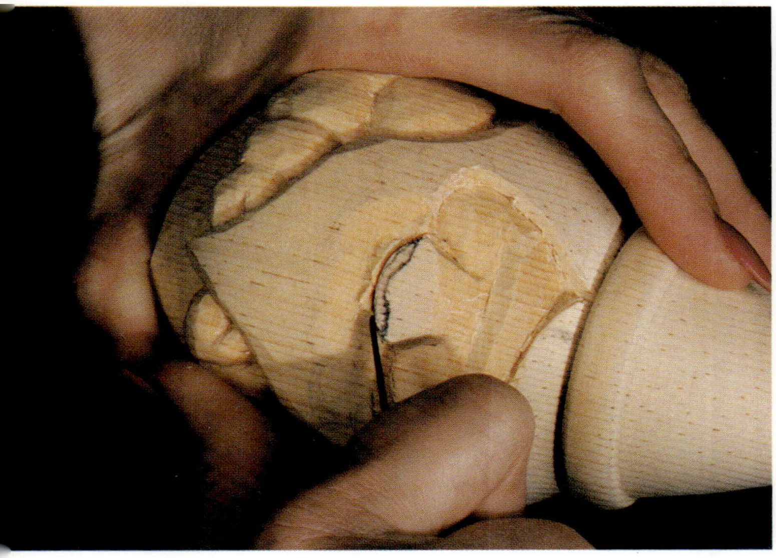

Rescore the line...

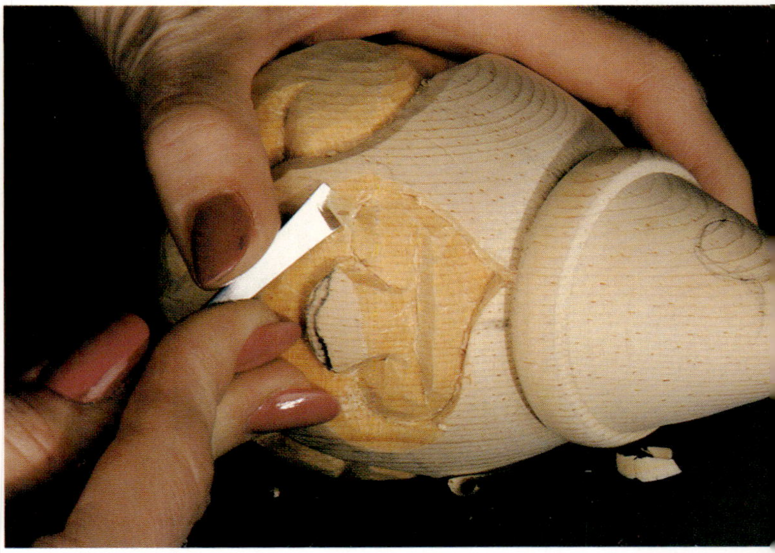

Do the same on the other side,

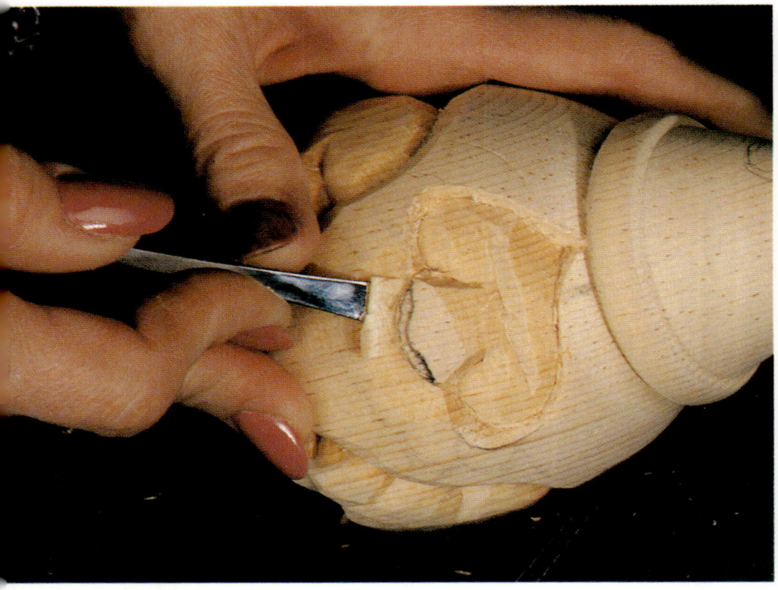

and chisel back to it to bring the nose out more.

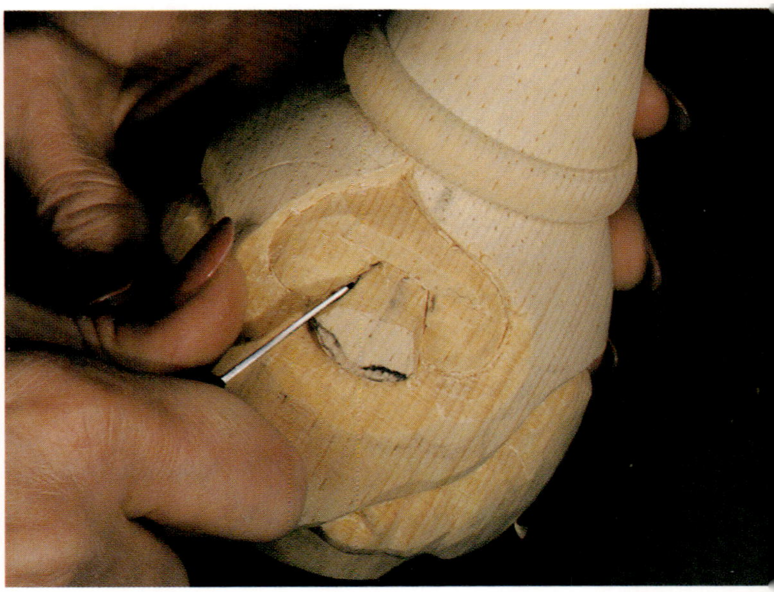

Extend the lines of the sides of the nose to the eyeline.

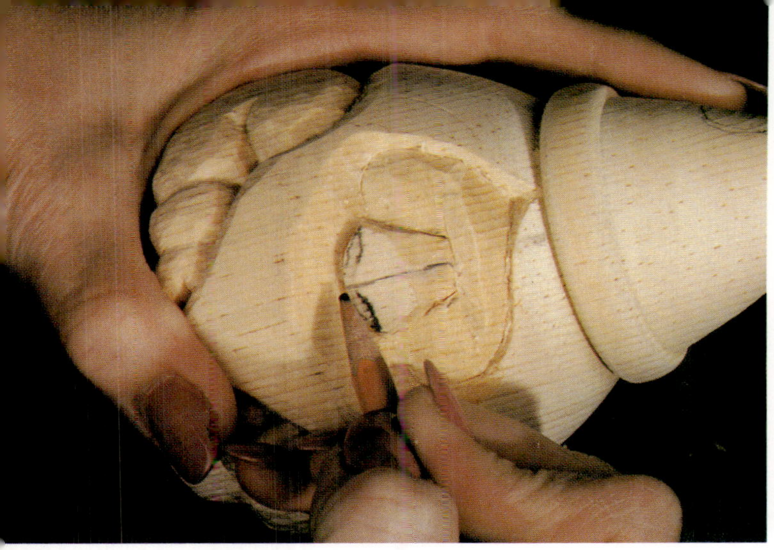

Draw in the ridge of the nose.

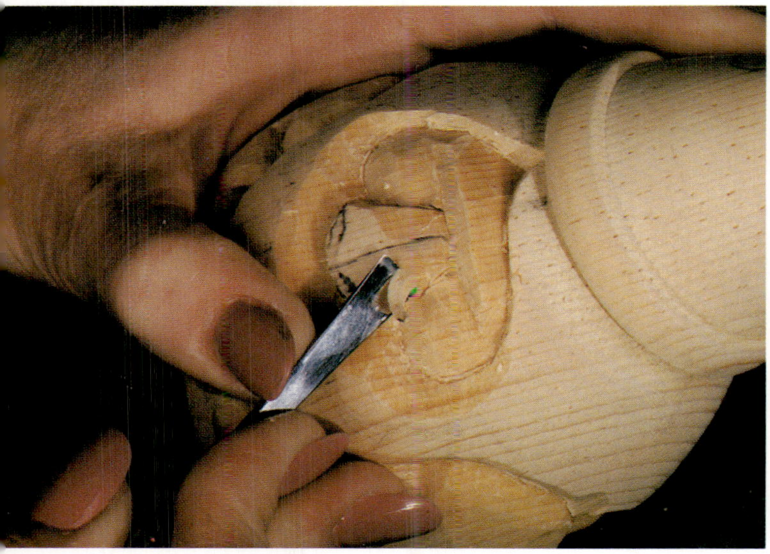

The nose is really several triangles in different planes...kind of a weirdly shaped pyramid. Slice from the nostril to the bridge of the nose, holding the chisel to the plane of the side of the nose.

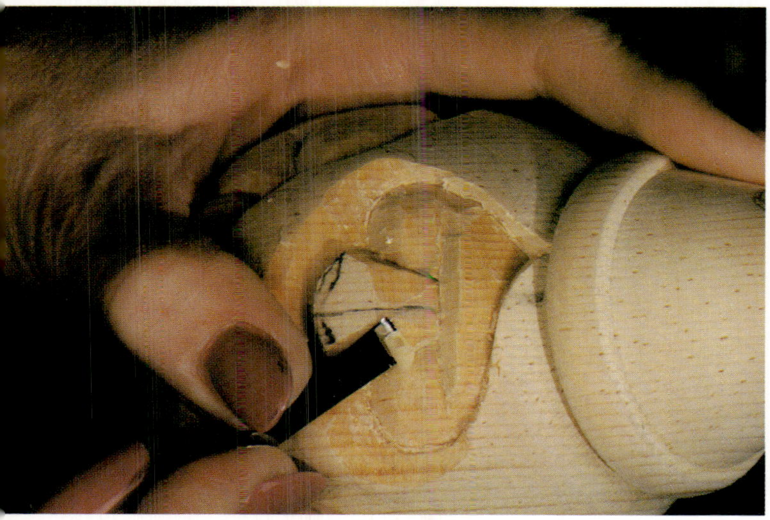

Repeat this cut until you reach the depth you desire.

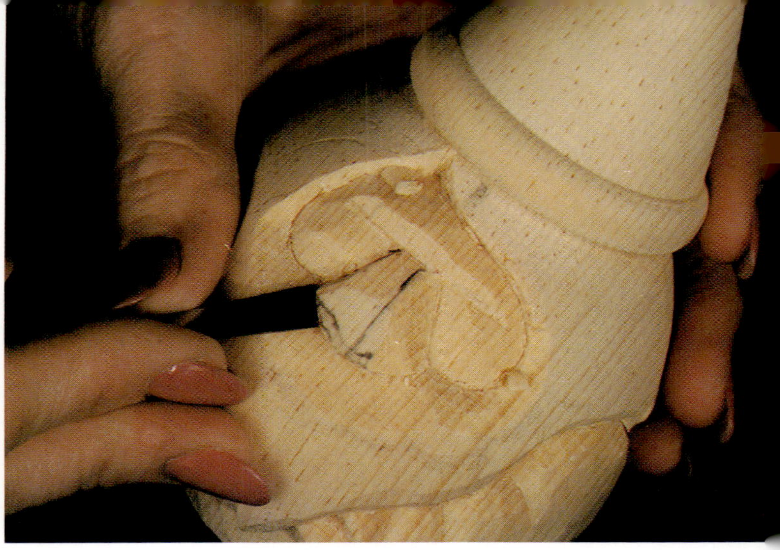

One side done and ready to repeat on the other.

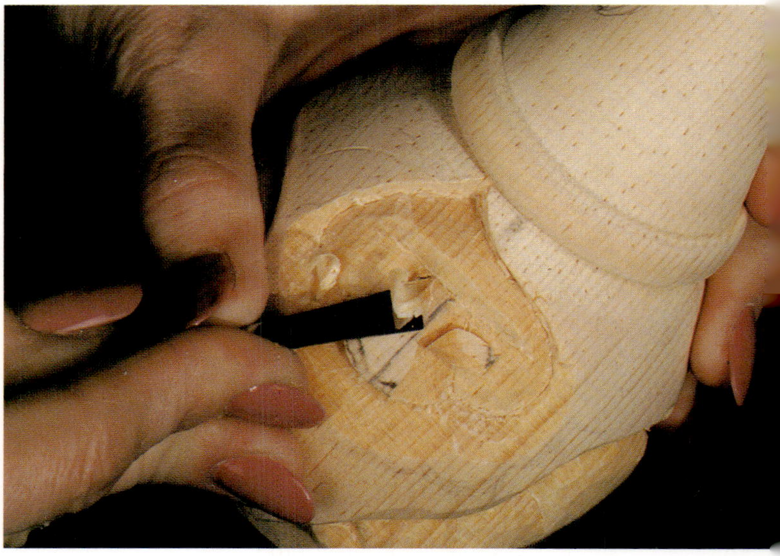

Follow the same steps on the other side.

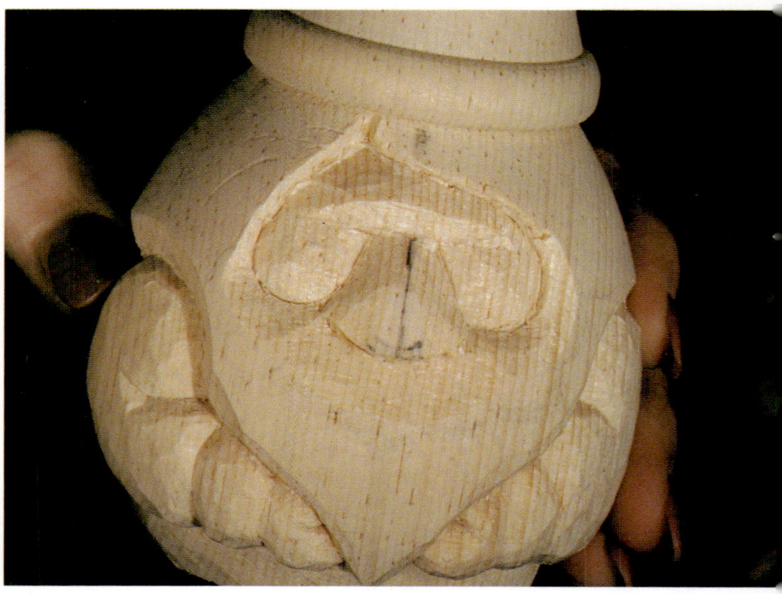

Progress.

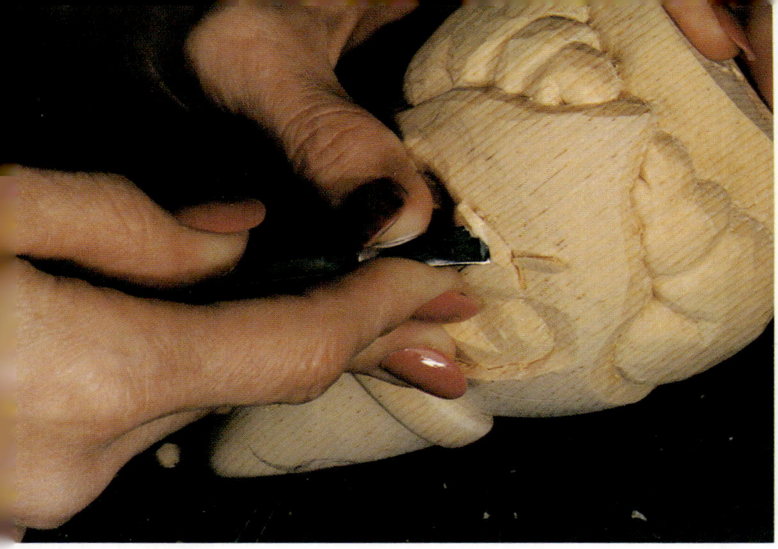

Round the end of the nose down to the moustache.

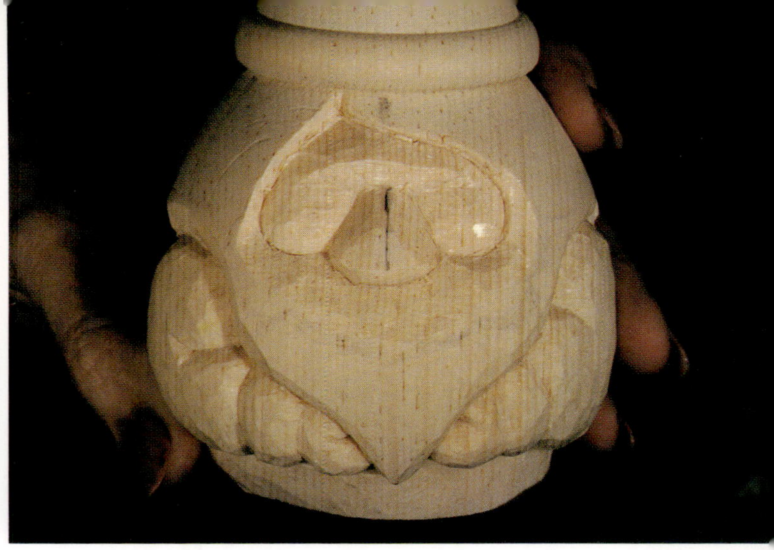

A good time to check again for symmetry.

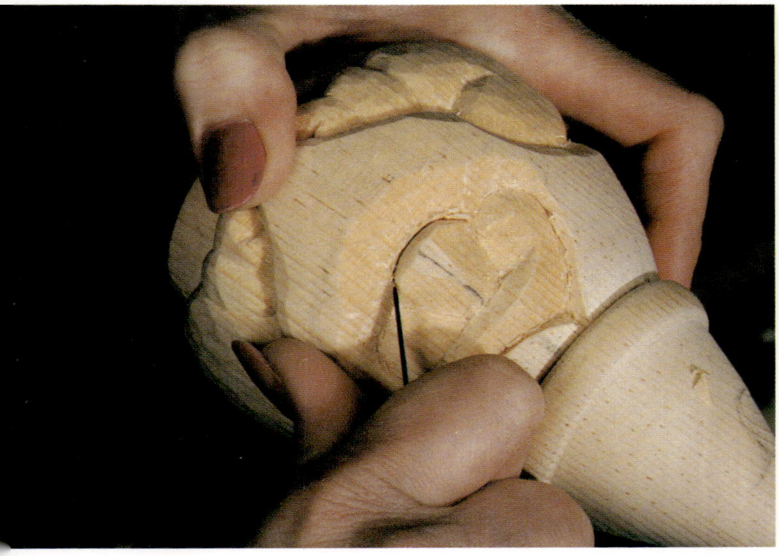

The nose needs to come out a little more so I deepen the score line under the nose...

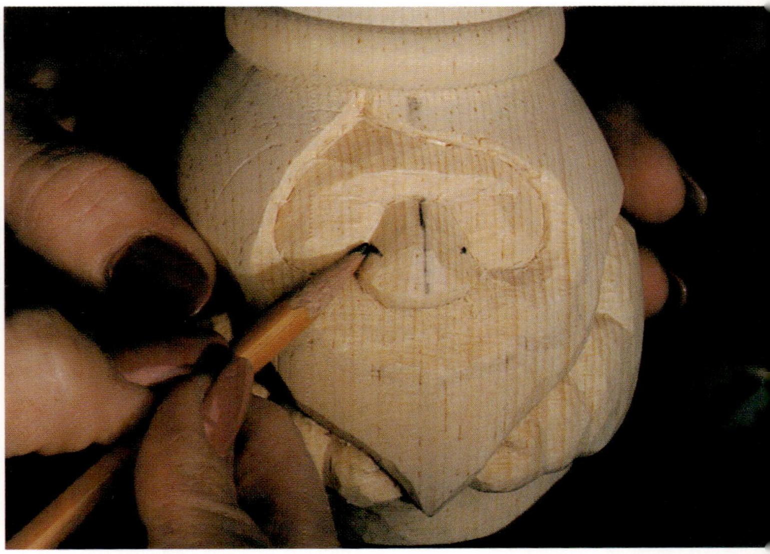

Make a mark at the top of the nostril, where it meets the cheek.

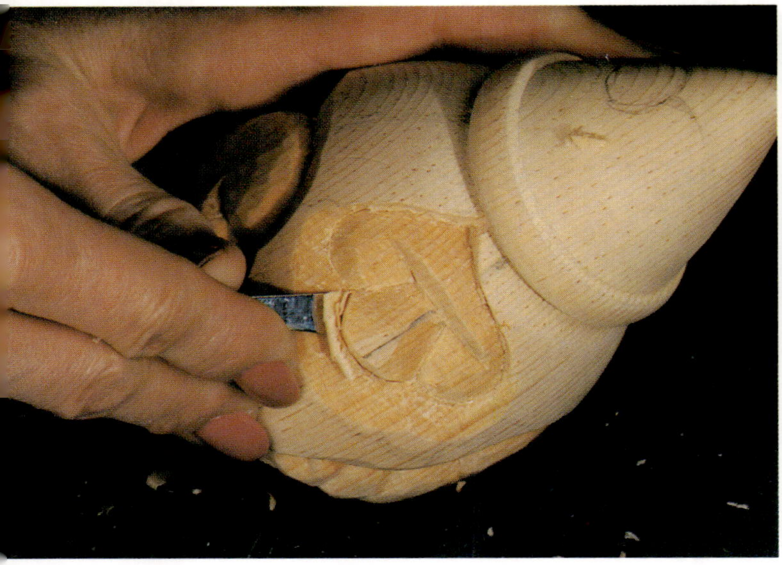

and come back to it from the moustache.

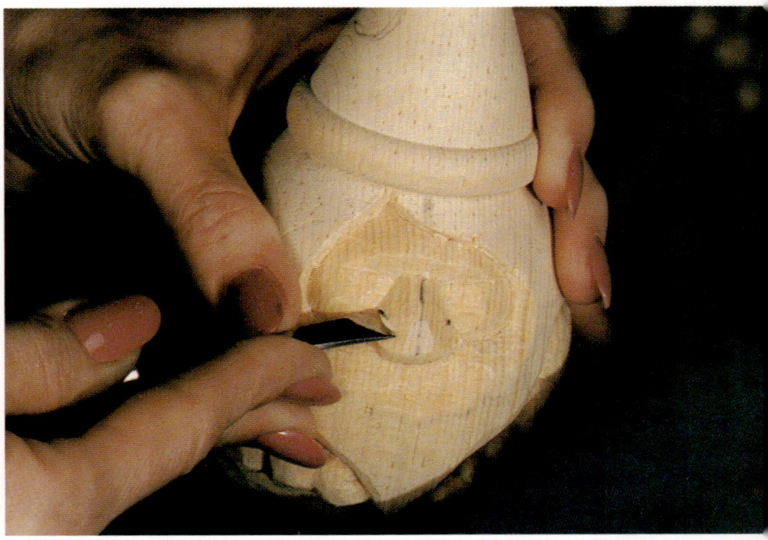

Place a corner of the chisel on the mark and angle the blade toward the tip of the nose. Push in...

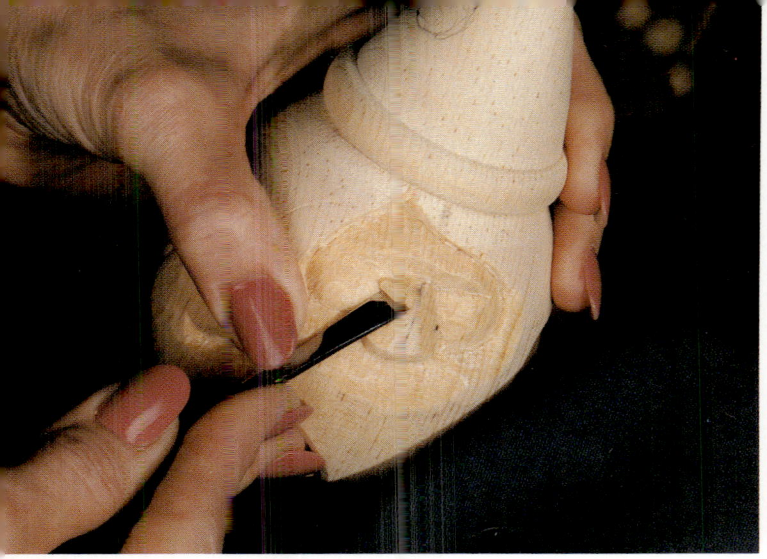

and cut up toward the bridge.

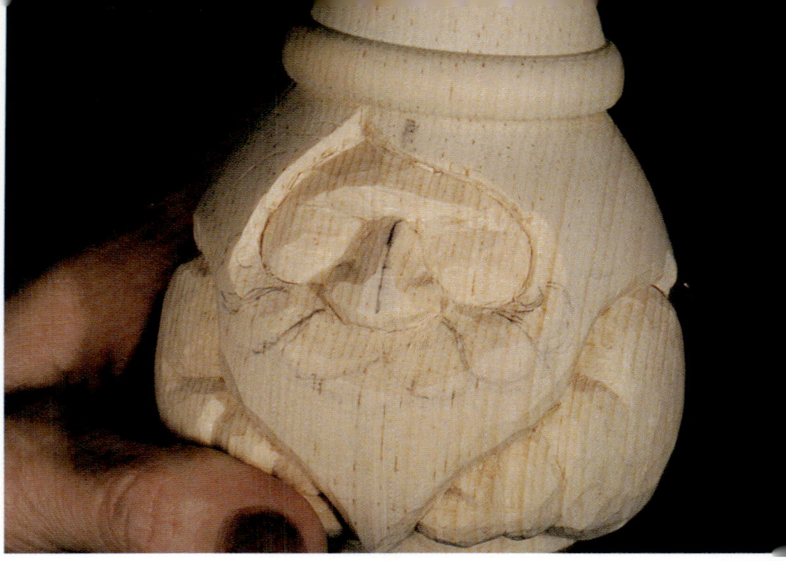

The result.

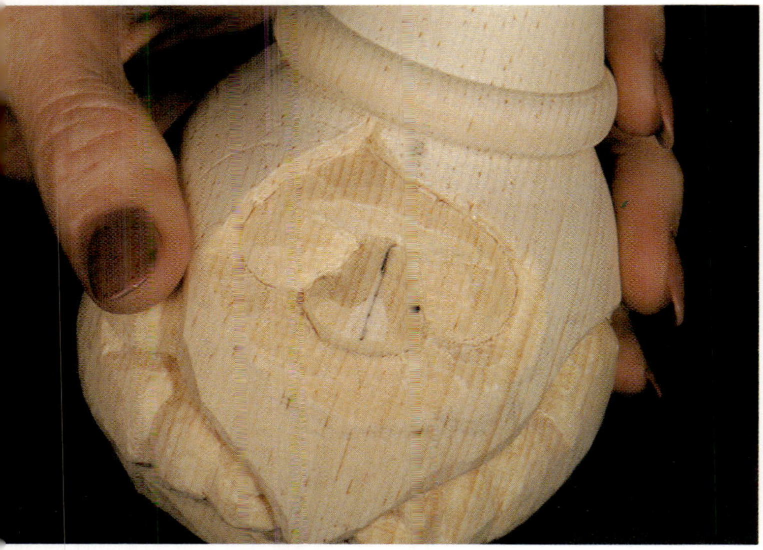

Repeat the process until you get to about this point.

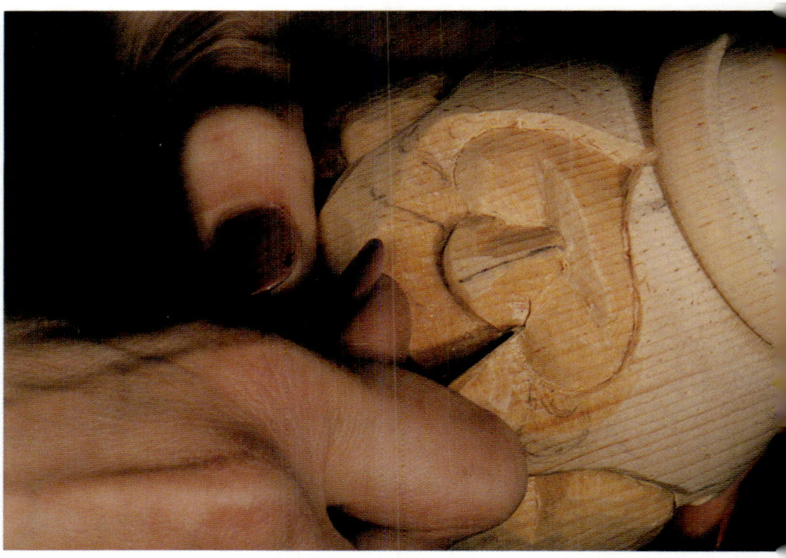

Score a smile line around the flange into the cheek.

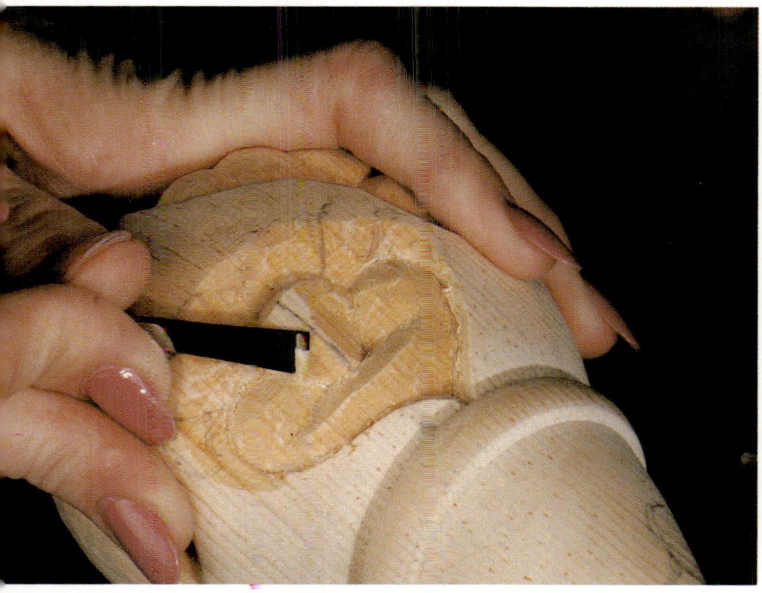

Repeat on the other side.

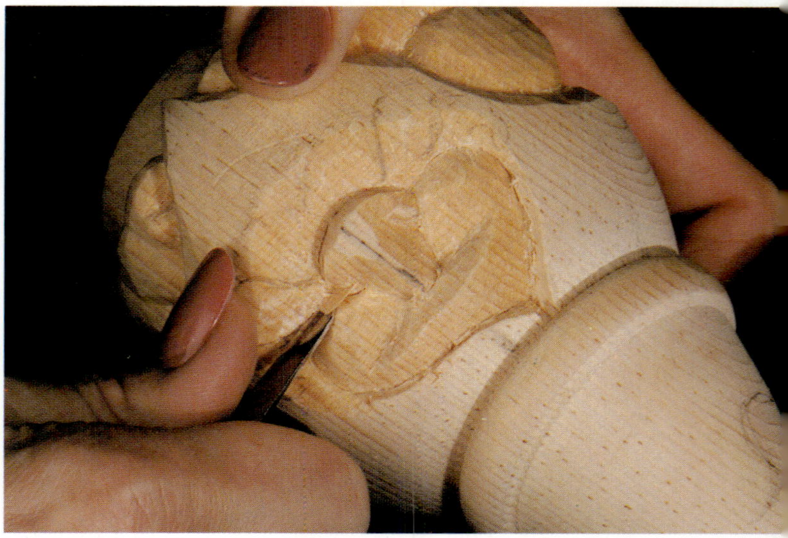

With the knife blade flat against the cheek slice back to the score.

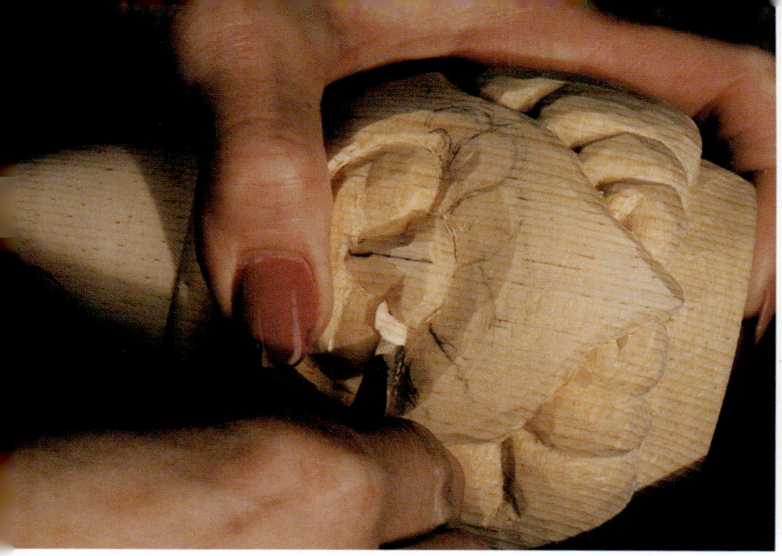

Repeat on the other side.

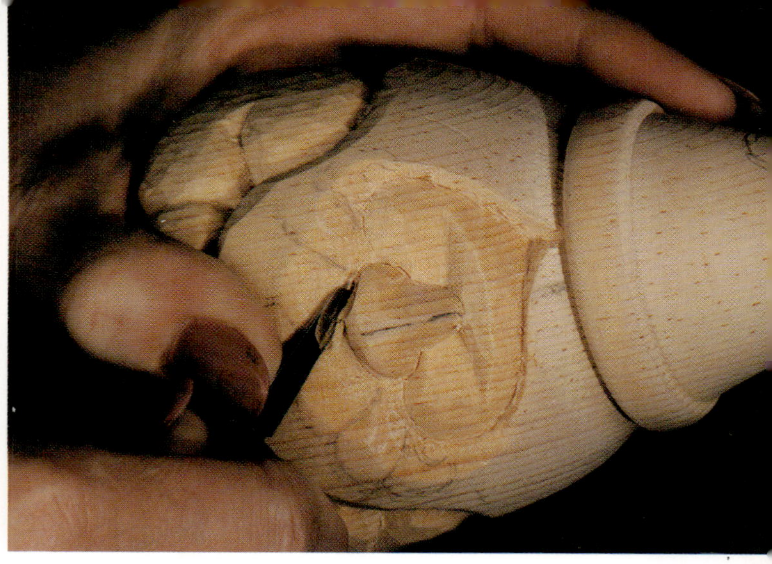

and come back to it from the moustache.

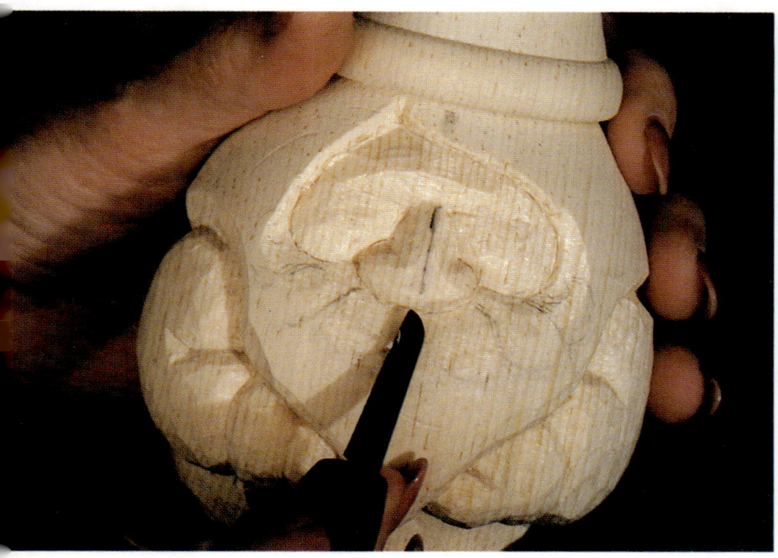

The result. Now we need to bring shape to the bottom of the nose.

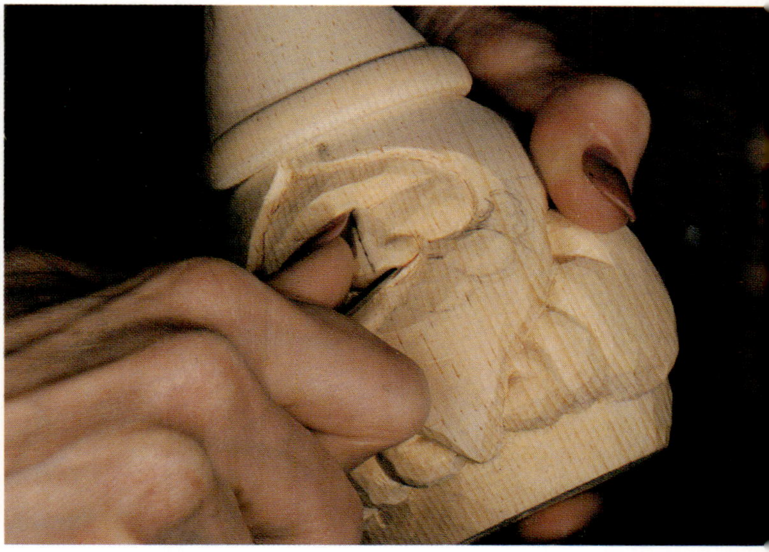

Repeat on the other side.

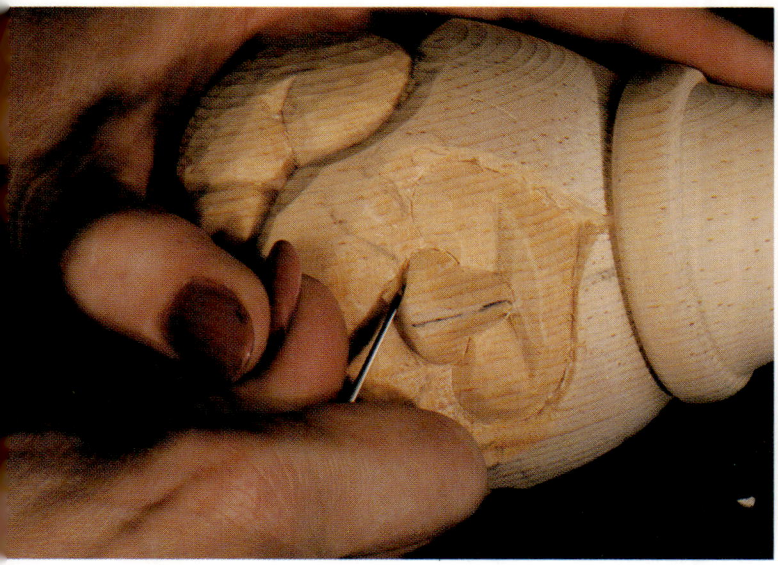

Cut the contour of the nostril straight in...

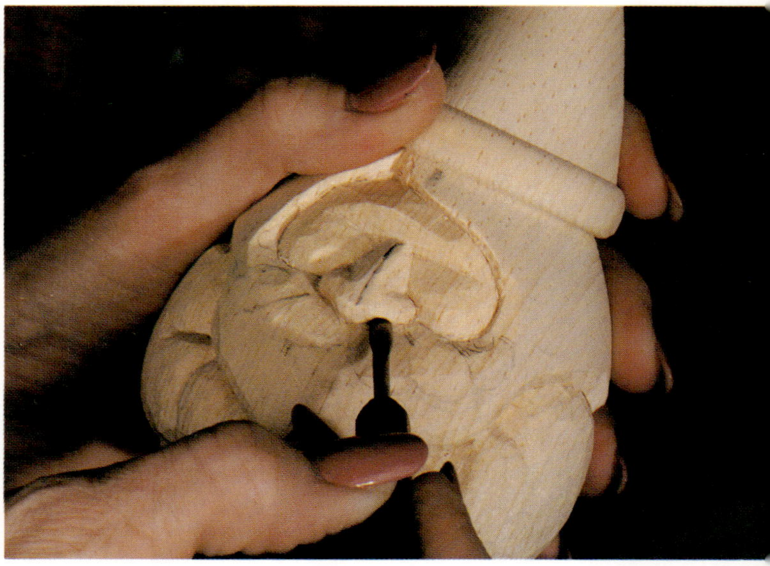

The final shaping of the nostril is done with a small curved gouge.

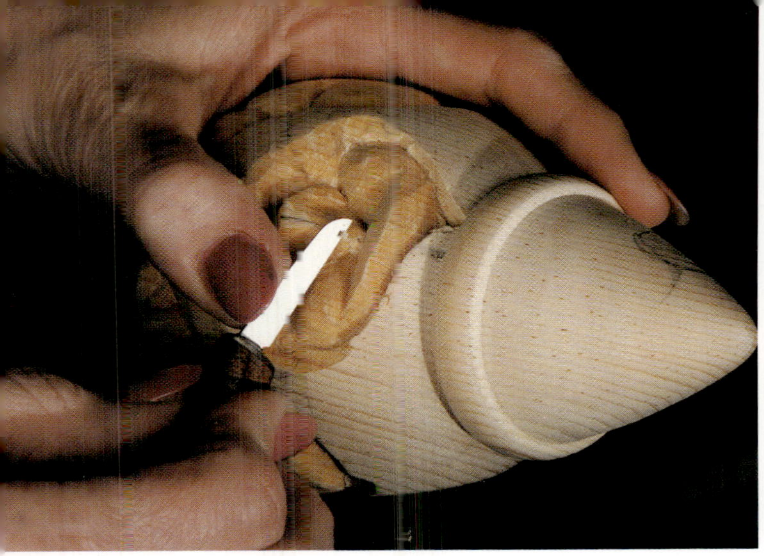

You can clean up the pencil mark down the middle of the nose with the knife

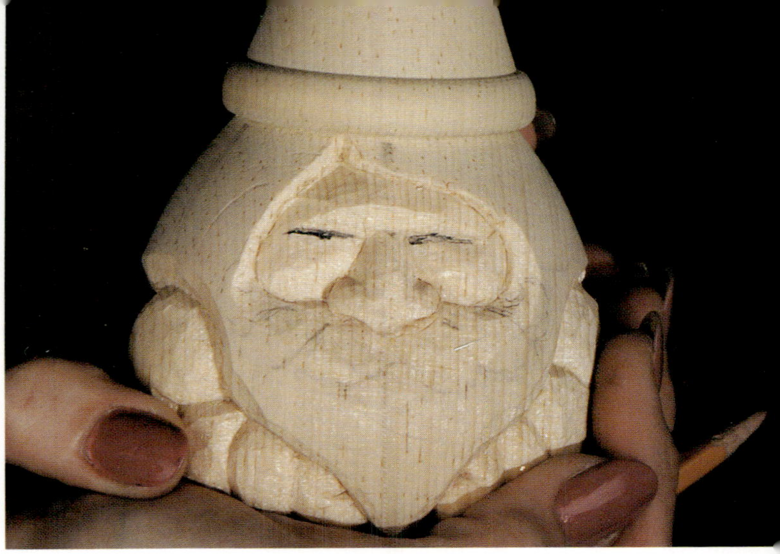

Better.

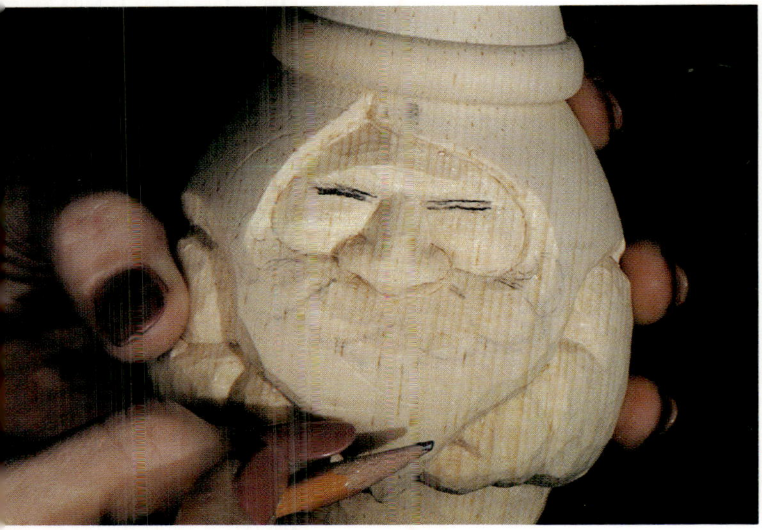

Draw the lines of the eyes to check for balance. There is a tendency for one or the other to go askew. Here Santa's left eye is slanted a little bit up

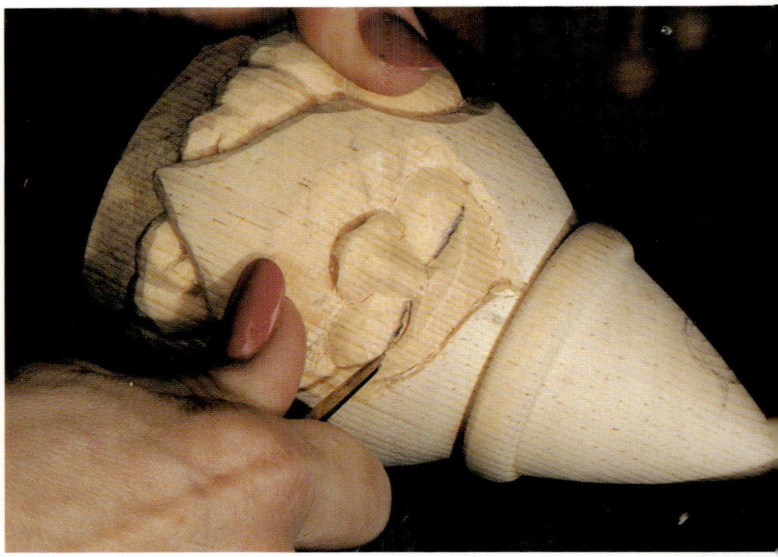

Score an arching line above the line of the eye.

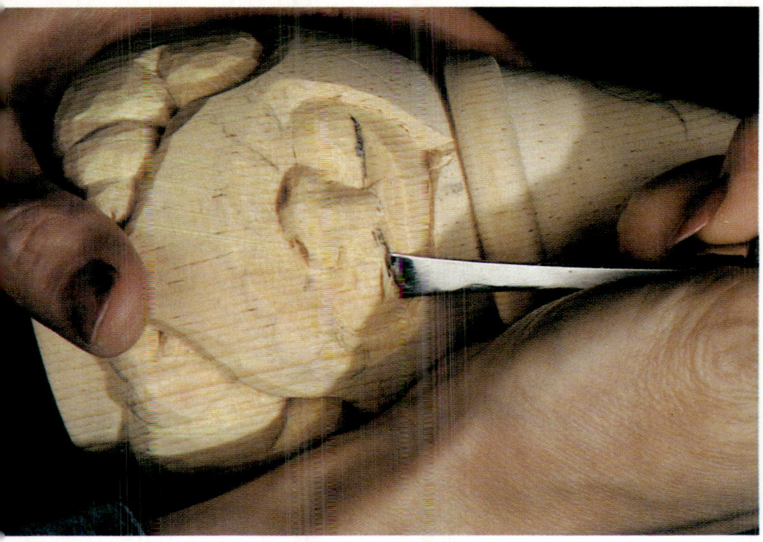

Drop the corner.

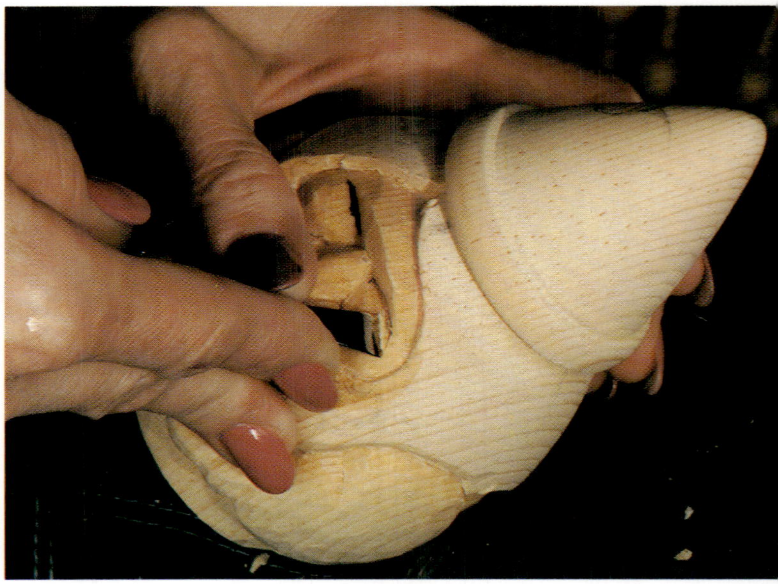

Chisel up to this line from the cheek.

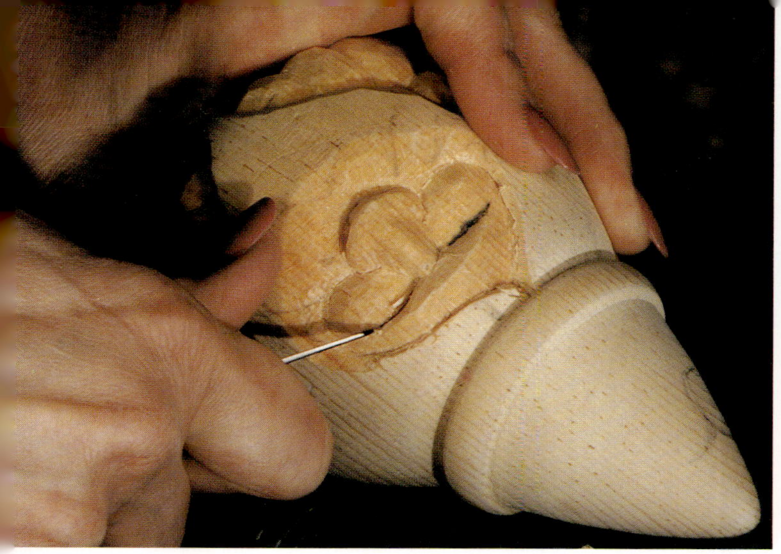

Repeat the process to deepen the eye.

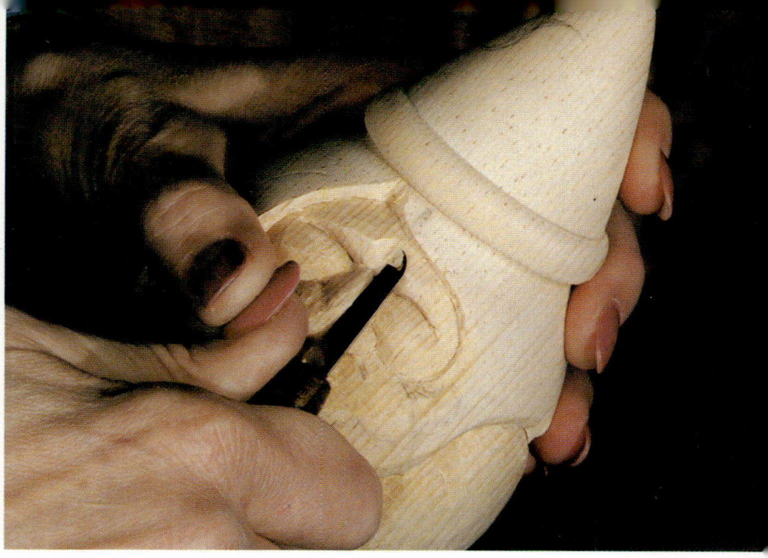

from both sides.

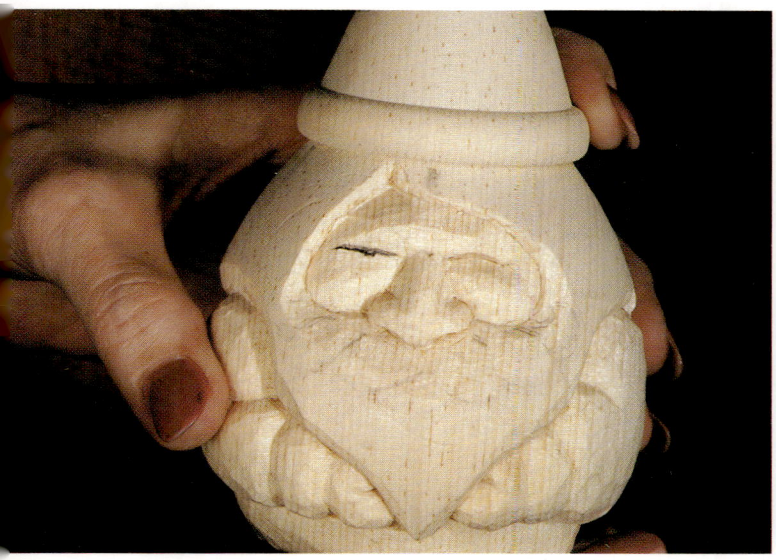

One side done. Repeat on the other.

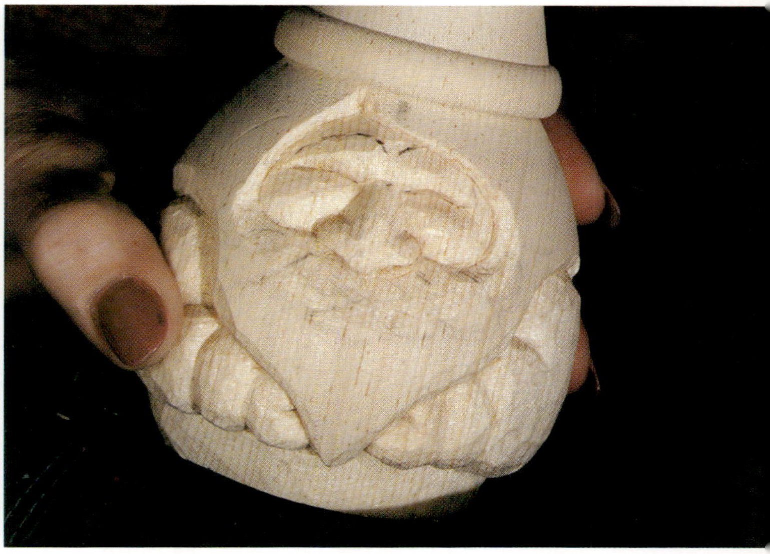

Here is the result. Draw the upper line of the eye brow.

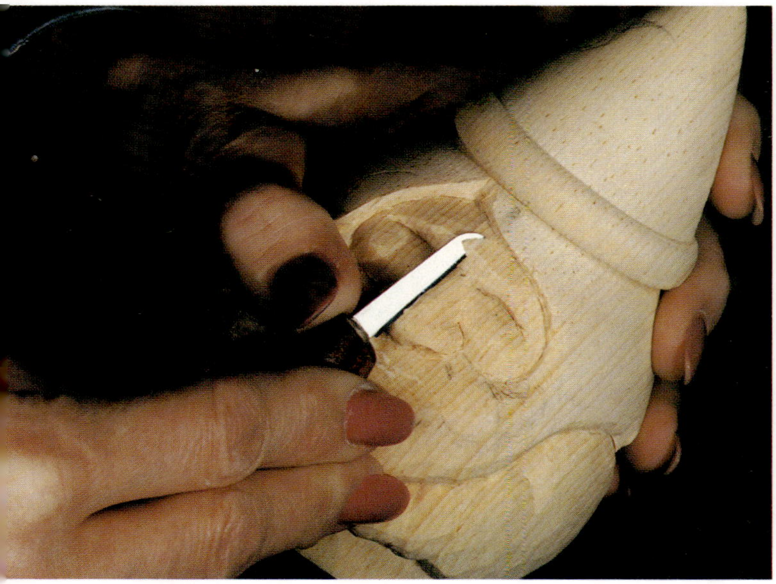

Scoop out between the eyebrows by coming...

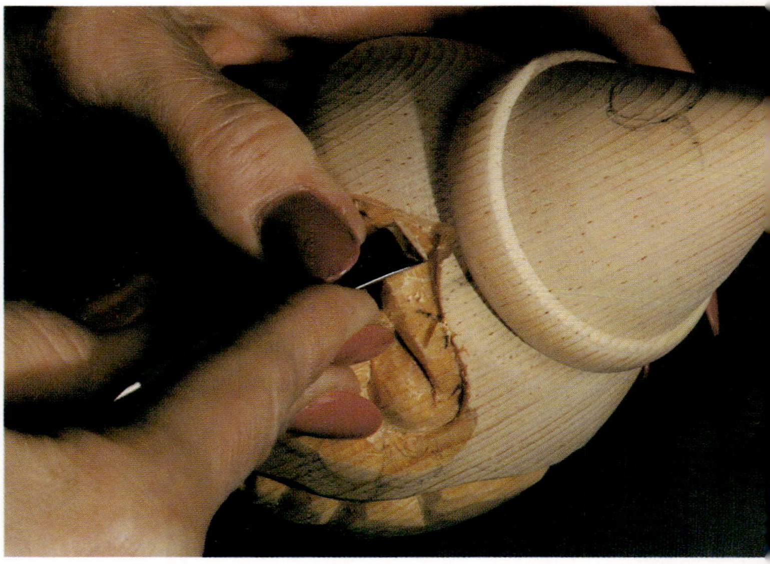

Go from the eyebrow to the hairline with a chisel, with a scooping cut that blends the brow to the forehead.

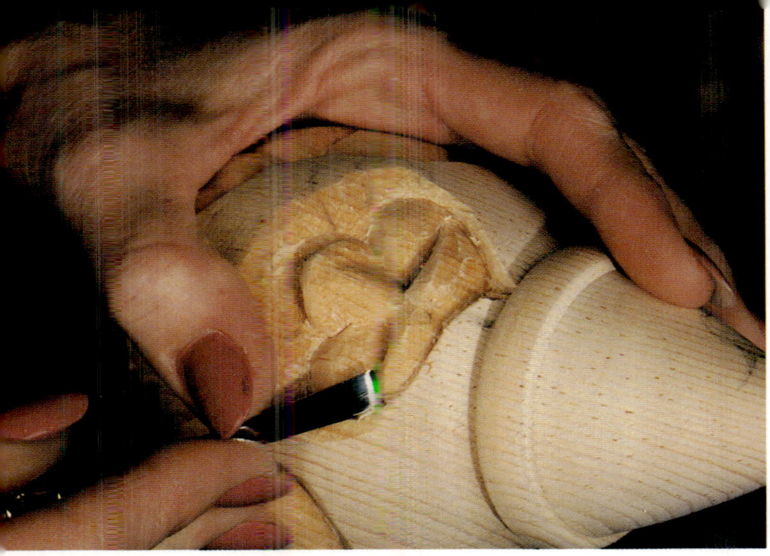

Much of the other brow is under the hair line, so there isn't as much carving.

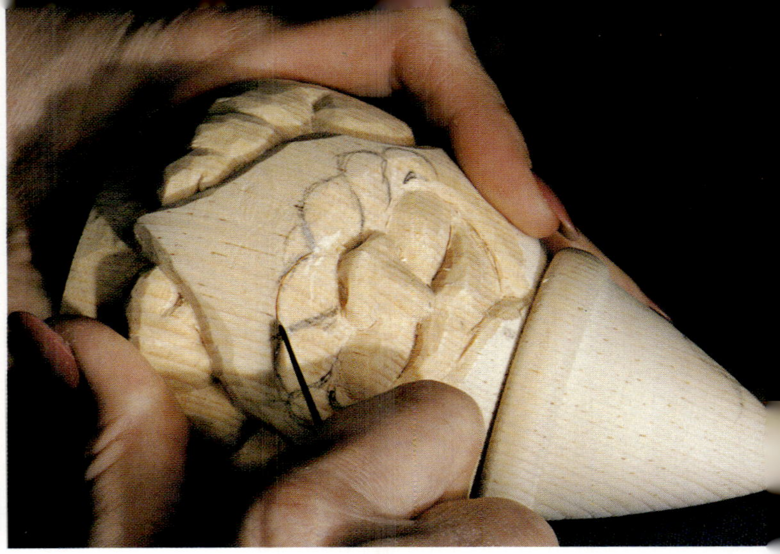

Score along the lower edge of the moustache...

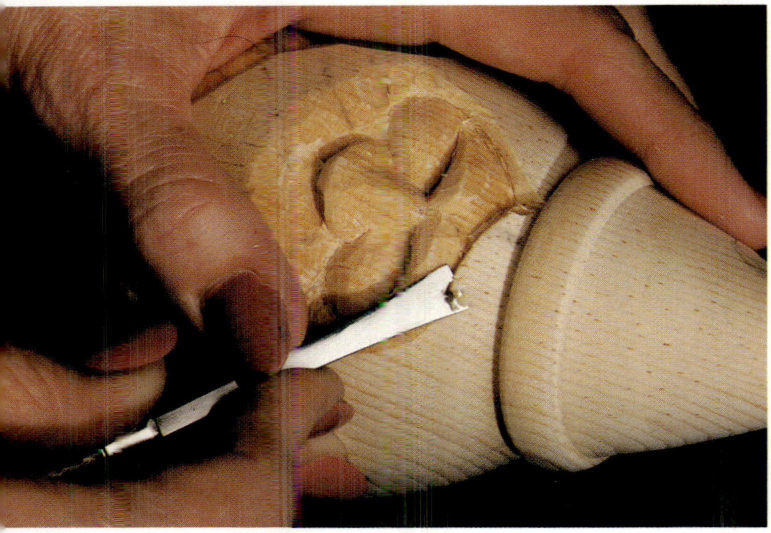

Round the edge of the hair around the face.

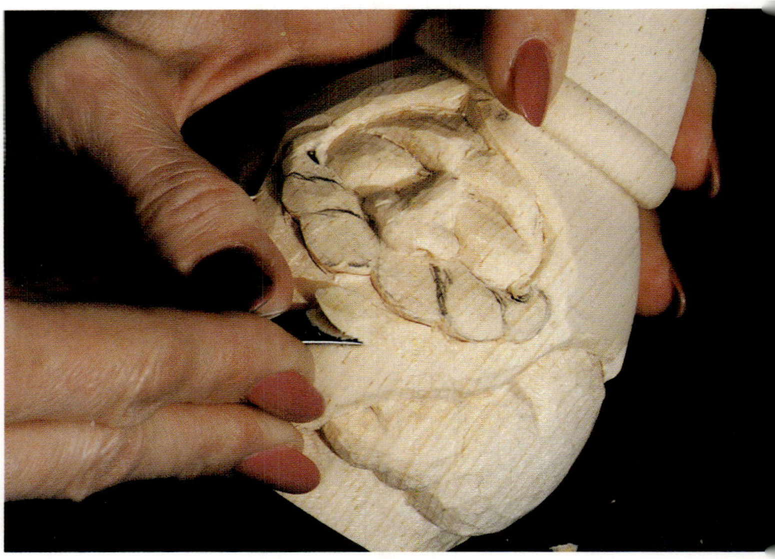

and trim back with the gouge.

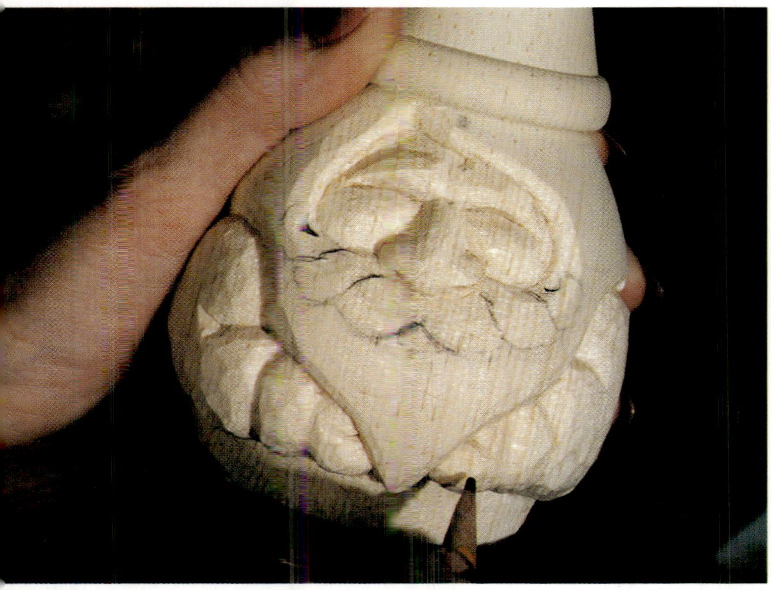

Redraw the segments of the moustache and the lower lip.

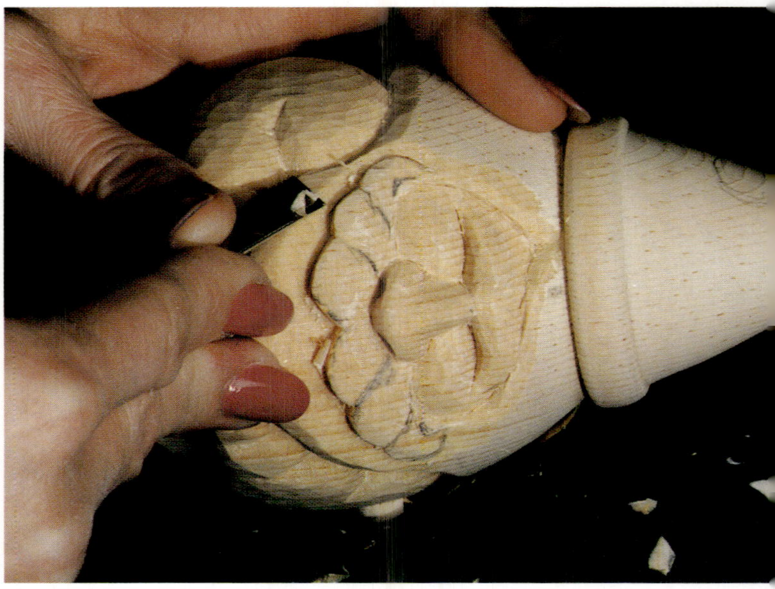

Shape the edges of the beard. Remember to cut down hill.

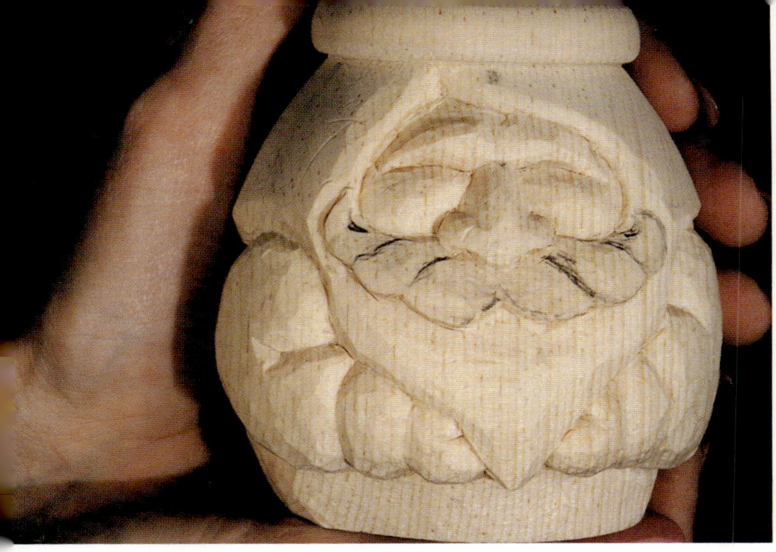

Progress. I have the shape of the beard and the depth of the moustache.

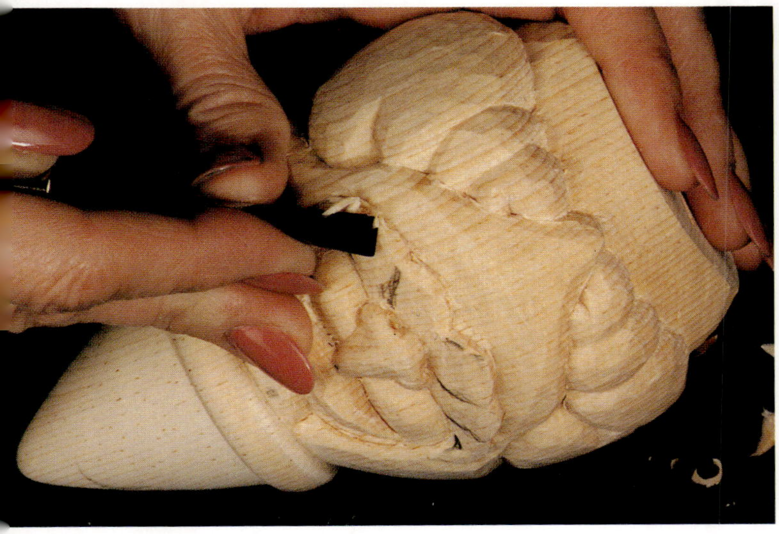

Round off the moustache.

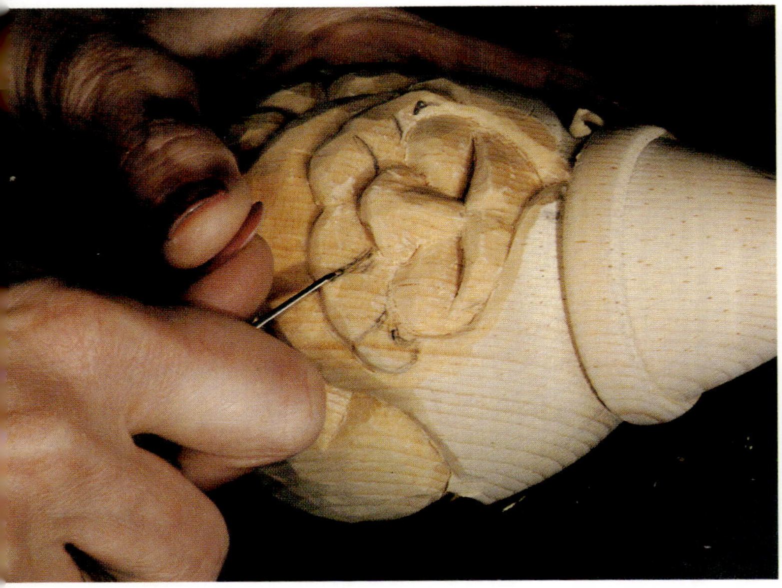

Score the segment lines of the moustache.

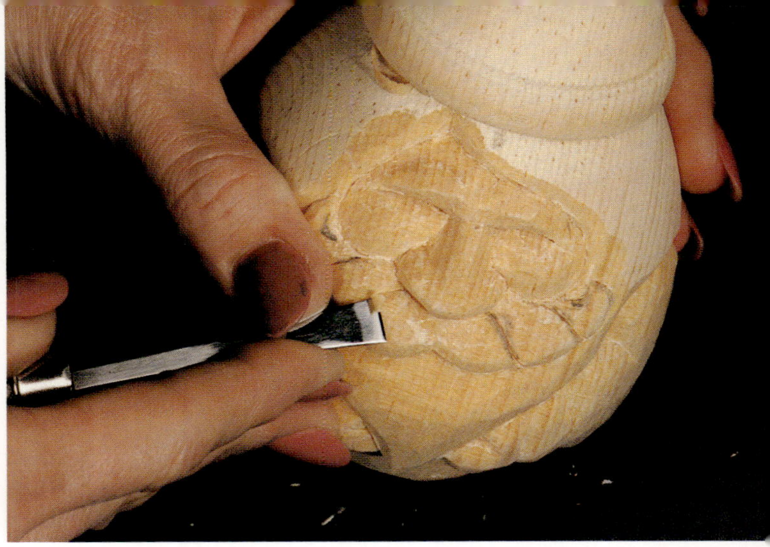

Round the edges of each segment back to the score line.

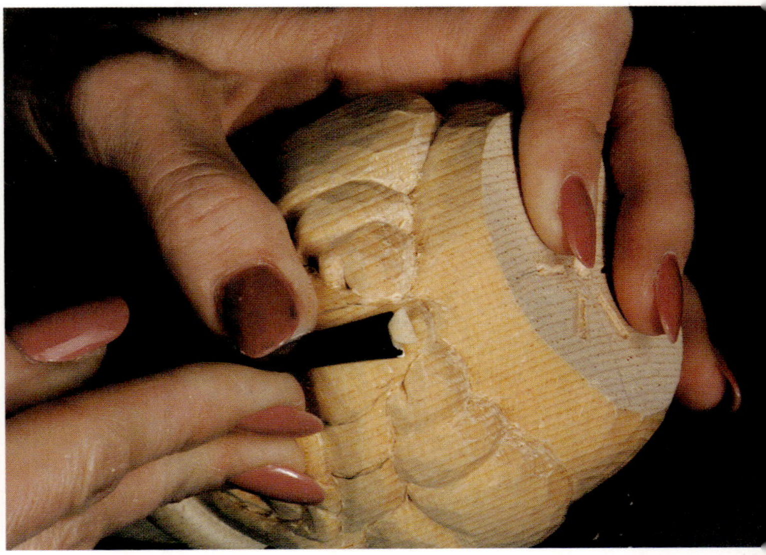

You can add a little curl to the end of the beard using a scooping cut with the chisel.

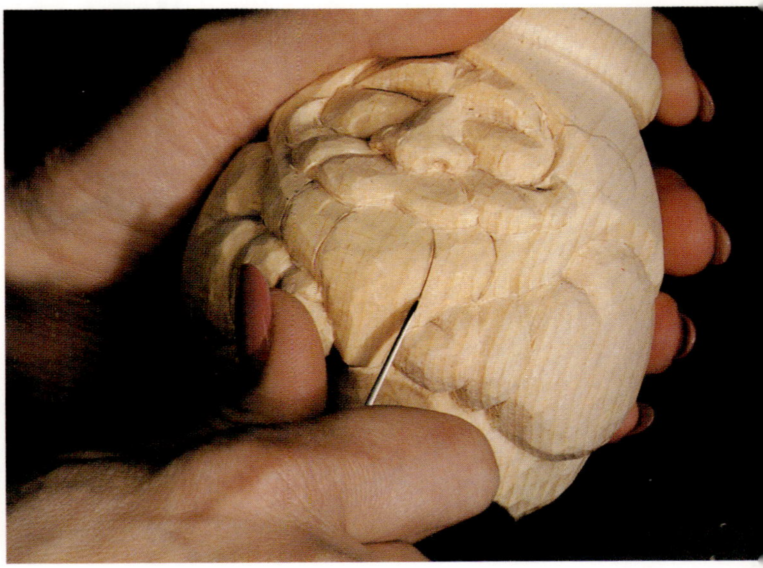

Scribe the segment lines.

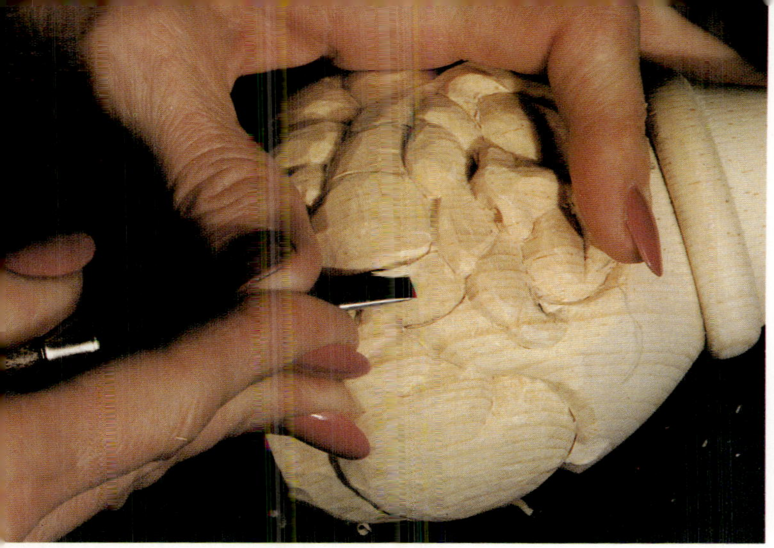

Round each segment of the beard back to the scribe lines.

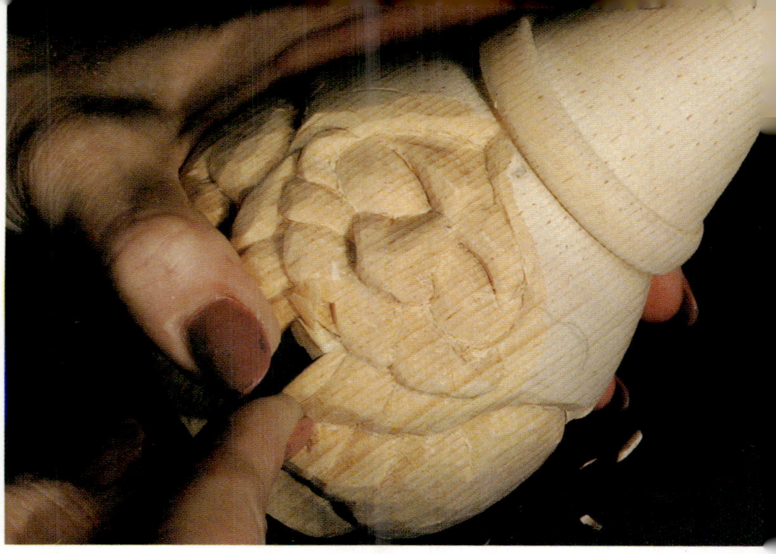

and cut back to it from the beard.

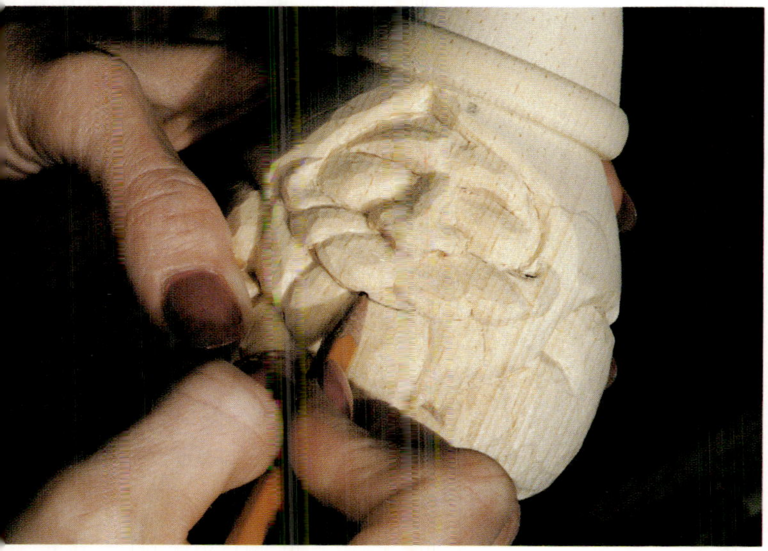

Redraw the lip.

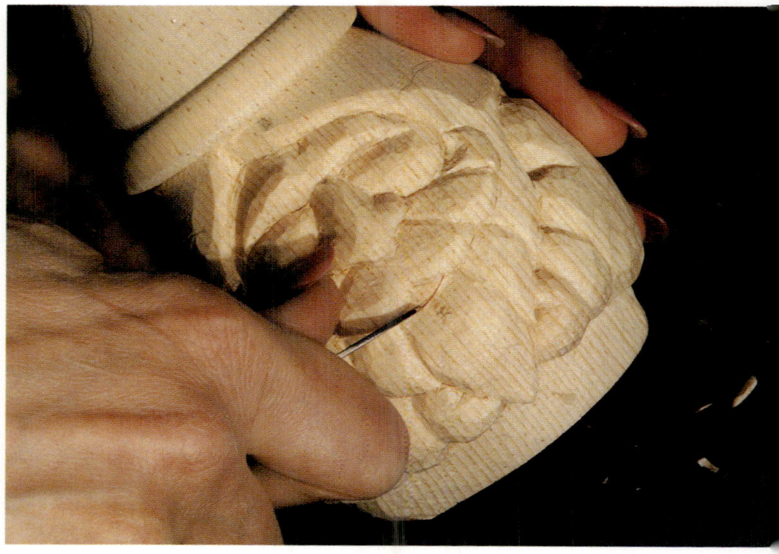

Deepen the cut until you like the result.

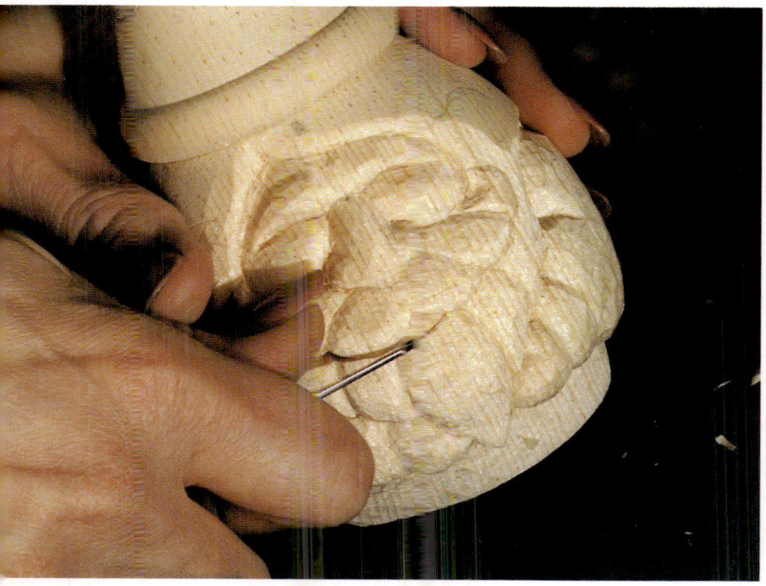

Score the line...

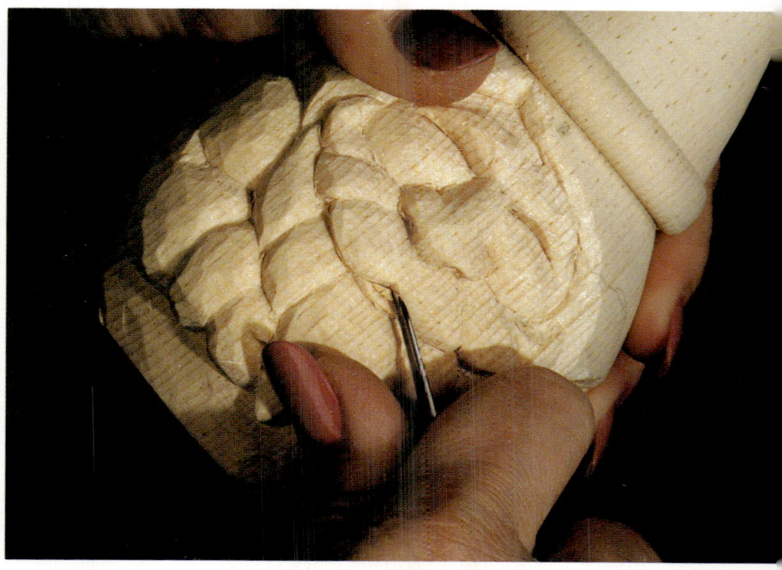

Open the mouth by scoring along one side of the moustache line...

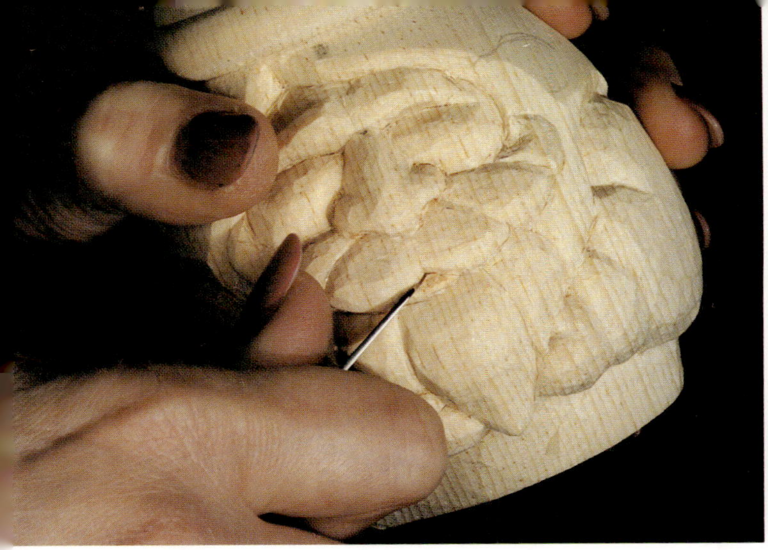

the other and clipping out from the lip.

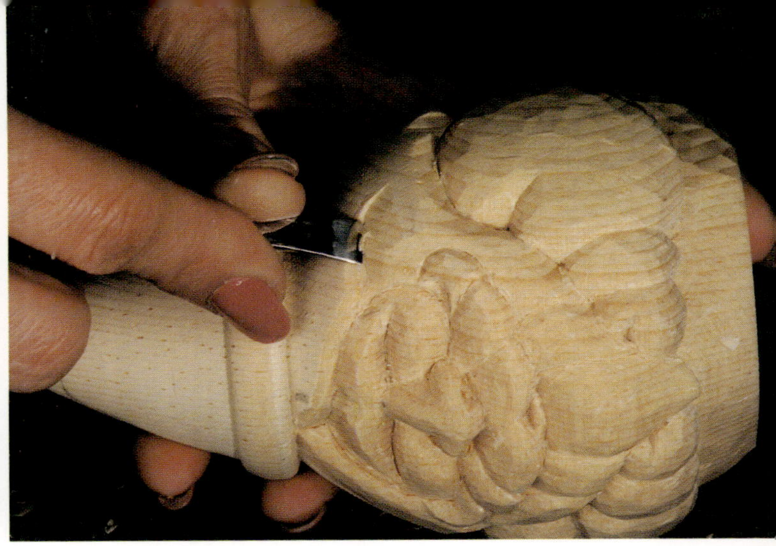

Then round off the wisp.

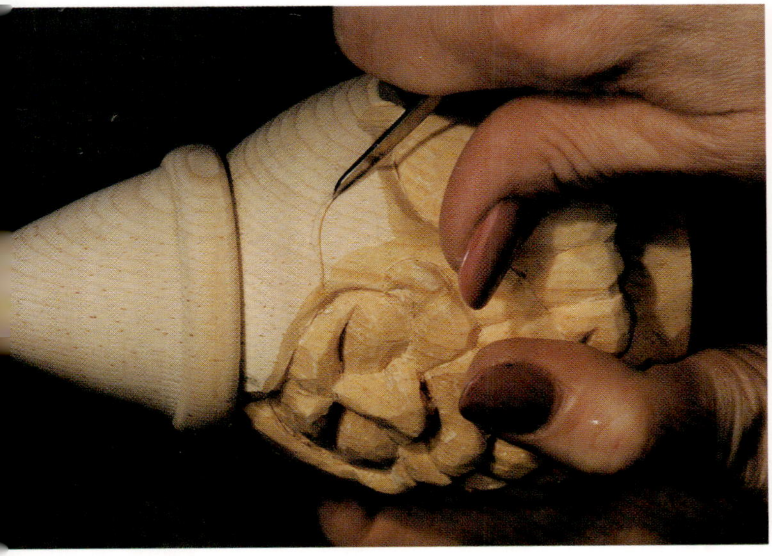

Score a line for the wisp of hair to the side of the face.

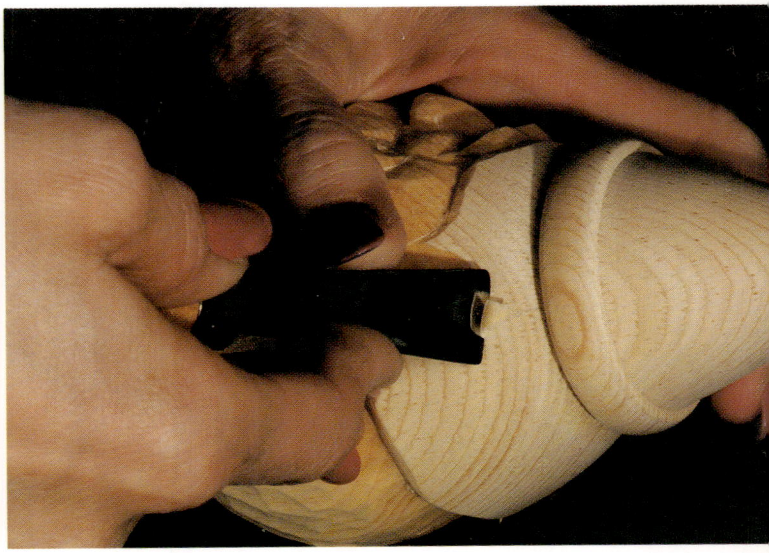

With a wide gouge, give texture to the hair.

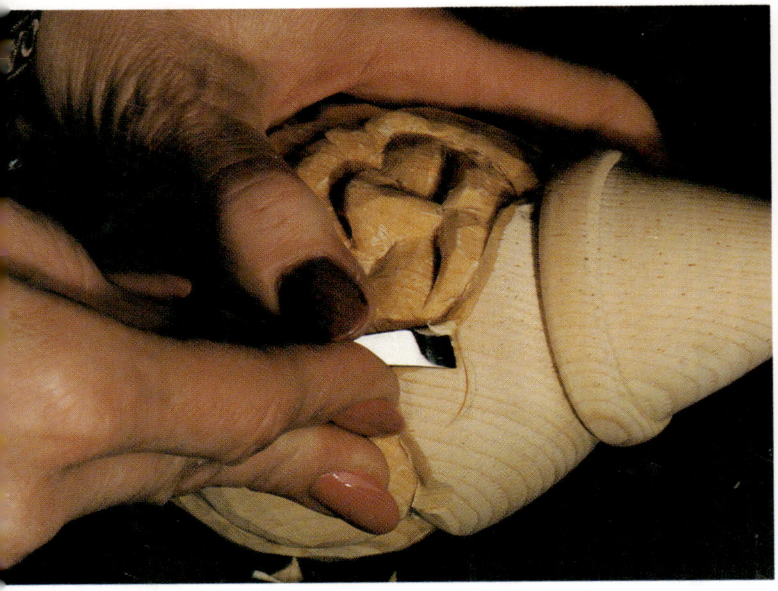

Cut back to it from below.

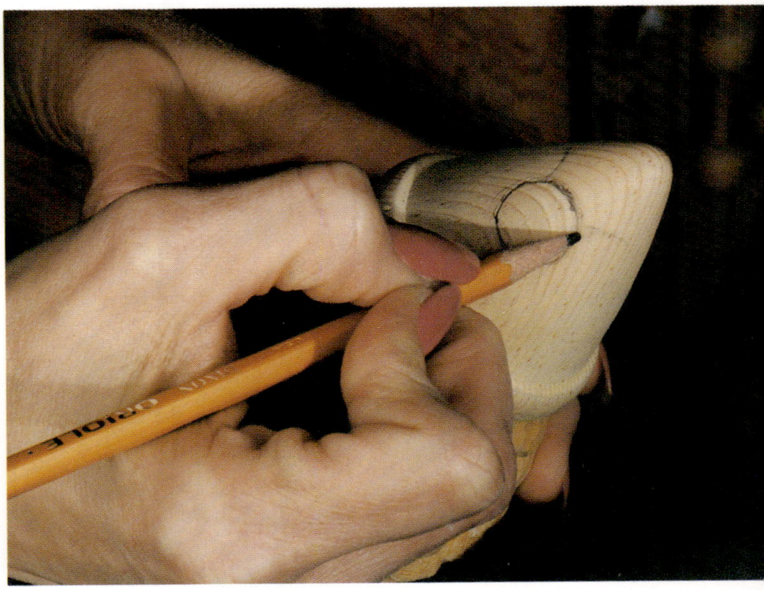

Draw in the pom-pom of the hat.

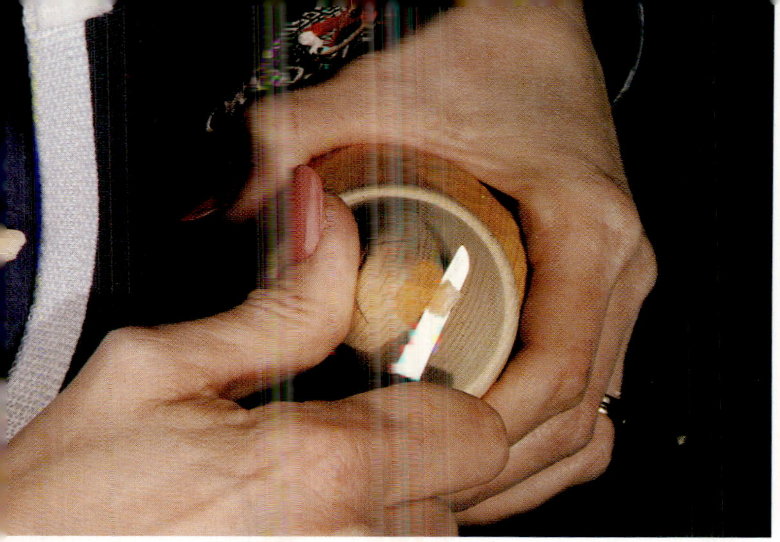

and round over the end of the hat.

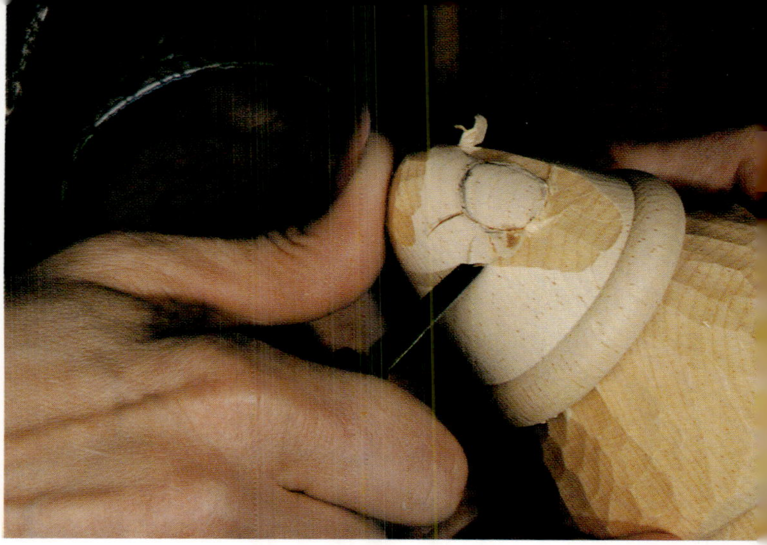

and along the sides.

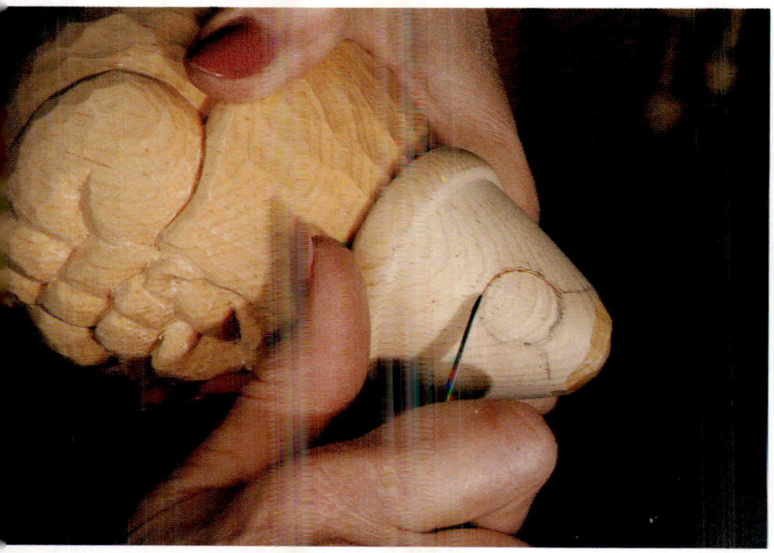

Score around the pom-pom.

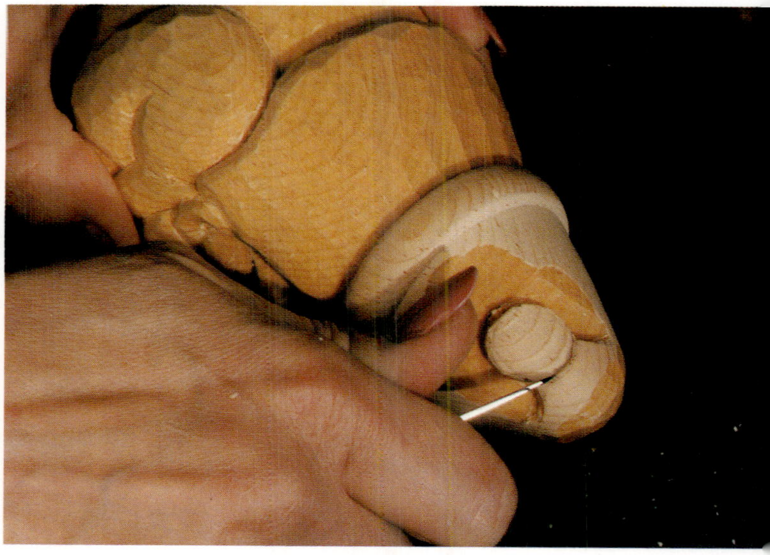

Score along the top of the pom-pom

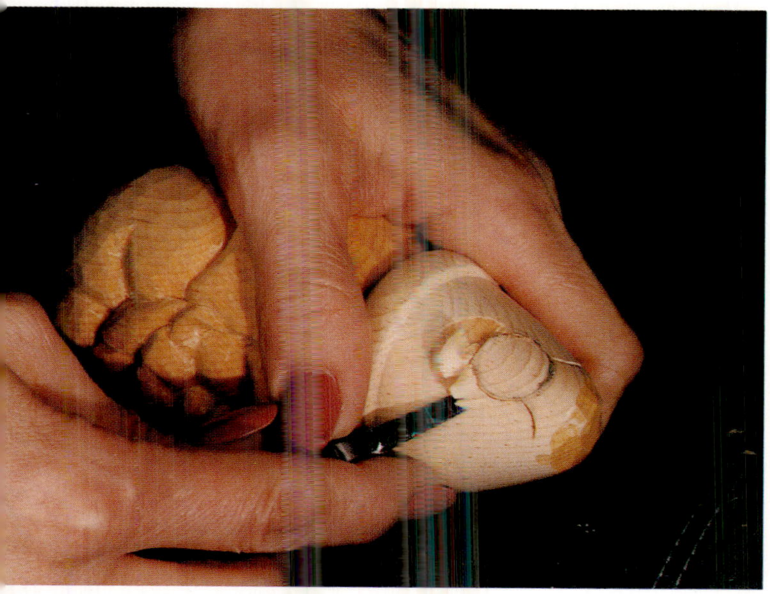

Cut underneath it...

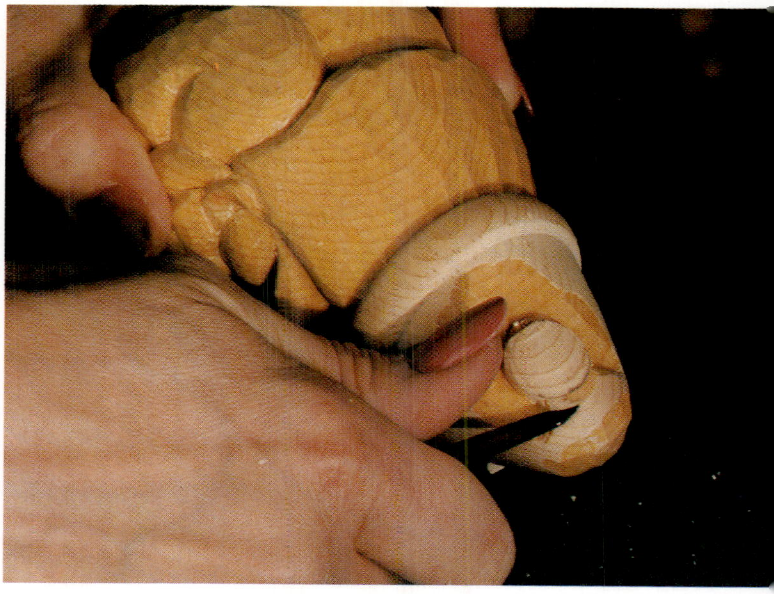

and trim back from the hat.

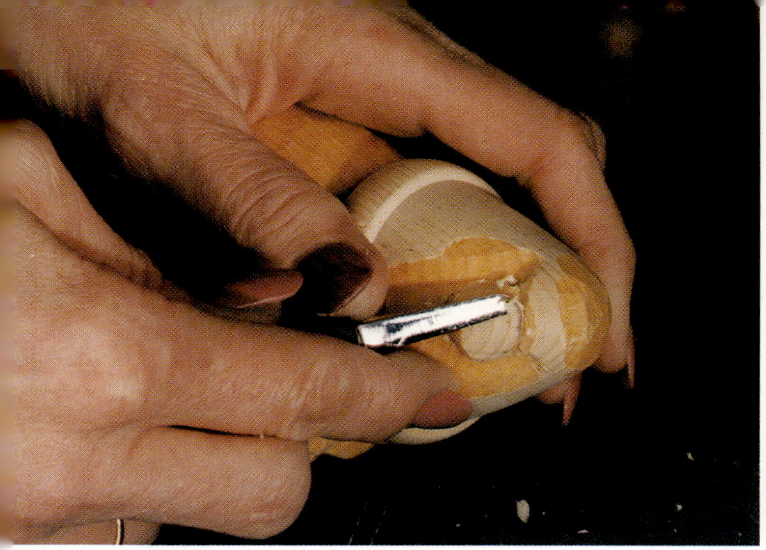

Round off the pom-pom.

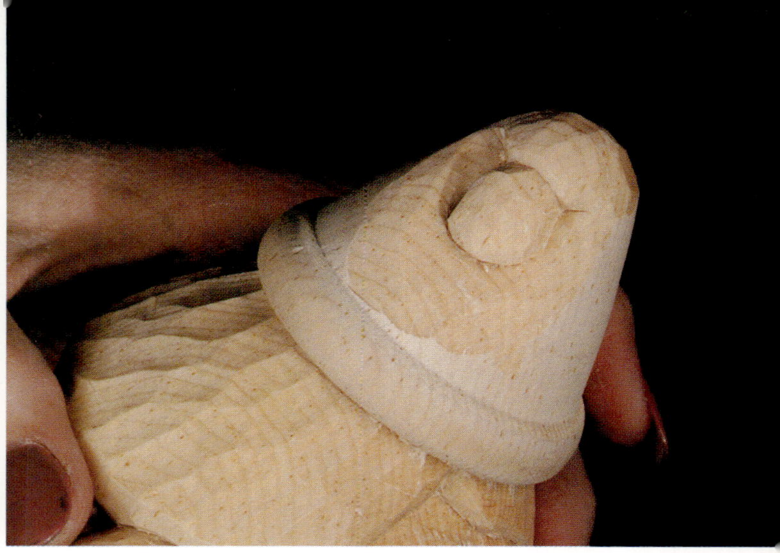

The result.

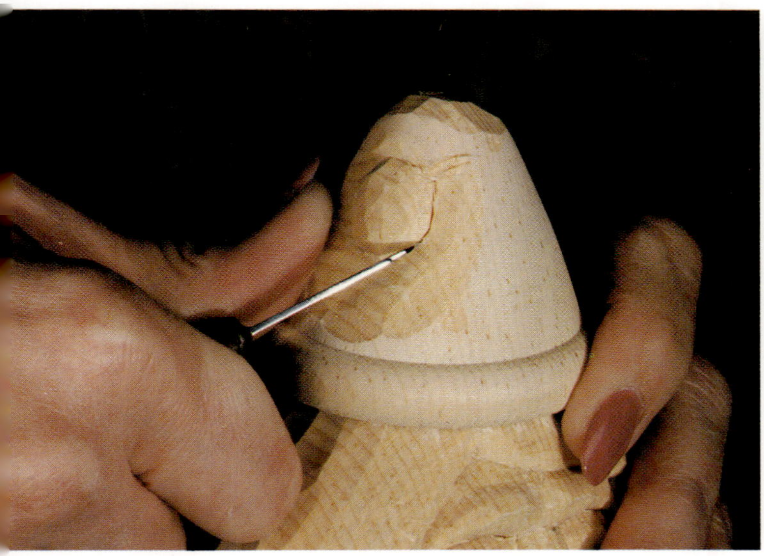

Underscore the pom-pom to make it seem as if it is sitting on top of the hat. In underscoring the cut should be angled under the element to be emphasized.

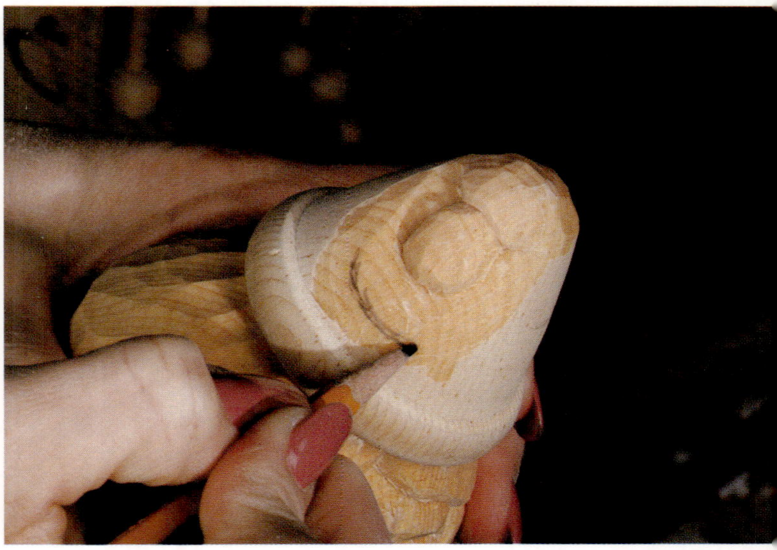

Some wrinkles around the hat...

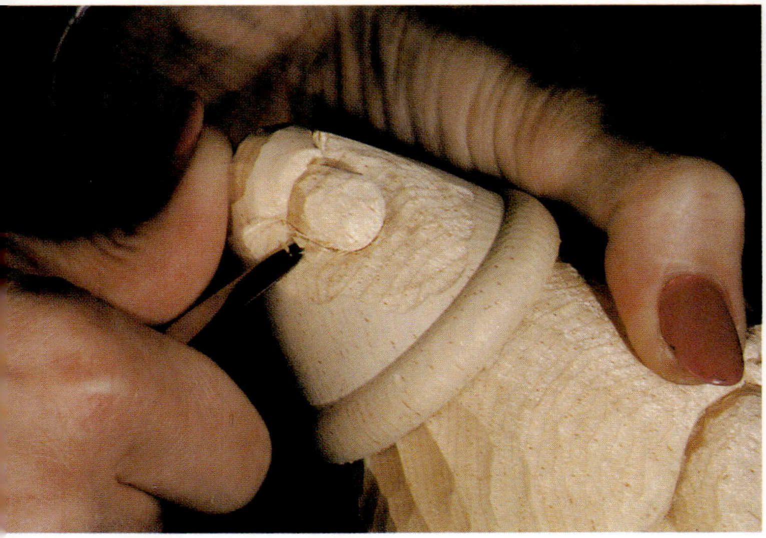

Trim back to it.

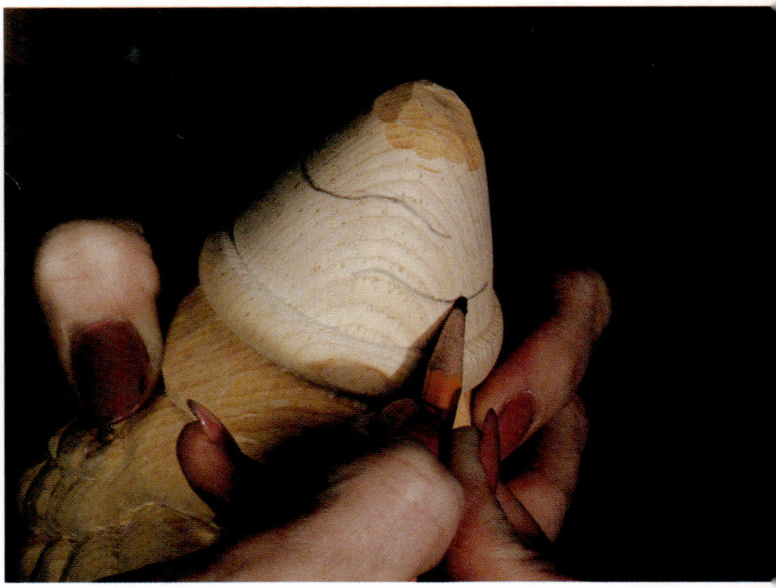

will add interest.

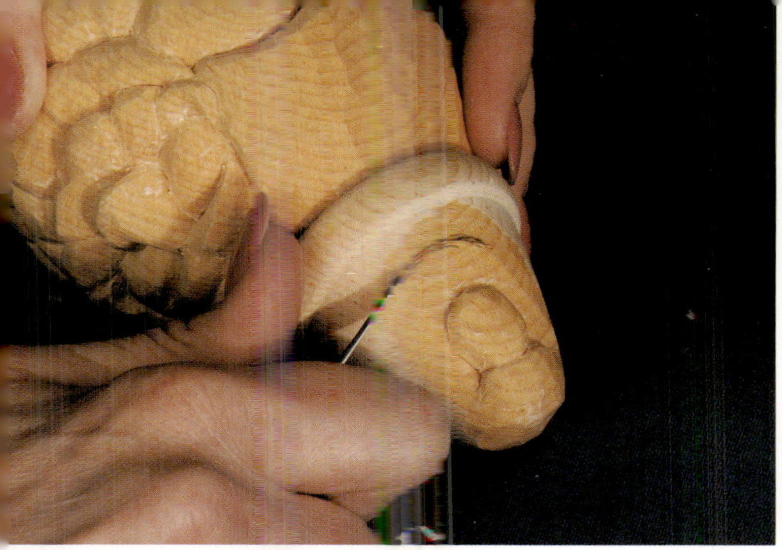

Score the wrinkle lines...

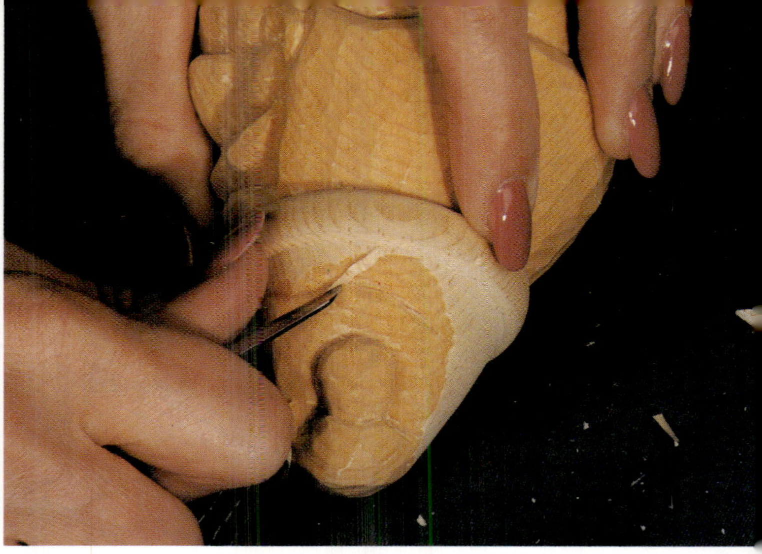

Round and blend the cuts into the line.

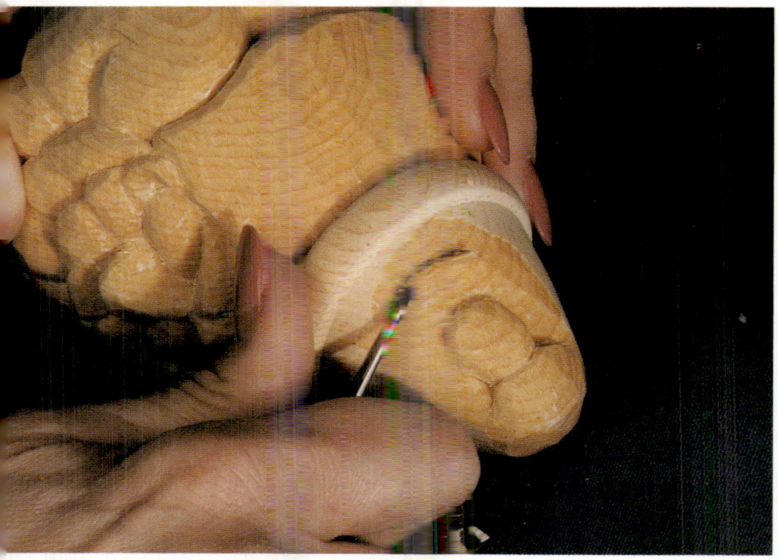

Wedge cut back to them from above...

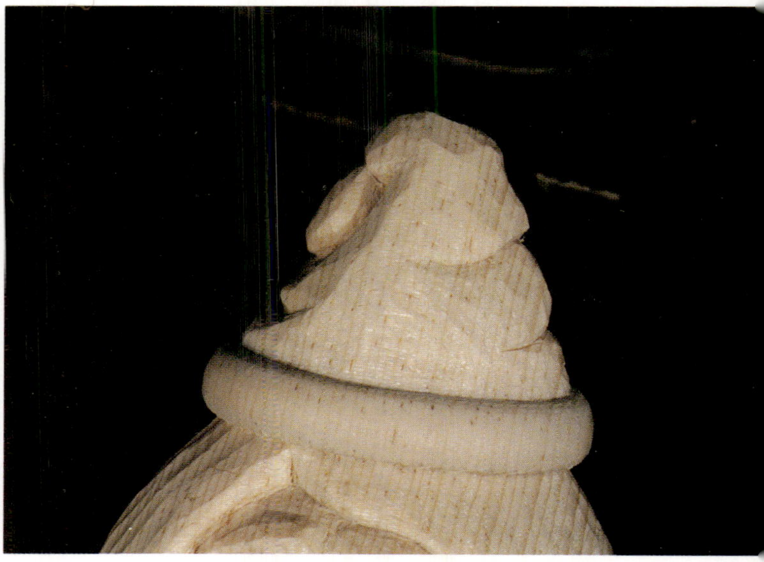

The result.

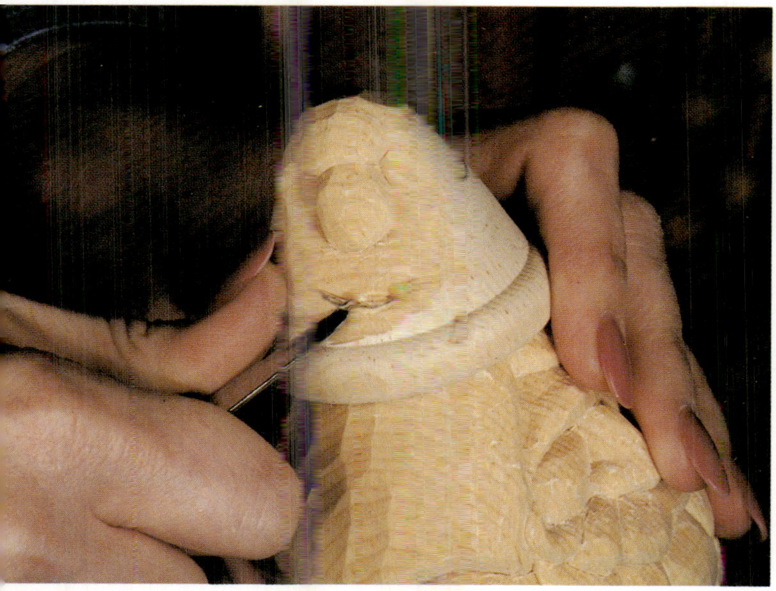

and below.

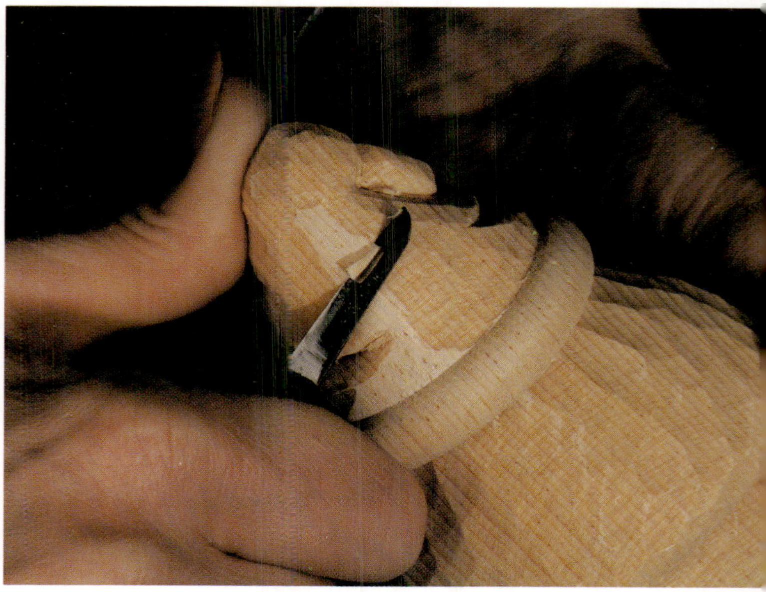

Clean up the smooth lathe surface.

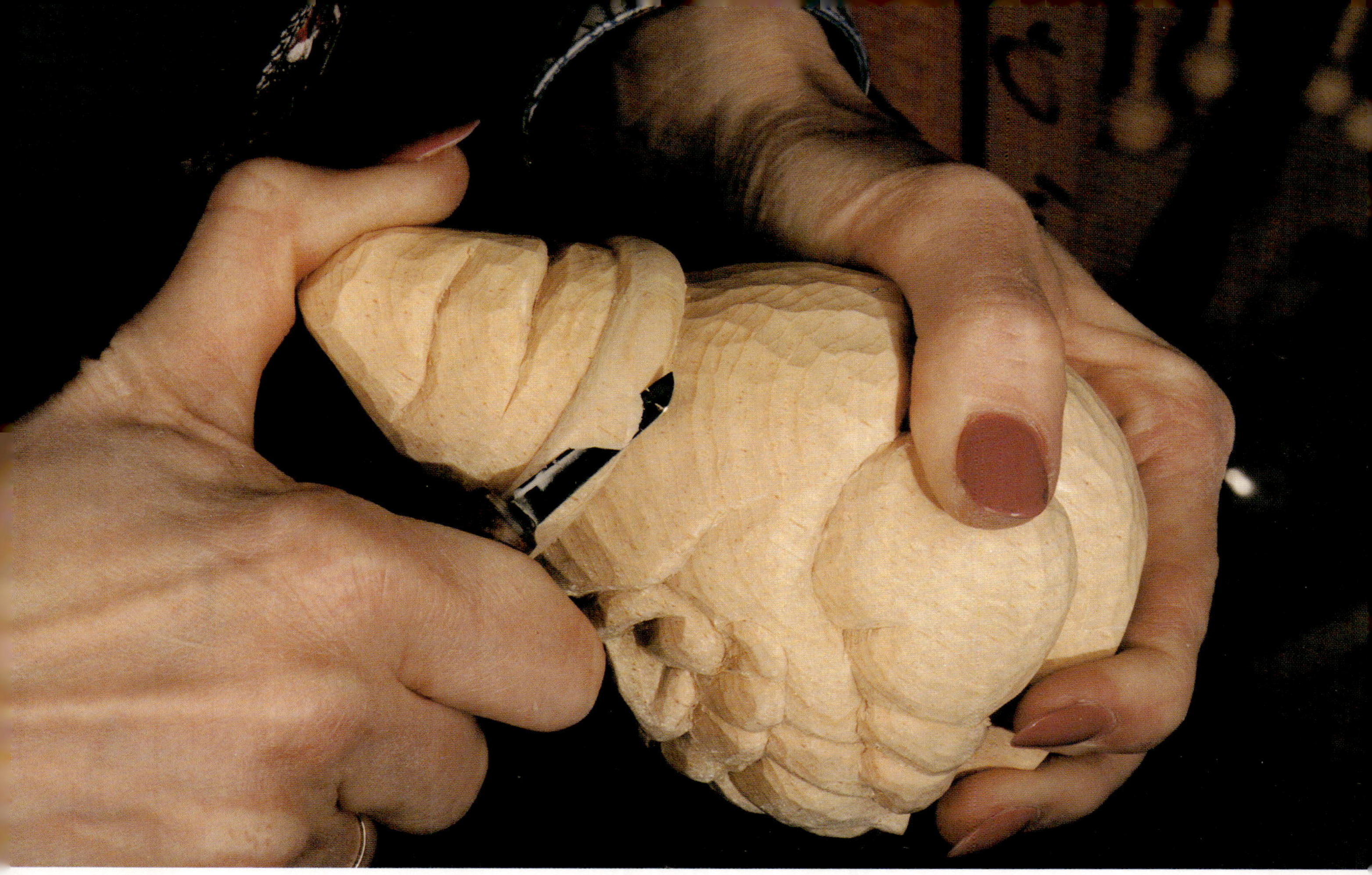

Leave the fur trim rounded or flatten it to create a decorative band.

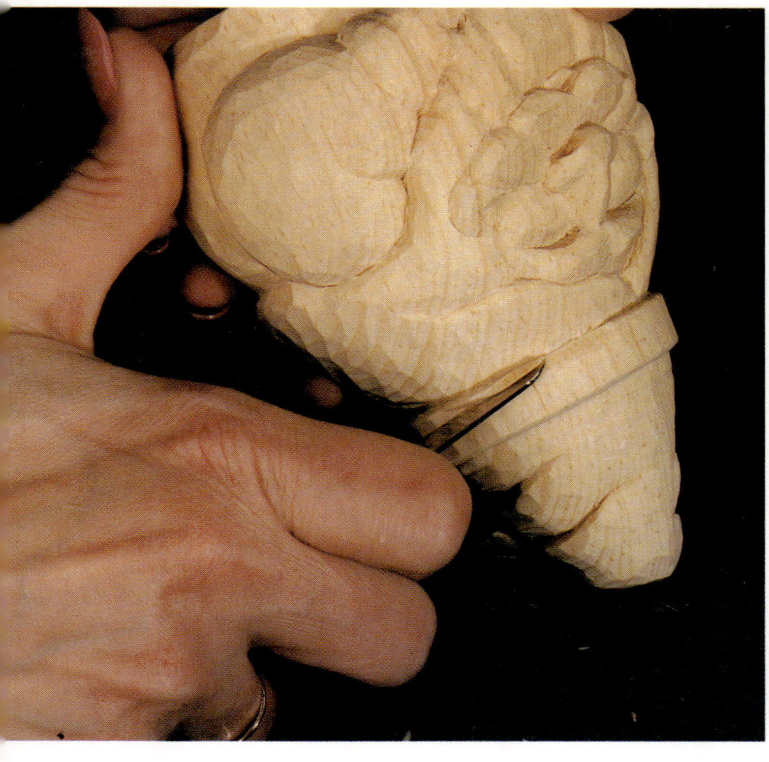

Round the edge of the band.

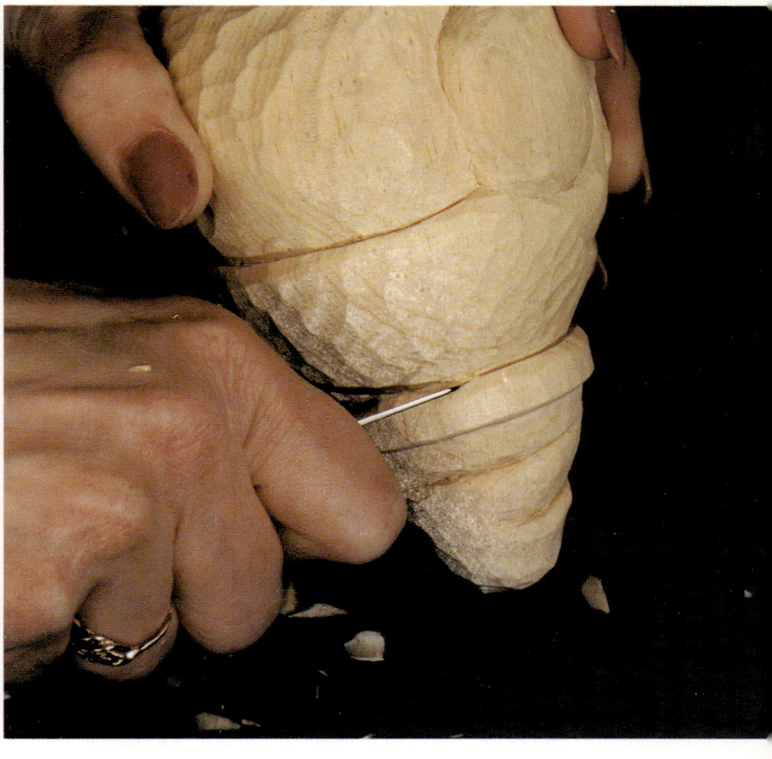

Undercut the bottom edge of the trim.

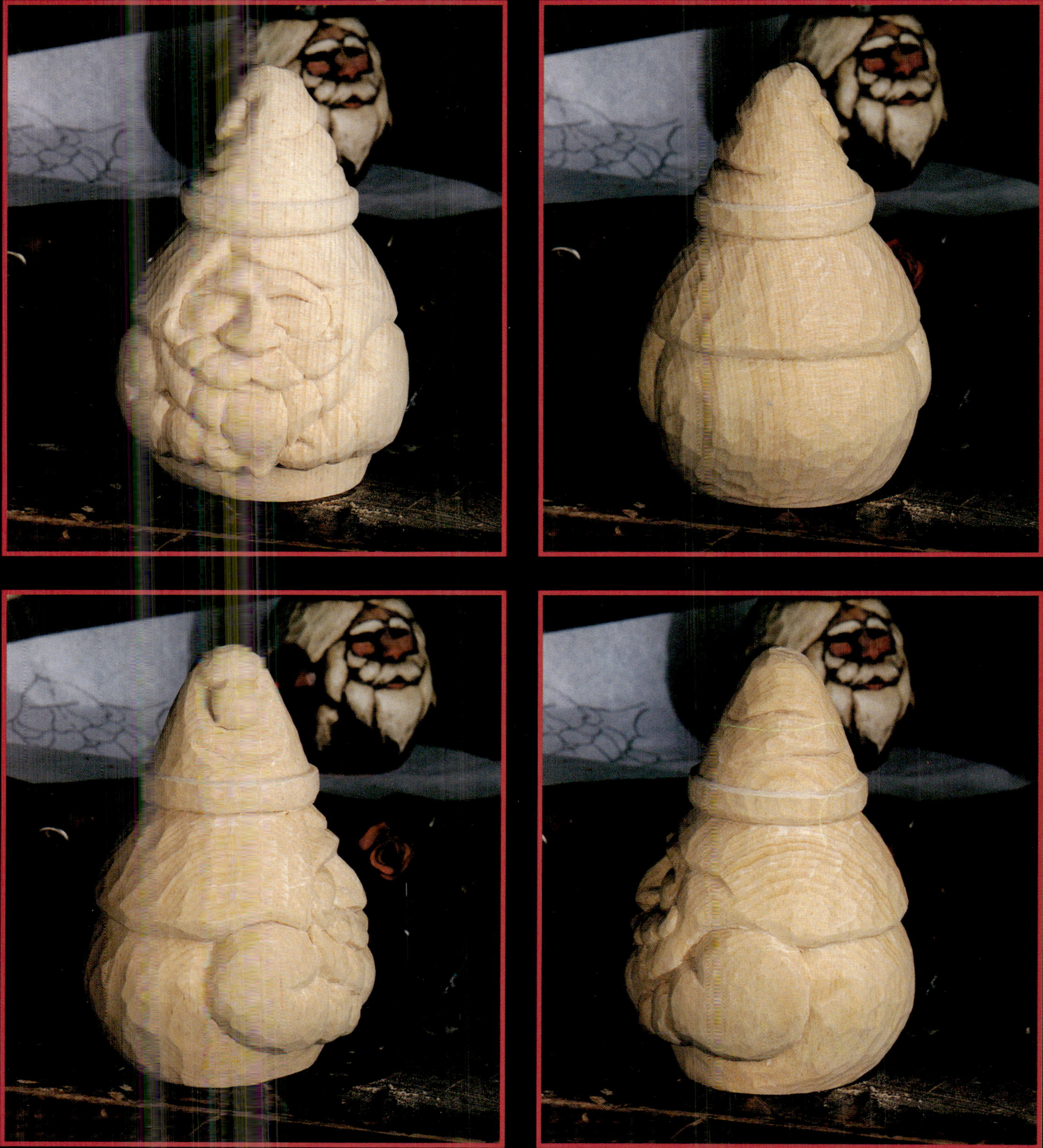

Ready for painting.

Carving the Tree

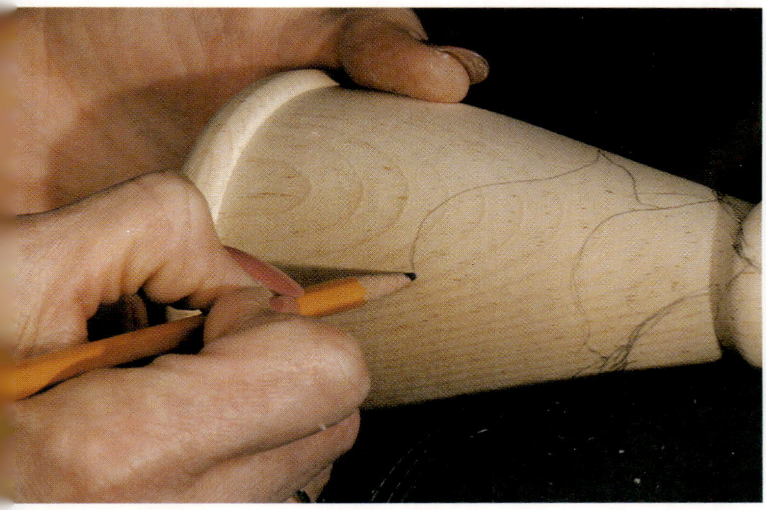

Draw some free-form patterns for the leaves of the tree.

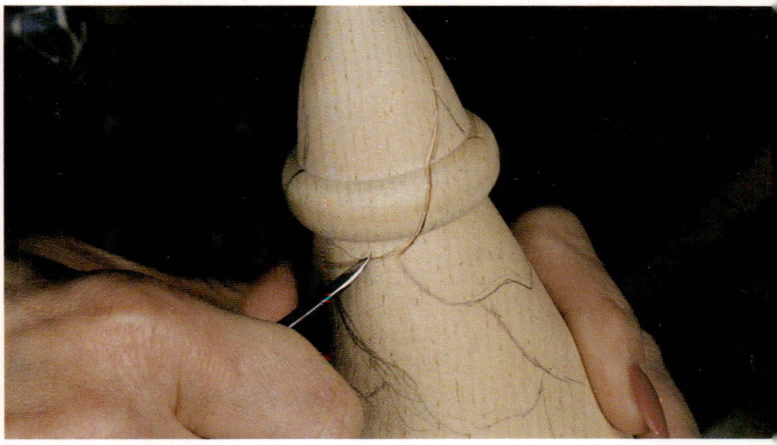

Start at the top and score the lines.

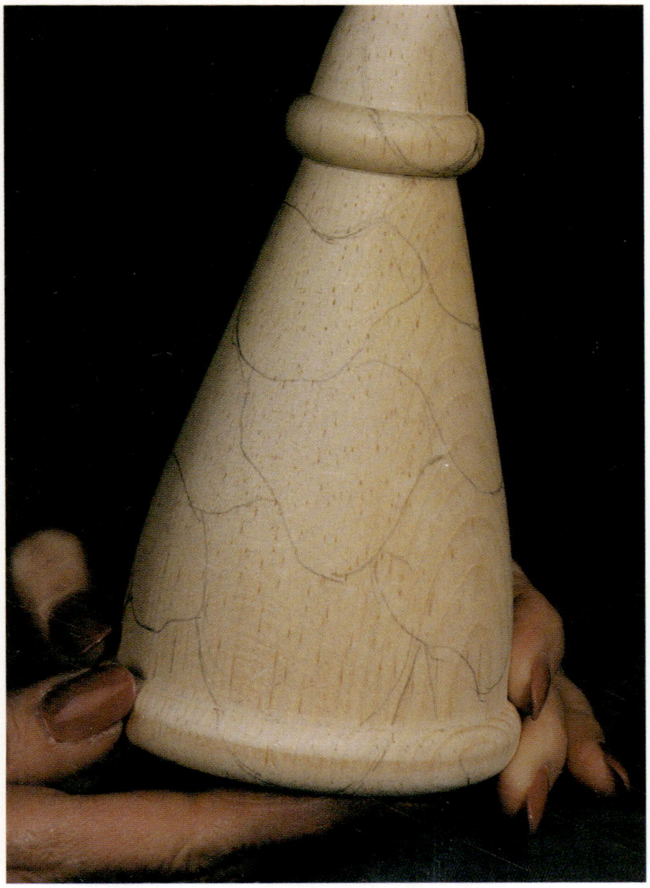

The pattern drawn.

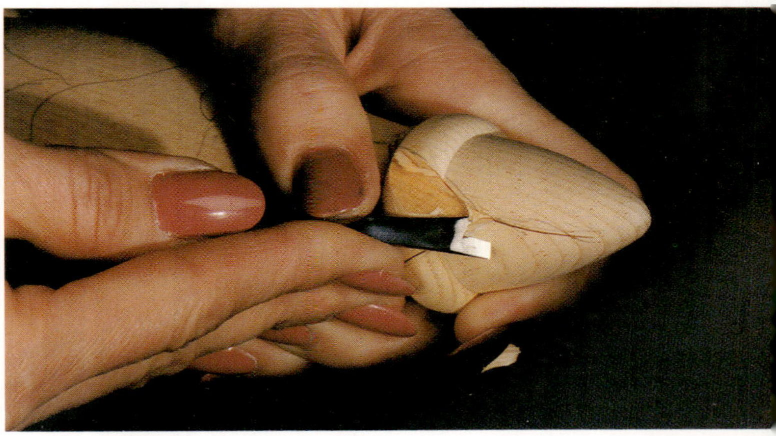

Cut back to the lines of the overlapping branches with a chisel.

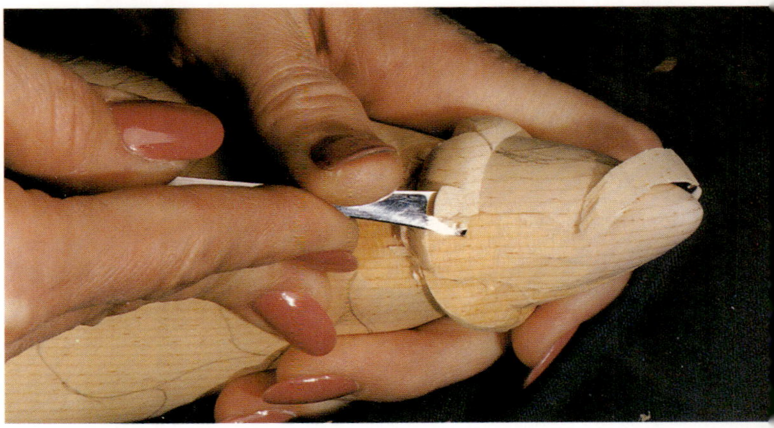

Scoop the surfaces of the branches to give them some shape.

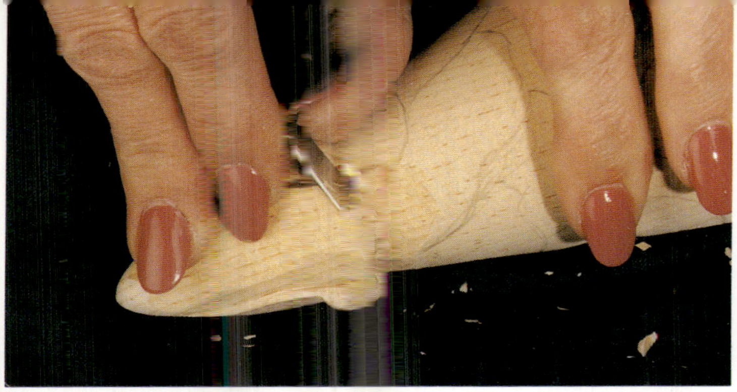

Round the bottom of the branch

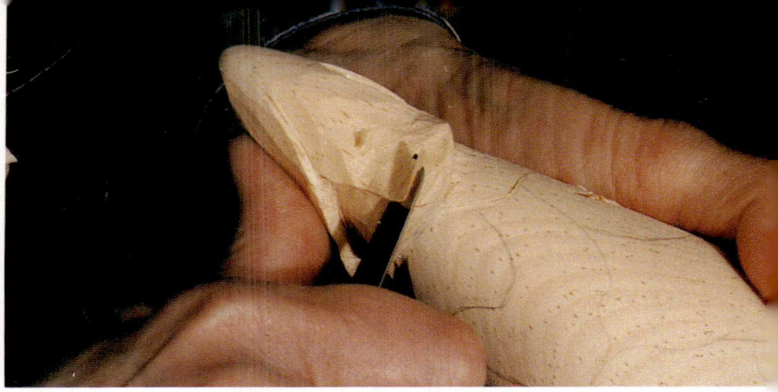

Continue around the top, slowly removing the turned line.

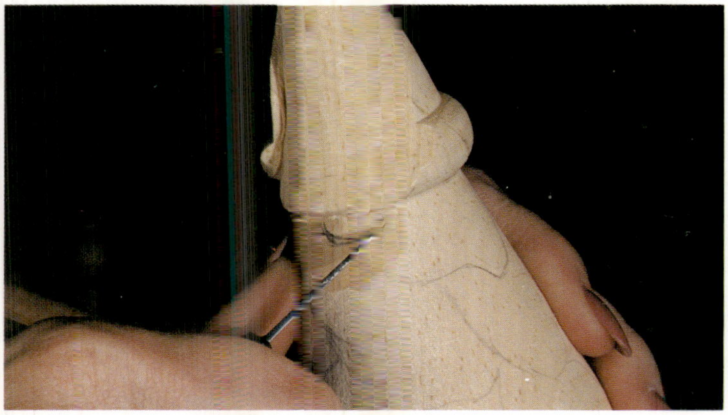

I don't want all the branches to end at the ridge so I want to bring a smaller branch below the line. Score it...

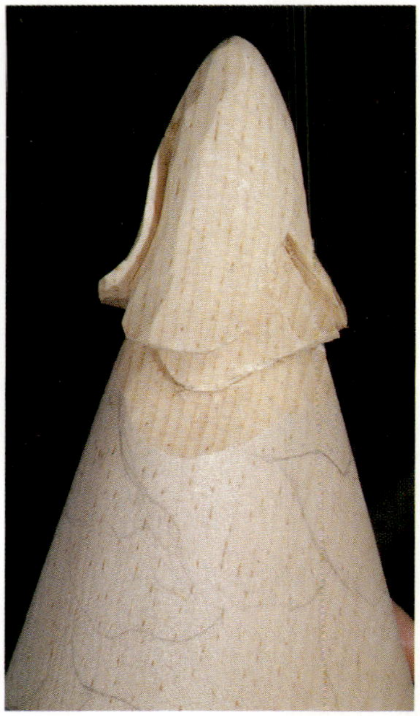

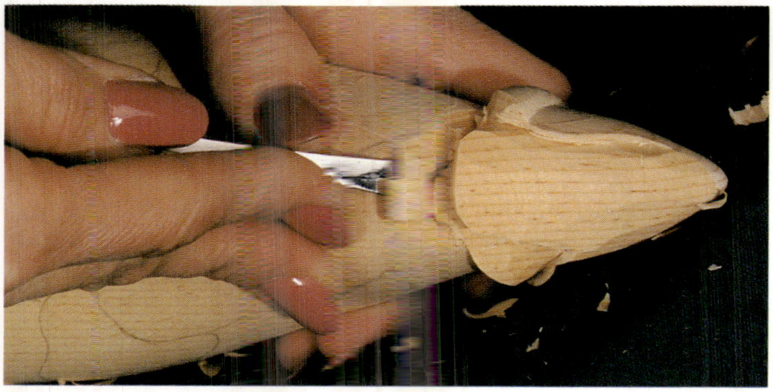

and trim back to it.

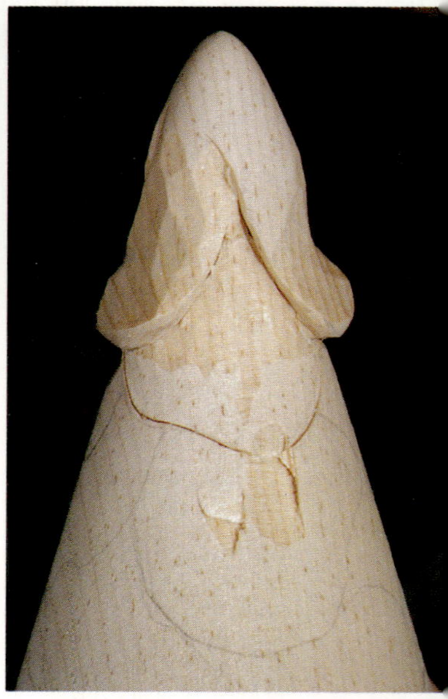

Progress.

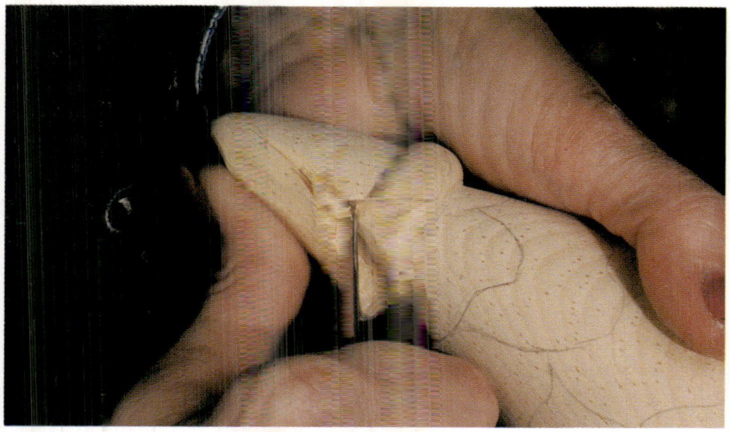

Shape the surface.

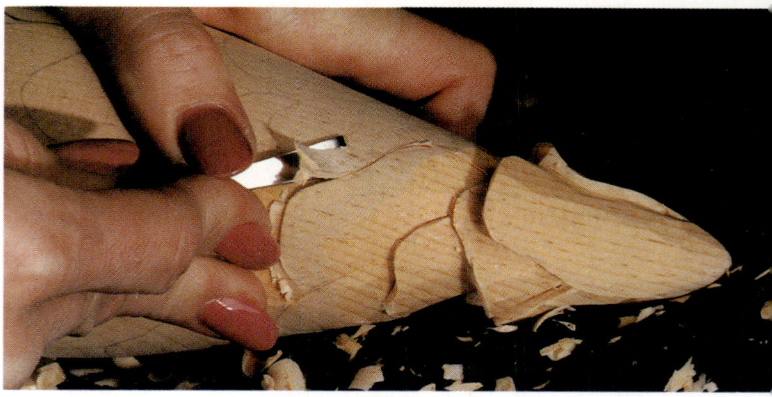

Work your way down the tree layer by layer, using the same method.

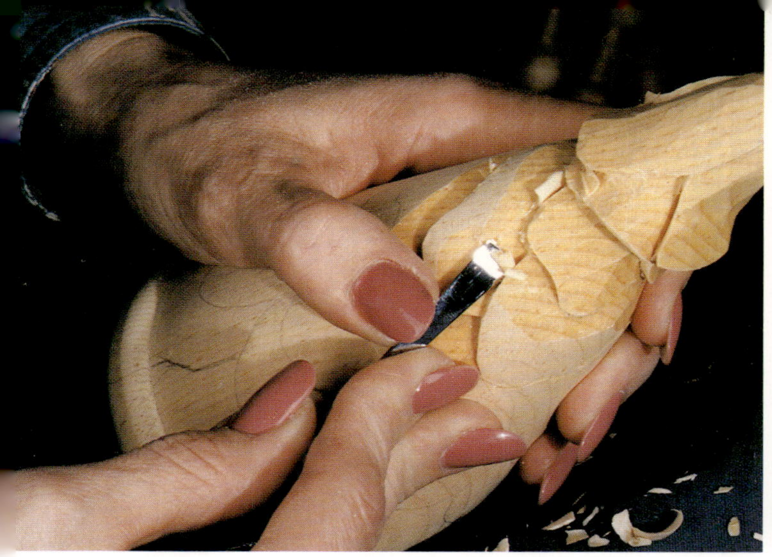

Where the branches overlap, you will get more dimension if you can tuck one under the other.

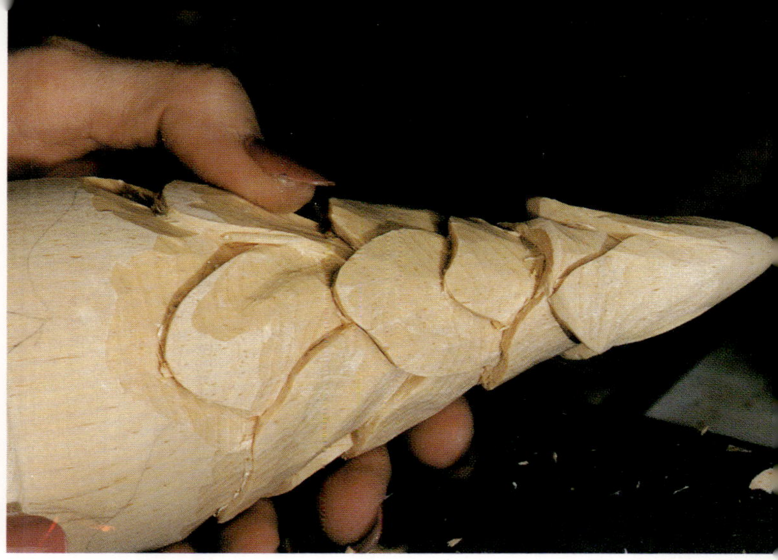

The result of one curl cut.

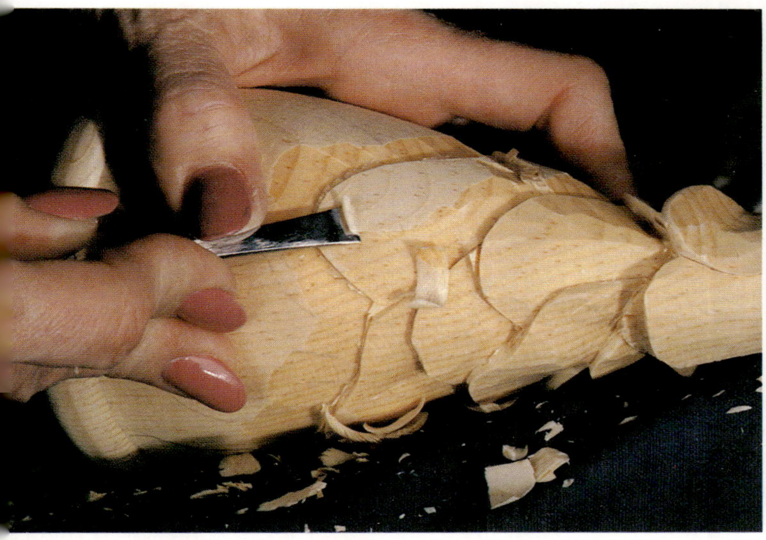

The lower you get on the tree, the bigger the branches will be.

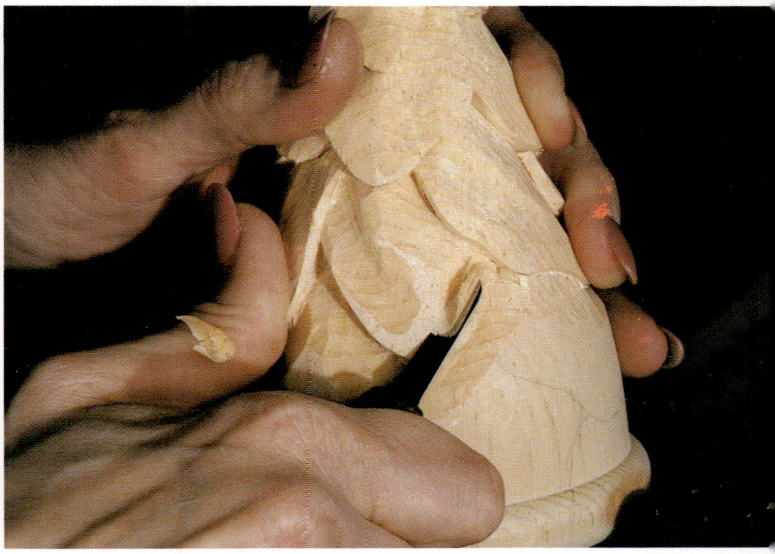

The same branch may have other contours like this.

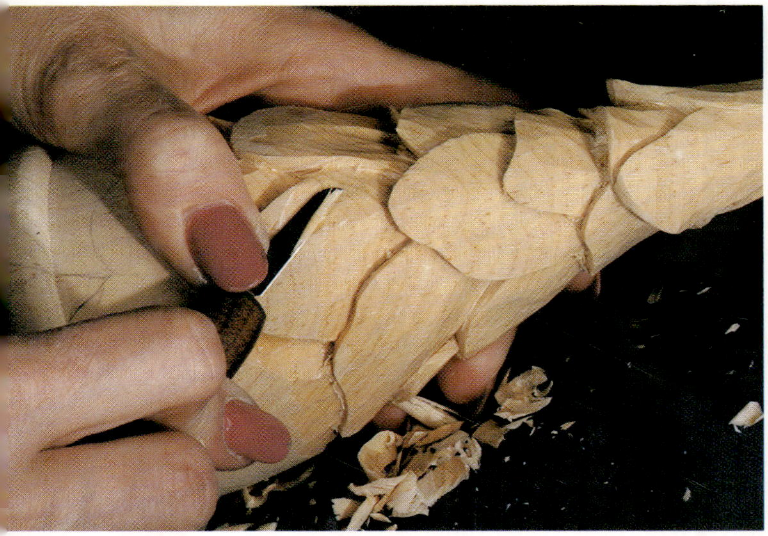

The branches are not flat. Some are gently curved and others have contoured ridges. Create this with a curl cut using your knife.

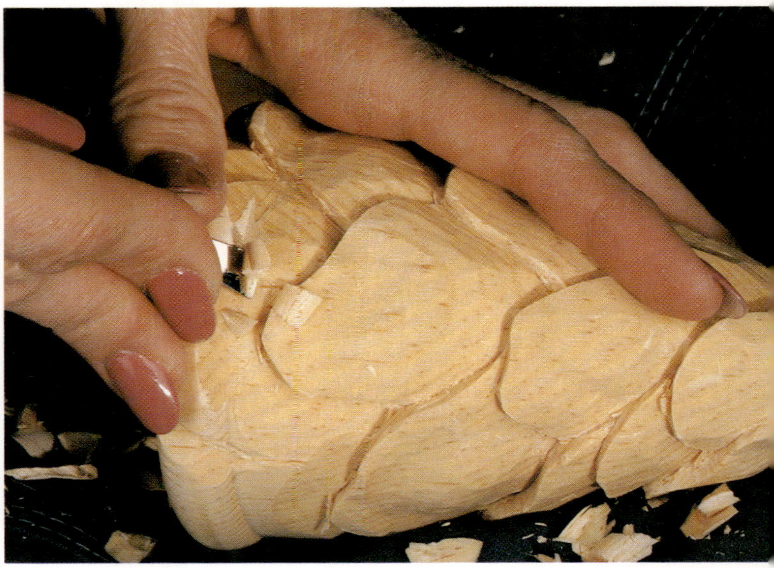

Use the bottom ridge of the turned blank to create some lift to the lower branches.

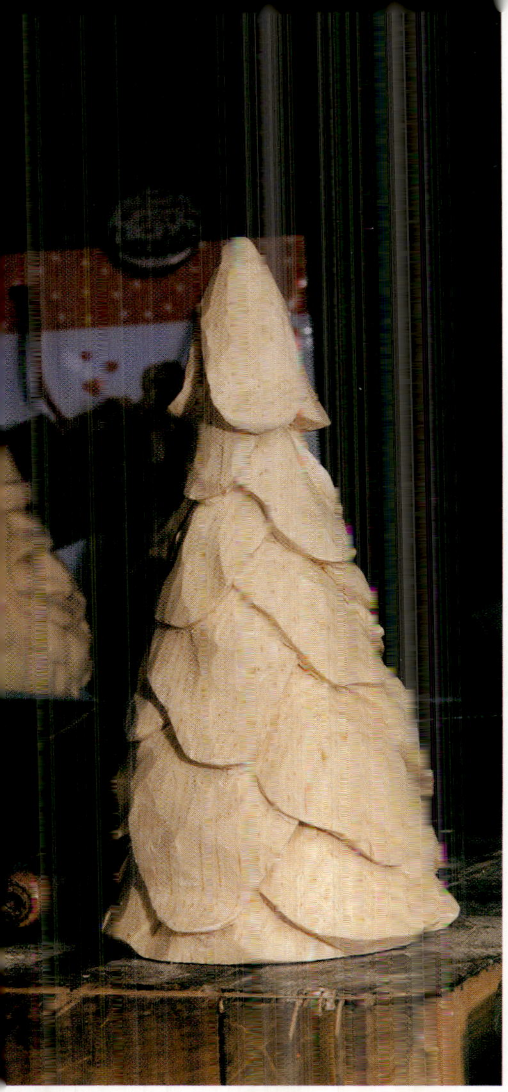

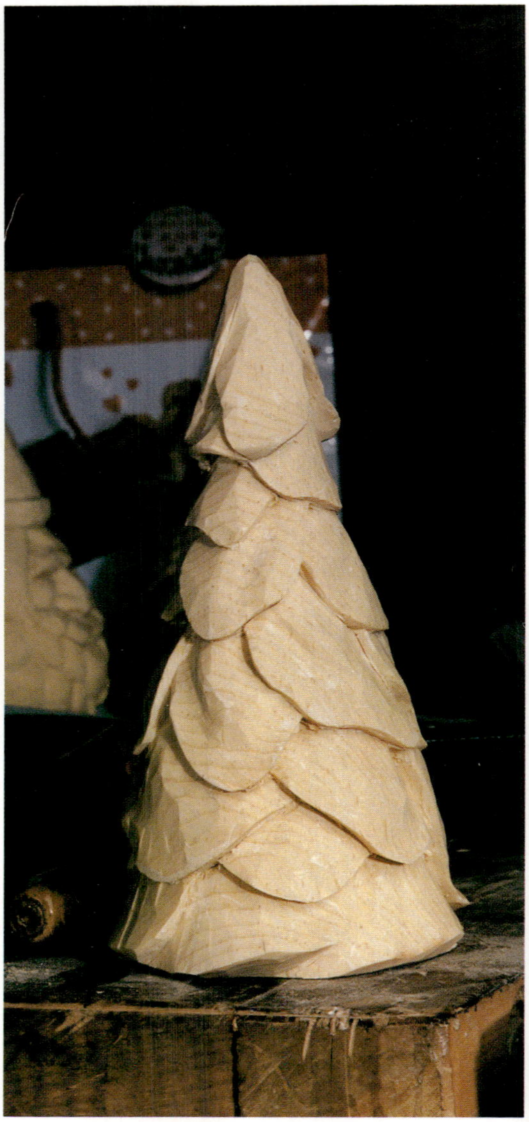

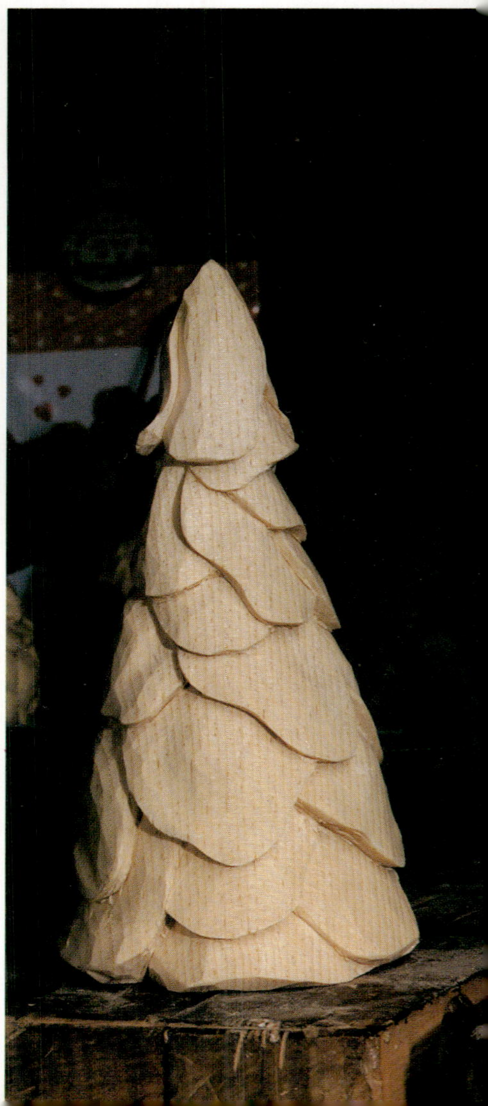

Ready for painting.

Painting the Projects

The Tree

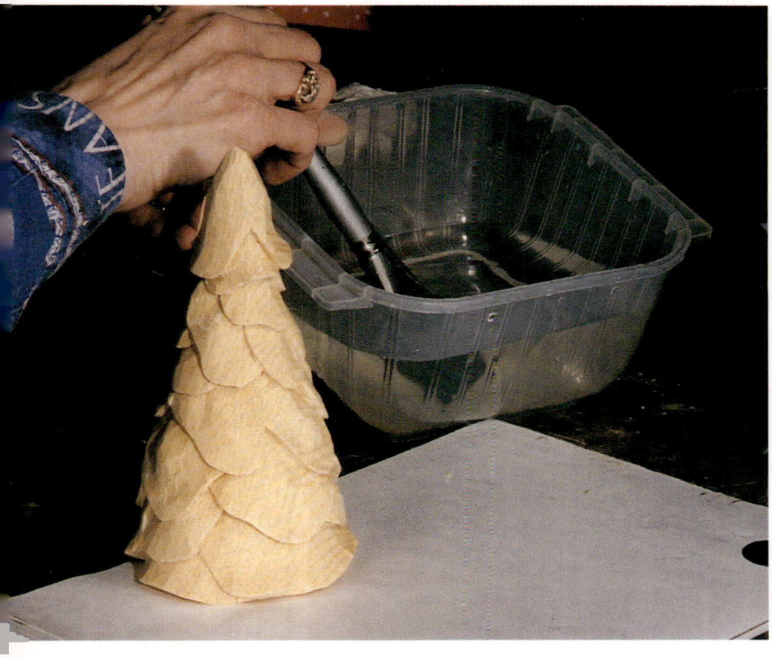

I use acrylic paints which come in bottles, and are available at most craft stores. Begin the tree with a dark blue green. Load the brush with water.

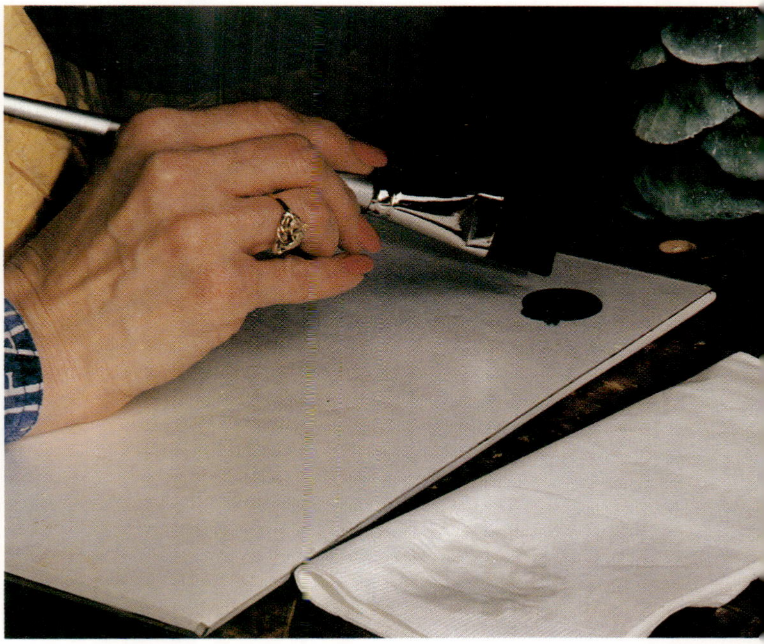

Corner load the brush by dipping one corner in the paint.

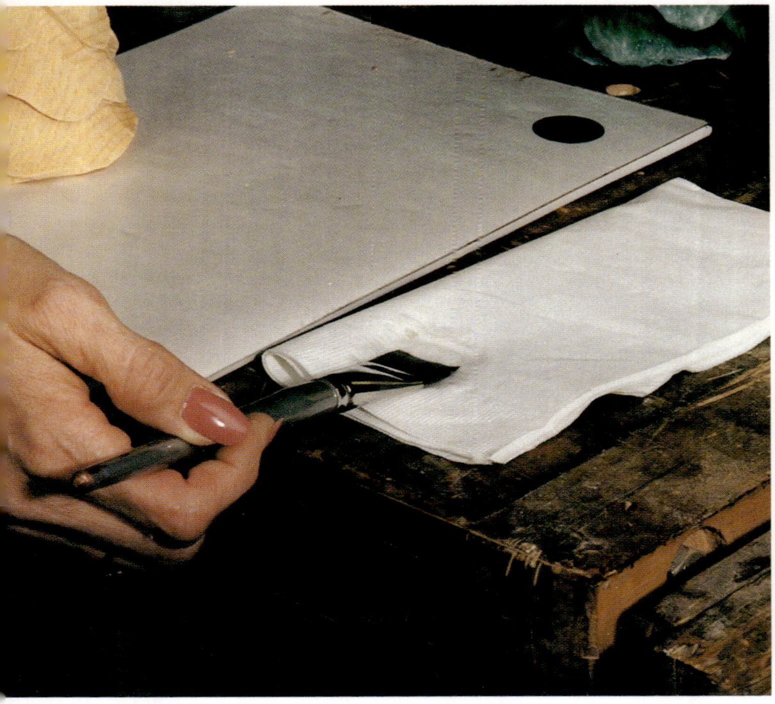

Lightly blot it on a piece of paper towel.

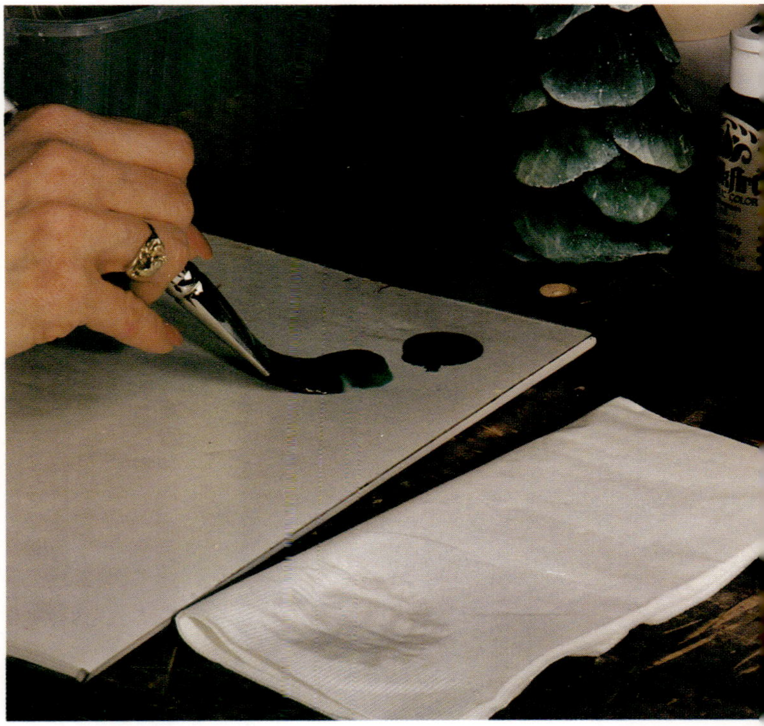

On the palette work the paint so one side of the brush is heavily loaded and the other has almost no pigment.

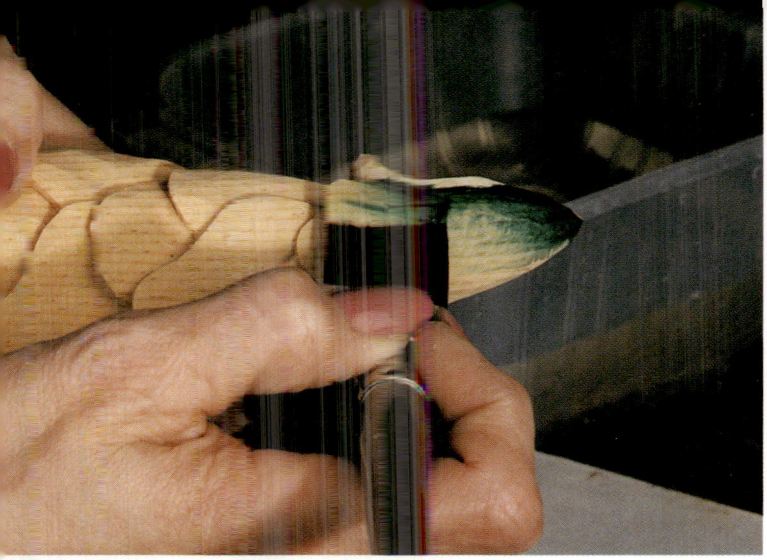

Apply the paint to the tree with the heavily loaded edge toward the top. This will create a lighter color toward the end of the branch where the snow covers it.

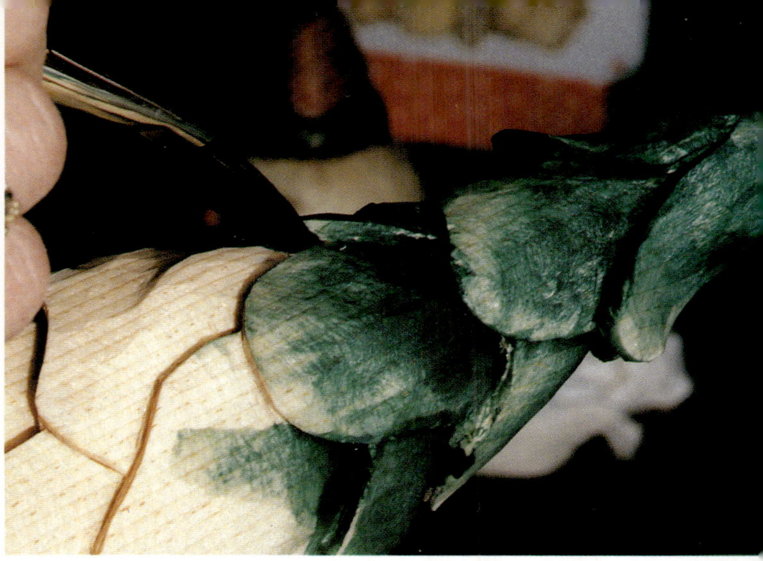

Paint the underside of the branches pretty heavily.

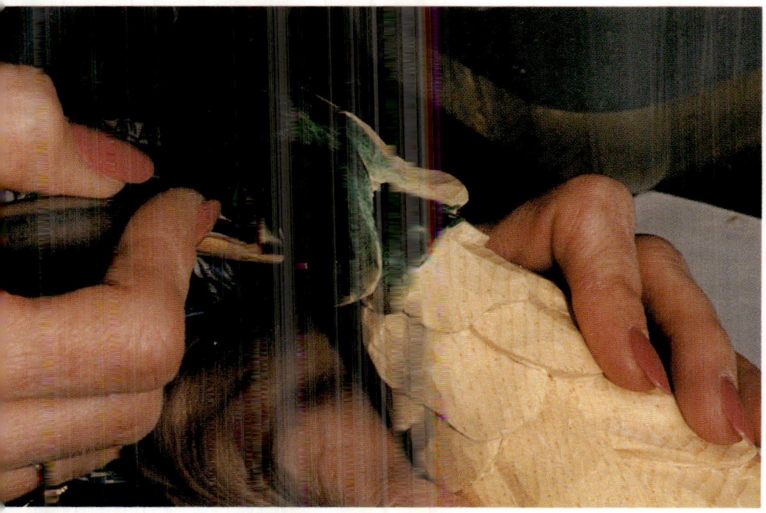

At the intersection of two branches the paint will be heavy, as it should be.

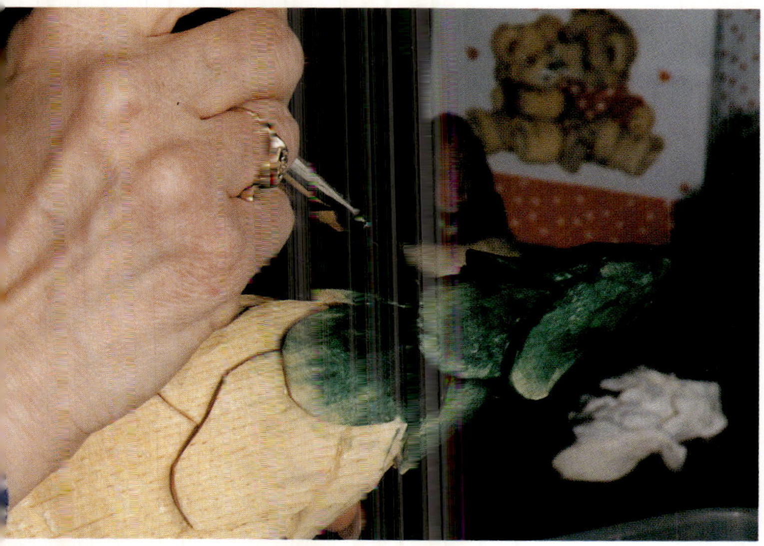

The effect of this is more apparent as you work down the tree.

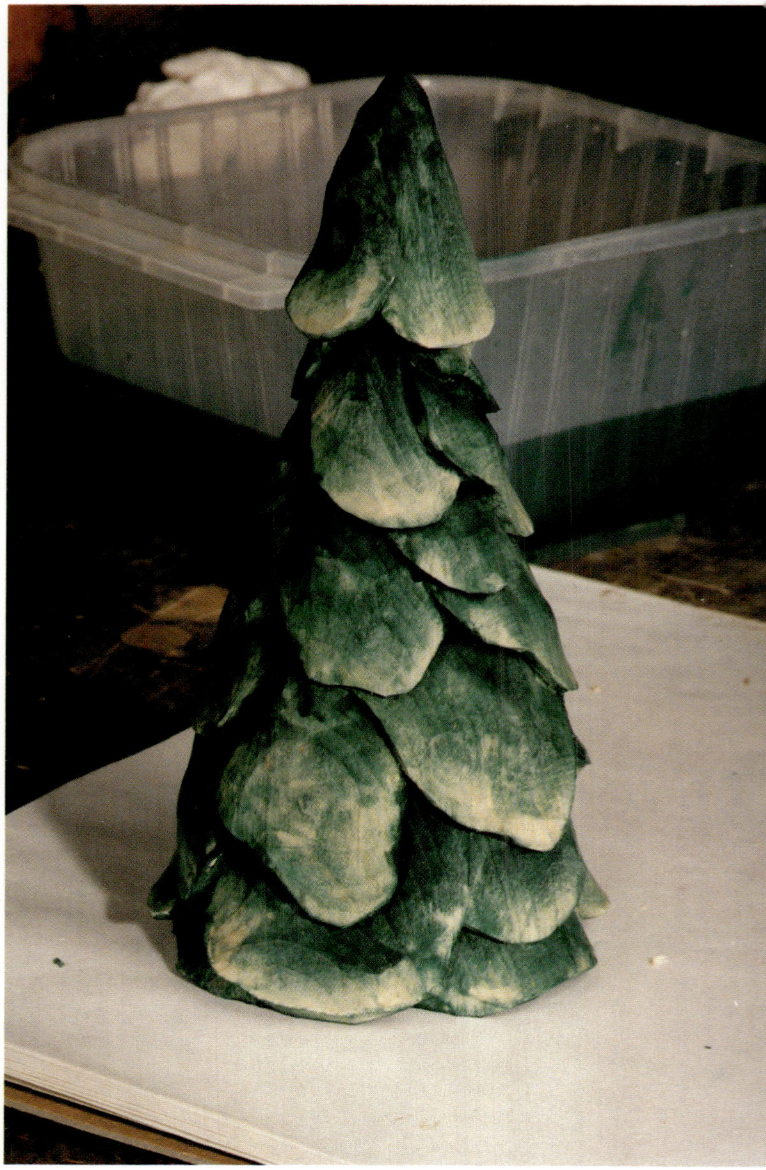

The tree is green.

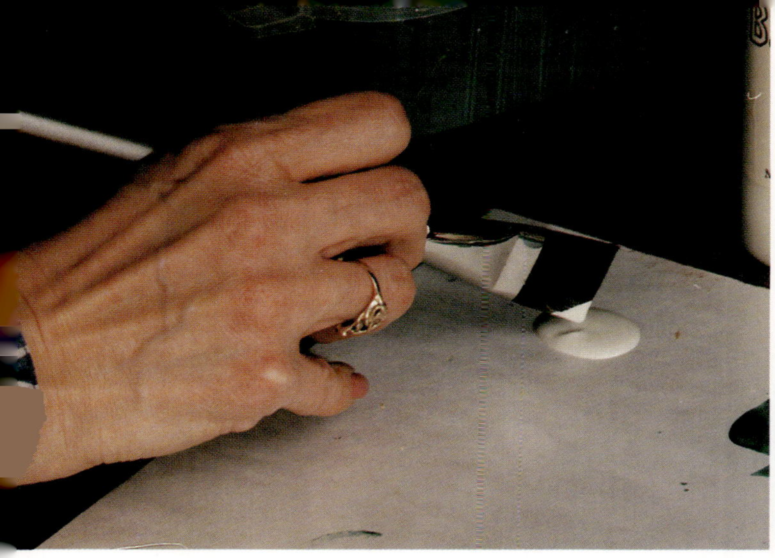

Start at the top again, and use a slightly off-white color to go over the tips of the branches. (For the folk art type pieces I never usepure white. With a blotted wet brush, corner load it with the off-white.

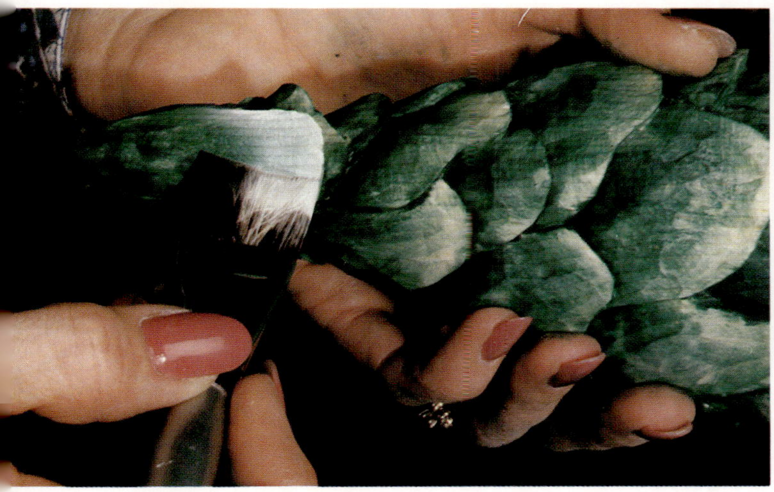

Apply it to the branches in the opposite way as the green, with the heavy pigment toward the ends of the branches.

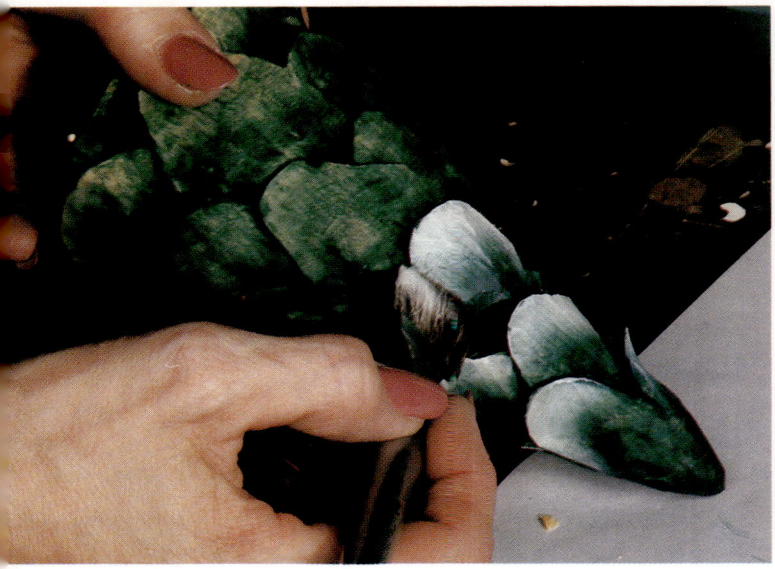

Once again work your way down the tree,

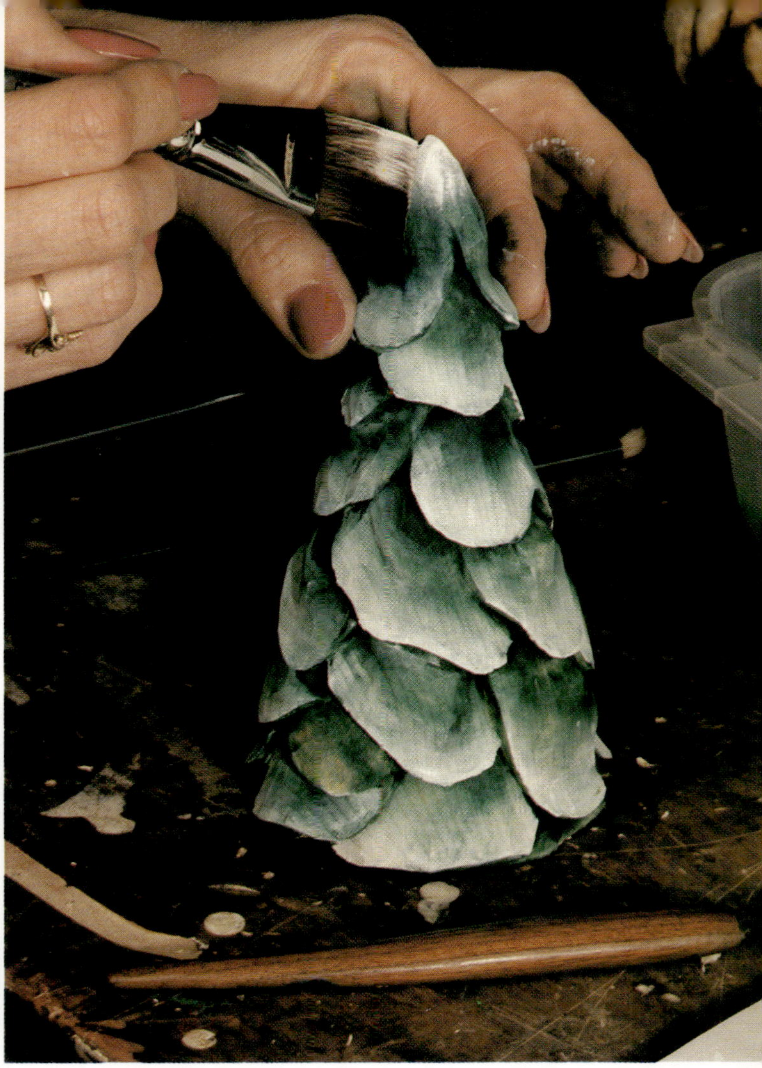

Apply white to the top of the tree. If you want a heavier look you can repeat this process several times. Notice that on some of the branches, where the snow would not reach, the branches are left unpainted.

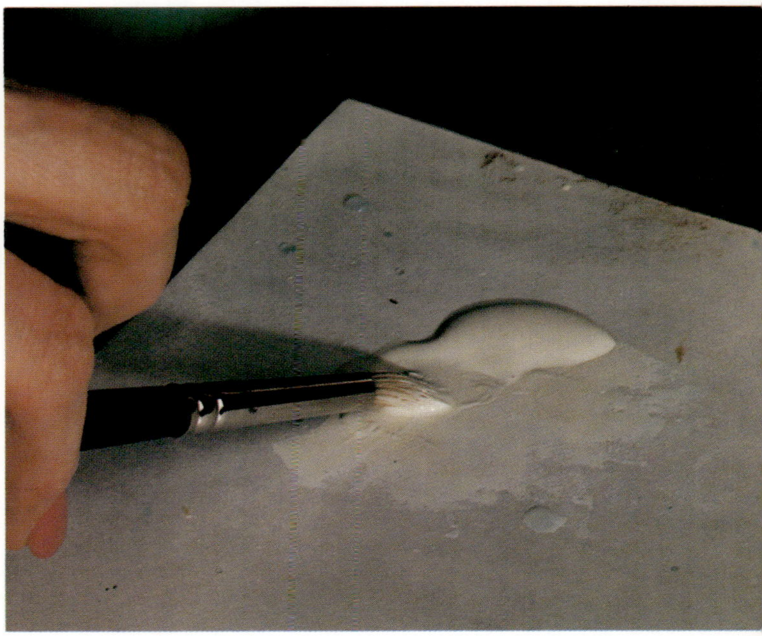

To add some splattered snow flakes load a stiff brush...

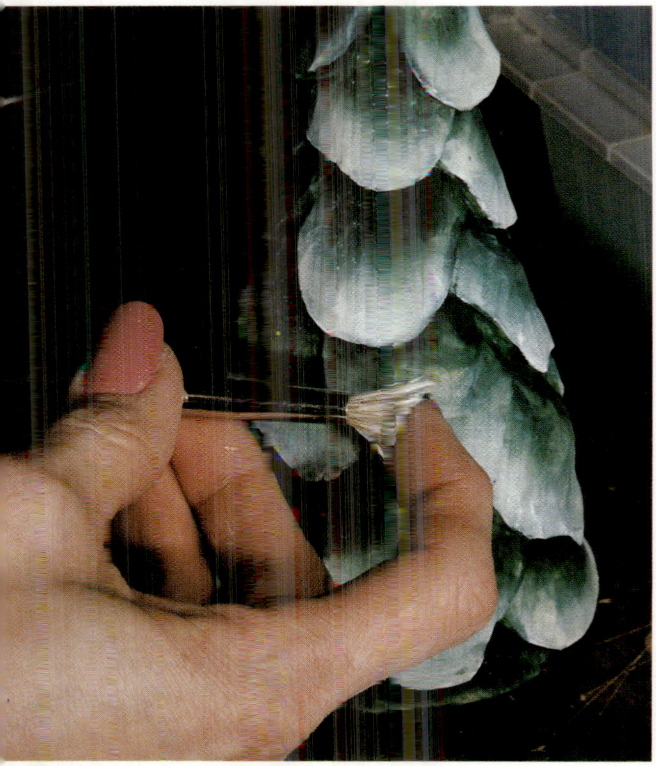

pull back the bristles with your fingers

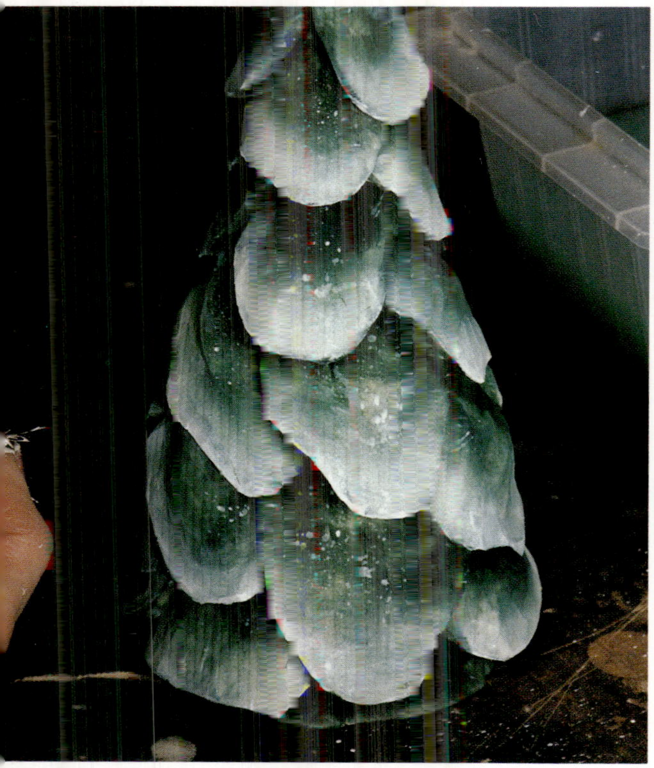

and let it go.

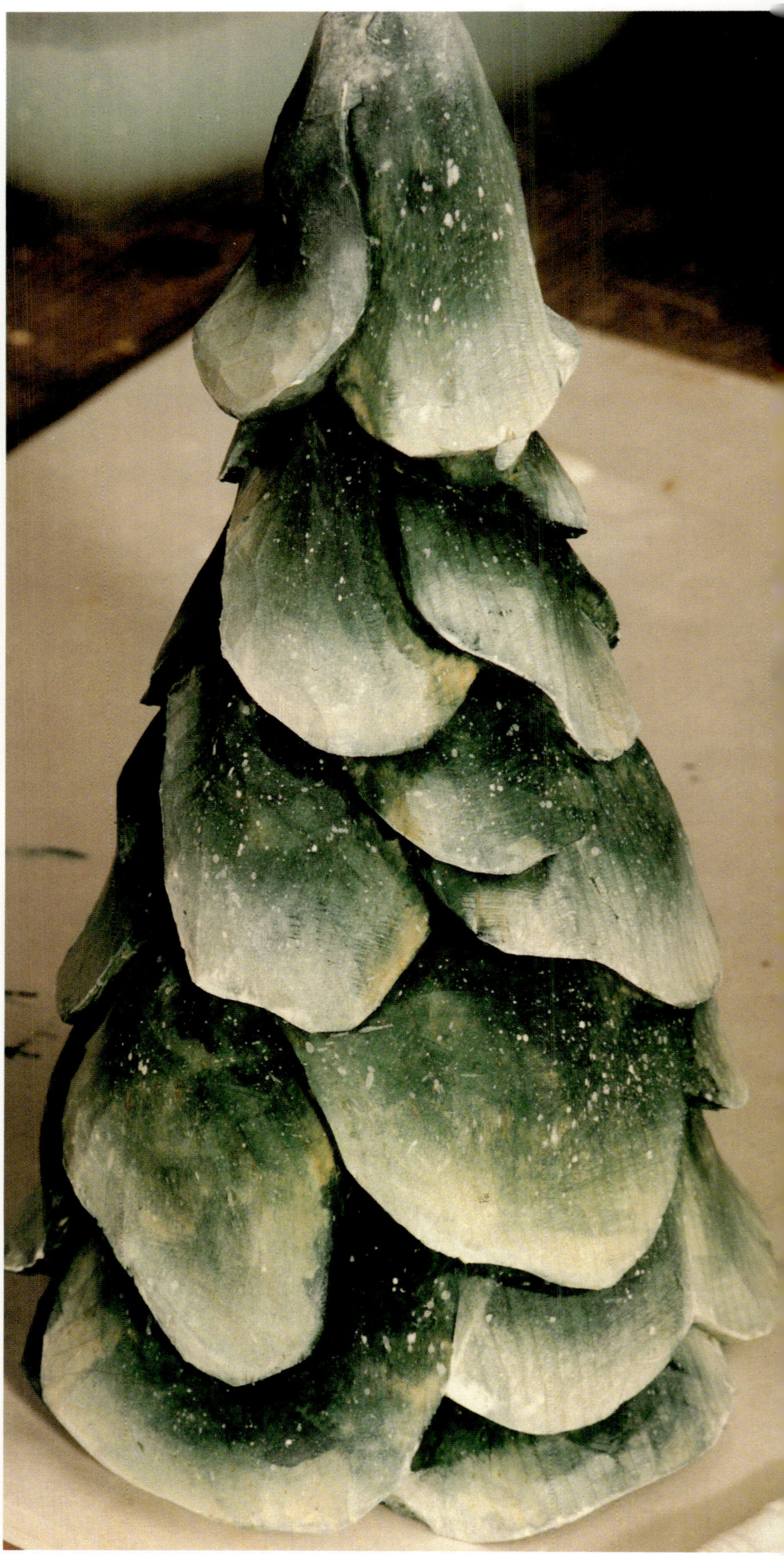

The result.

The Santa

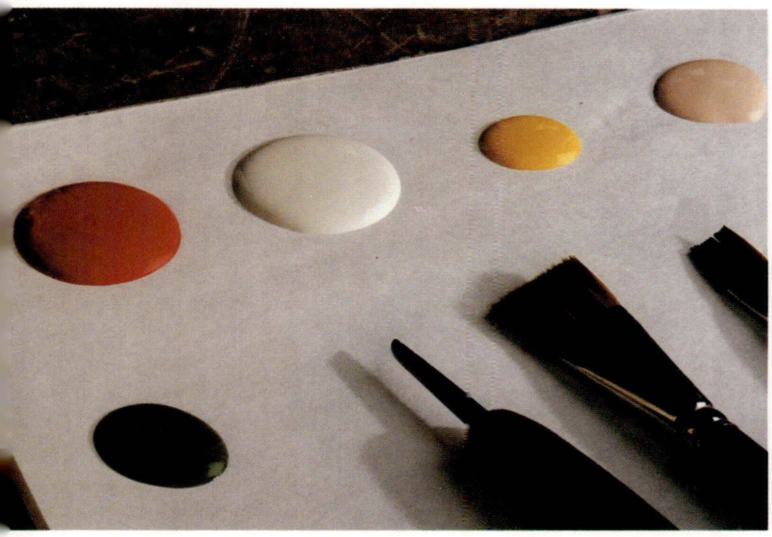

The palette for the Santa includes cardinal red, a medium flesh tone, off white, Christmas green, and bright yellow.

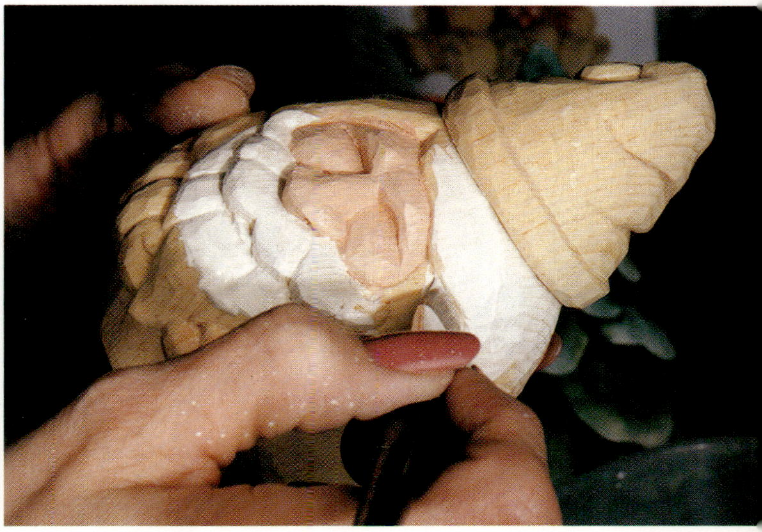

hair...

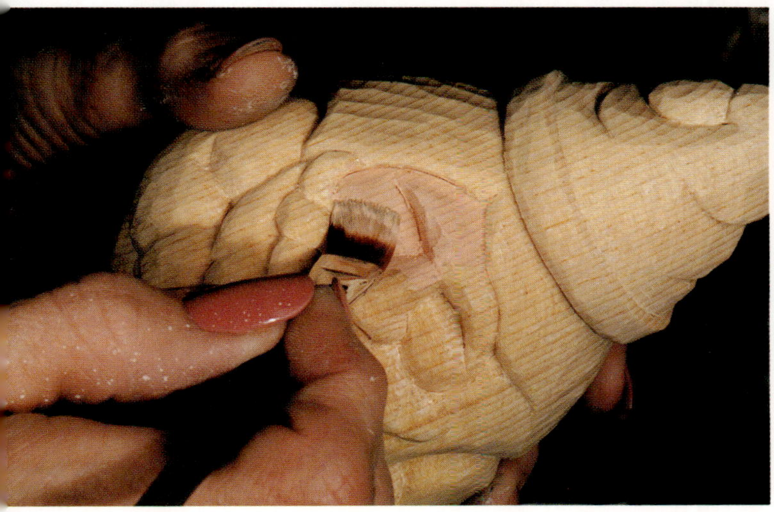

Use a chisel brush to apply undiluted flesh to the whole face. This brush has a nice sharp edge to get into corners and edges.

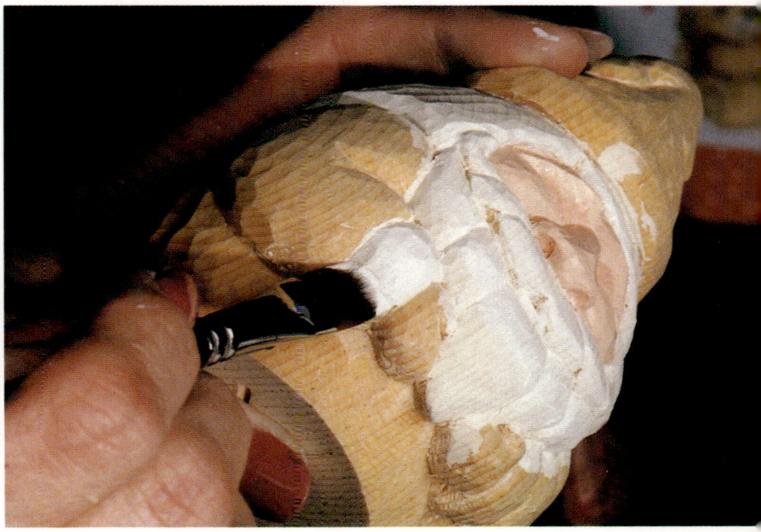

the fur trim at the wrists...

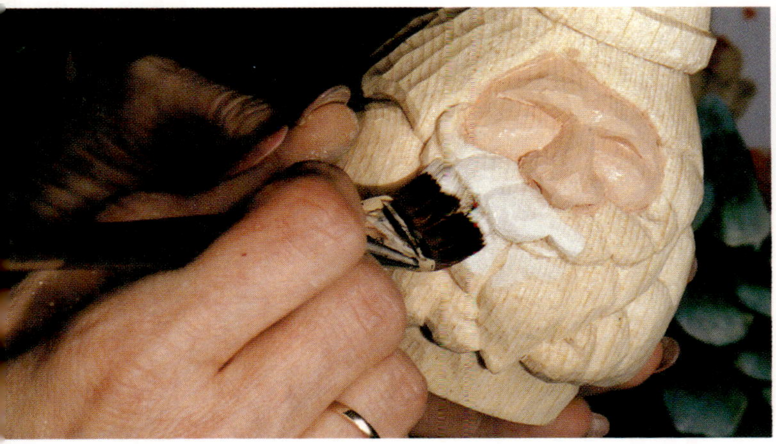

Apply white to the moustache and beard...

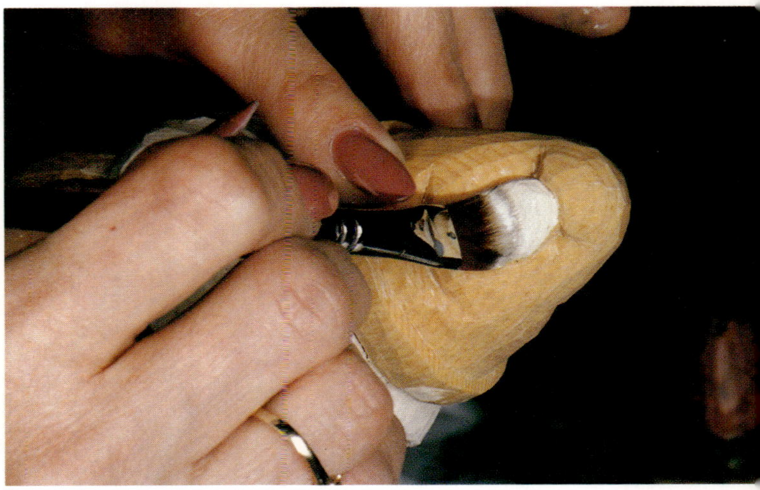

and the ball of the cap.

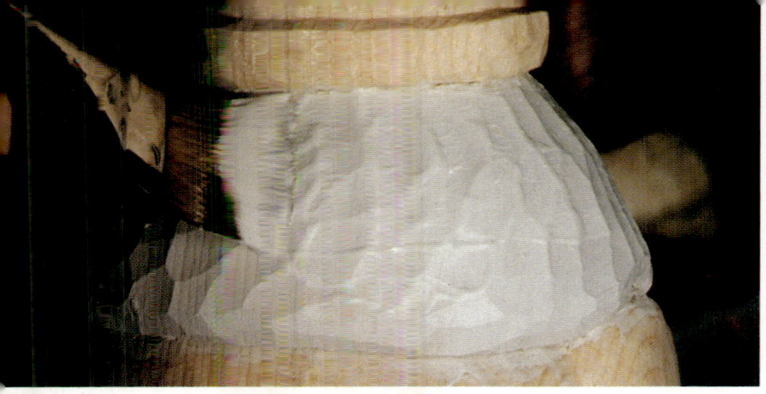

You may need to go over things again to get the coverage you need for antiquing. If it is too thin the wood will soak up the antiquing and you will not have the control you need.

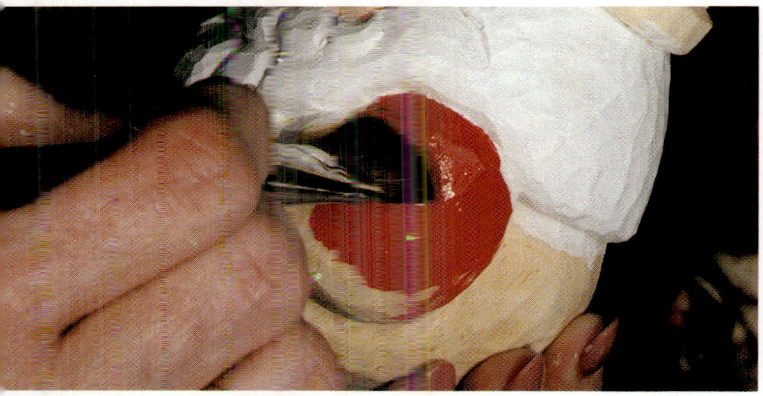

Apply red to the jacket...

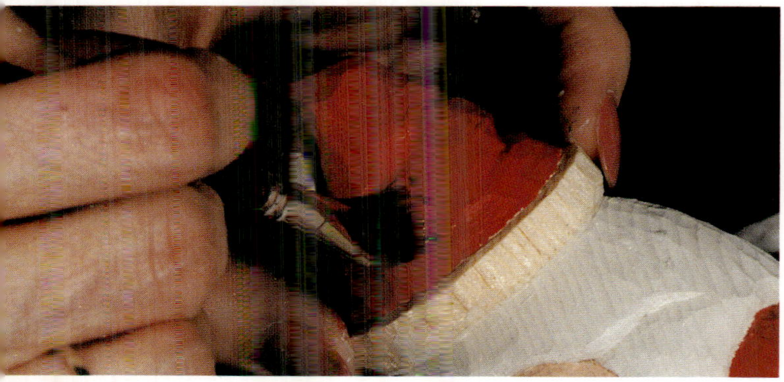

and the hat.

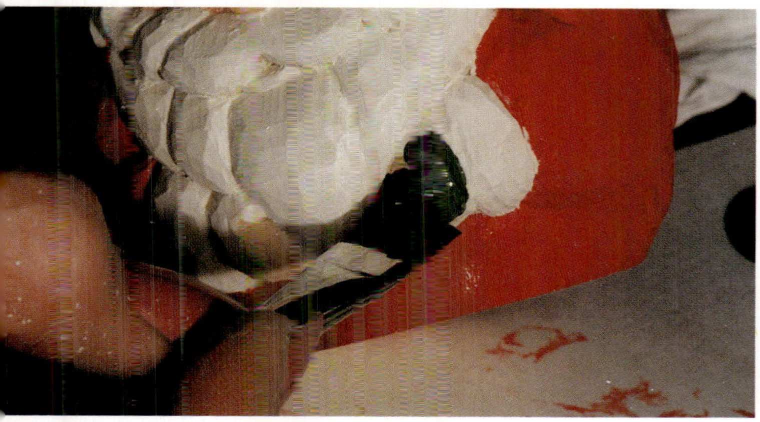

Apply green to the gloves...

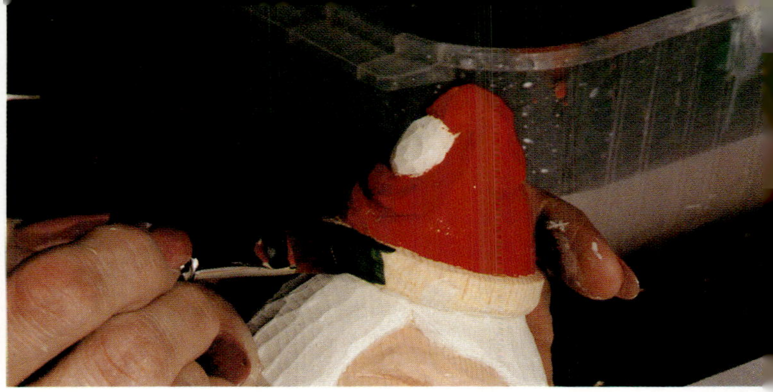

and the trim of the hat.

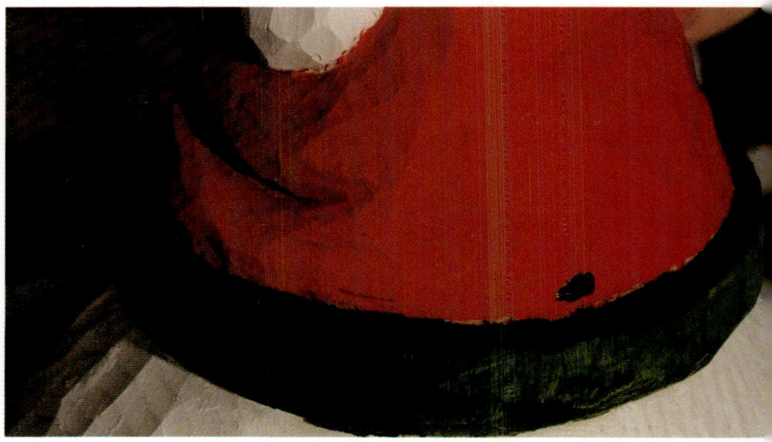

If you get some color were it doesn't belong, like this spot of green on the red...

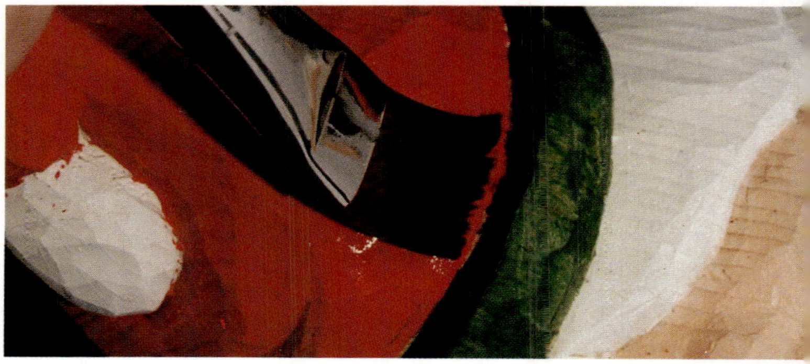

it can usually be removed with a wet brush.

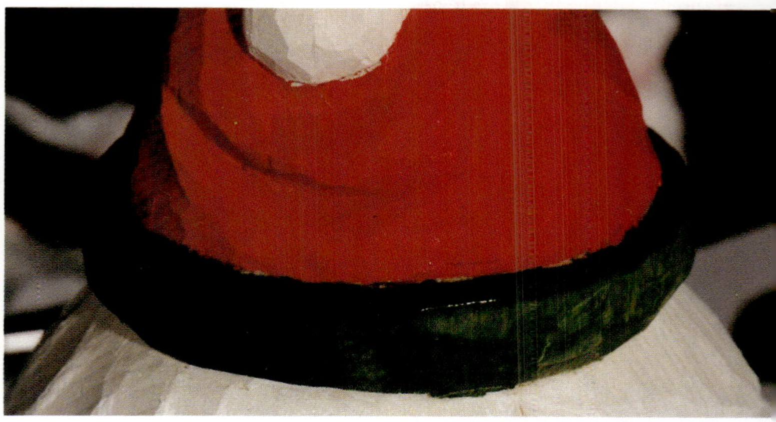

The result. Sometimes you may need to touch up the color.

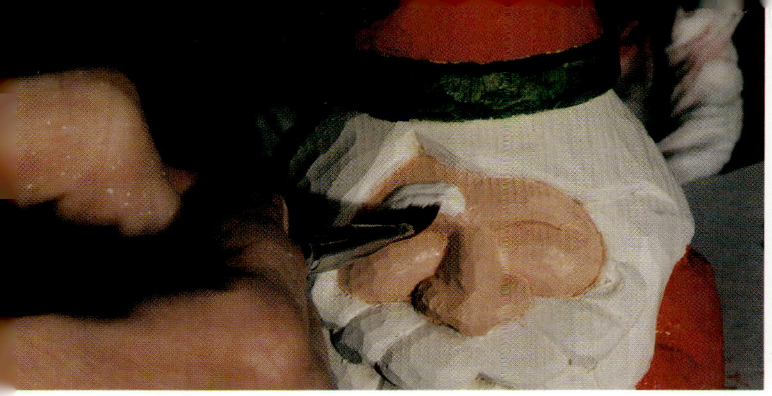

Don't forget the eyebrows.

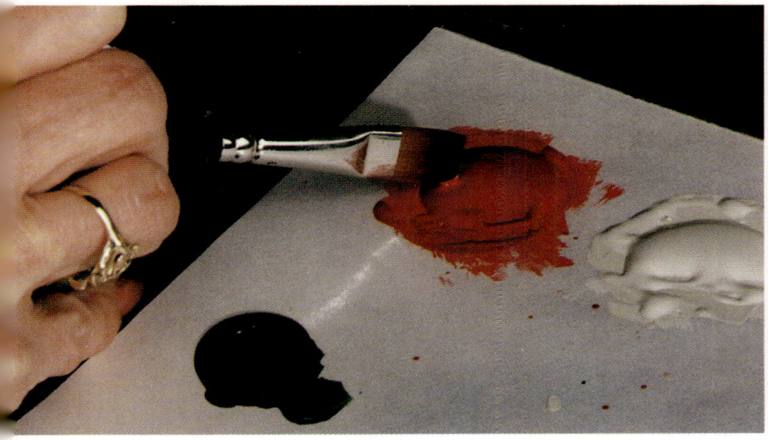

We need to add some blush to the cheeks. Do this with a wet brush that has been blotted. Corner load it with red paint.

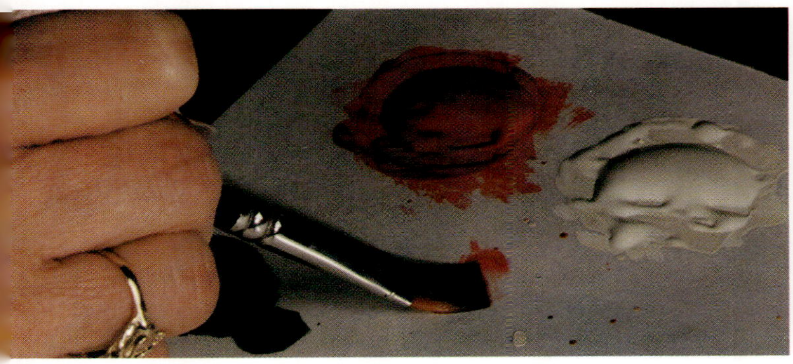

Work the paint into the brush so one side is heavy and the other has almost no pigment.

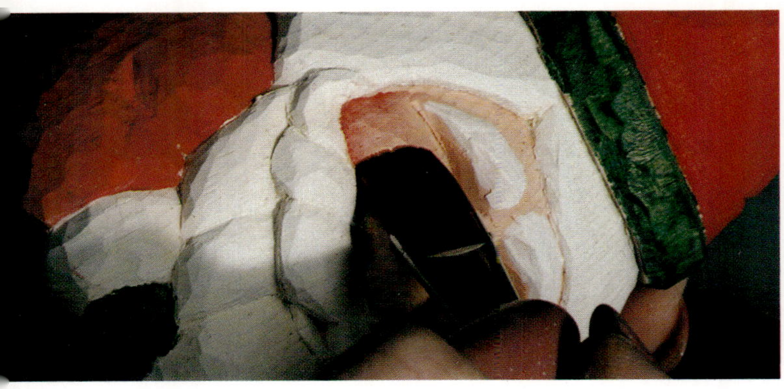

With the heavy pigment side against the beard line, go across one cheek...

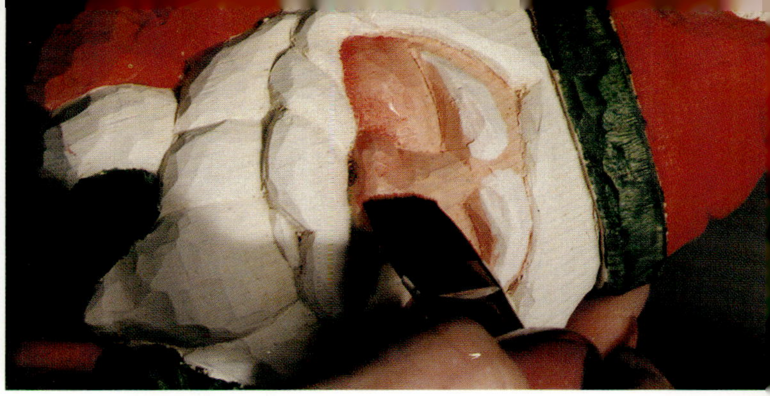

the nose and the other cheek.

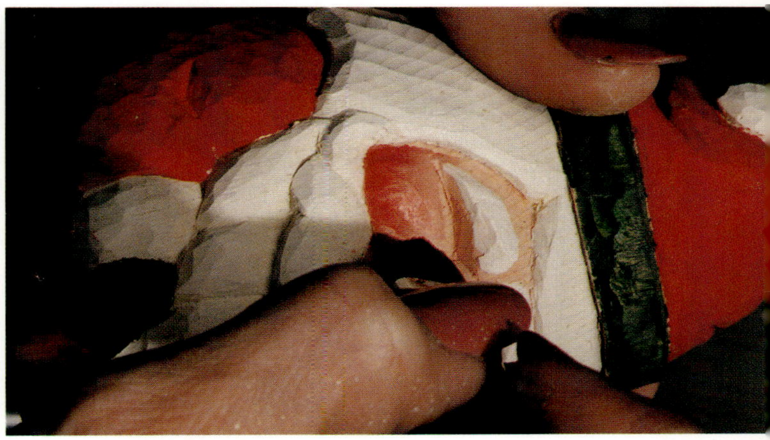

Because the antiquing will take away some of this color we need to repeat the blushing.

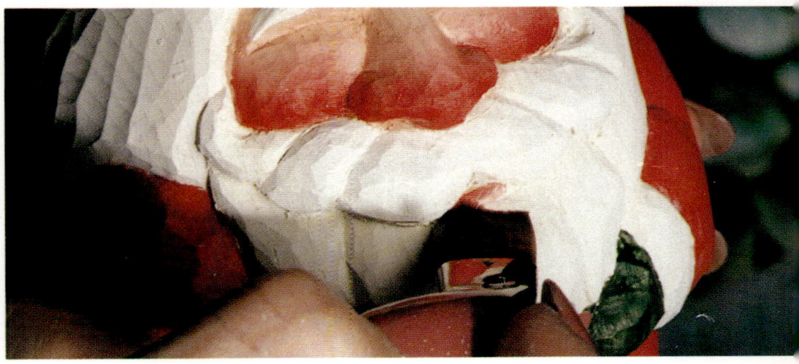

Add some blush to the lip.

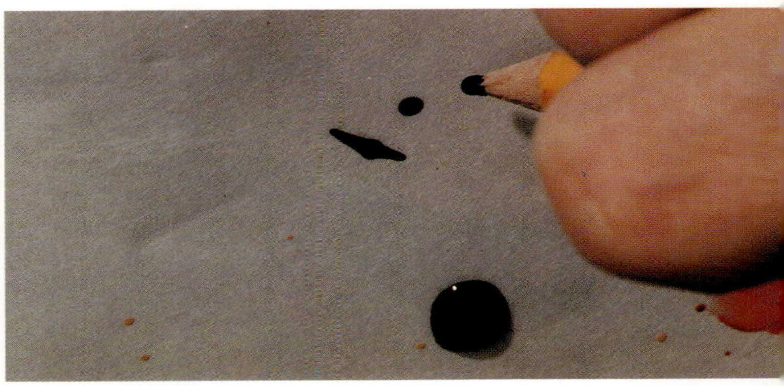

The point of a pencil works well with the eyes. Practice on the palette before trying the eye itself. Pick up some black paint on the point and make a dot.

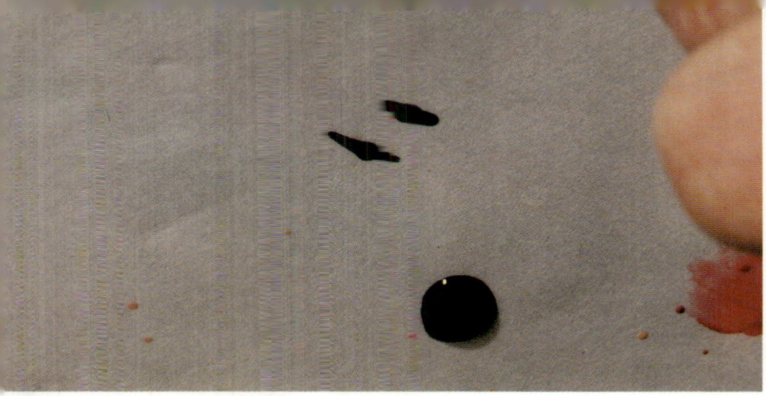

Pull the dot in each direction to elongate.

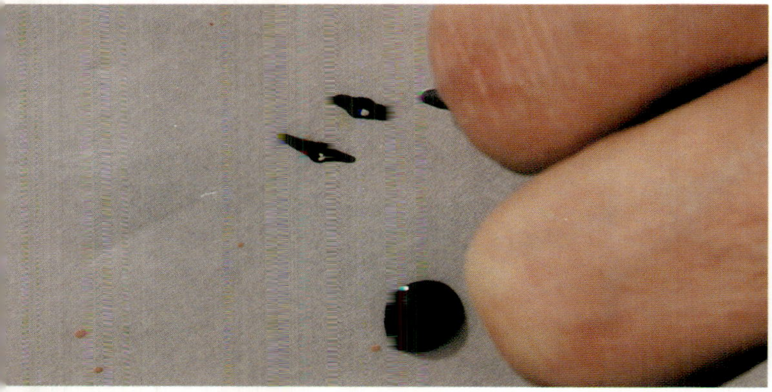

A dot of white highlights the eye and brings it to life.

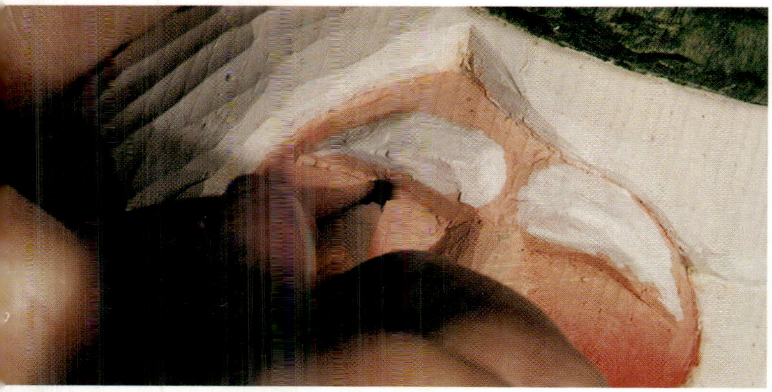

Now that I've practiced I will do the real thing on Santa. First the dot place right up from the center of the cheek...

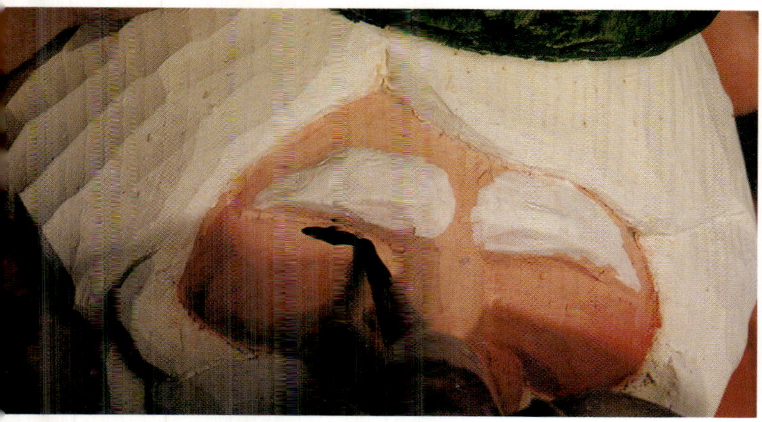

and elongated.

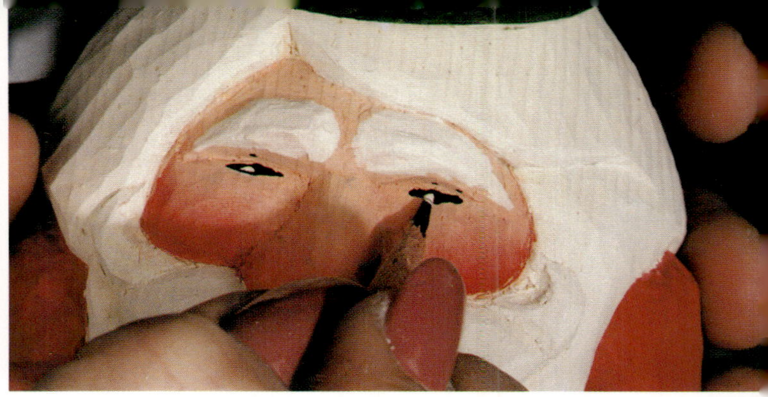

Add the white dot.

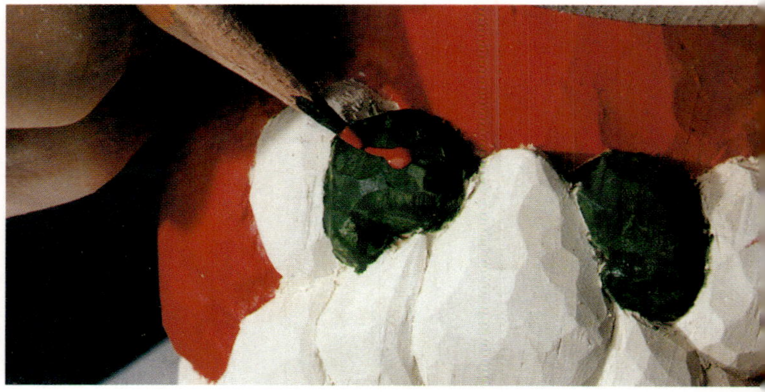

The decoration on the mittens is one large dot in the middle pulled toward the wrist.

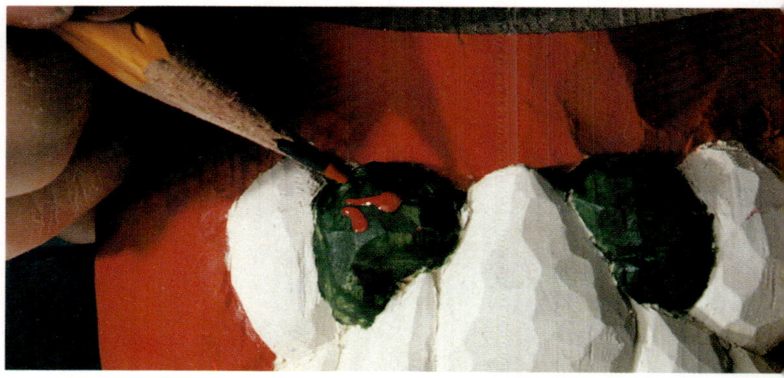

On each side of this dot do another smaller dot in the same way. First one...

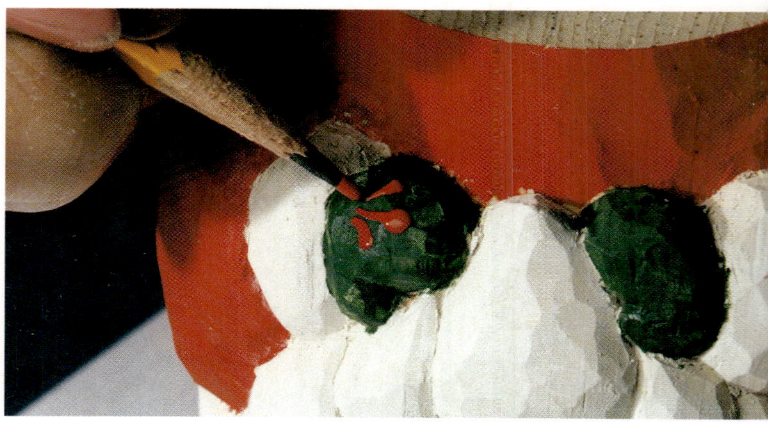

then the other.

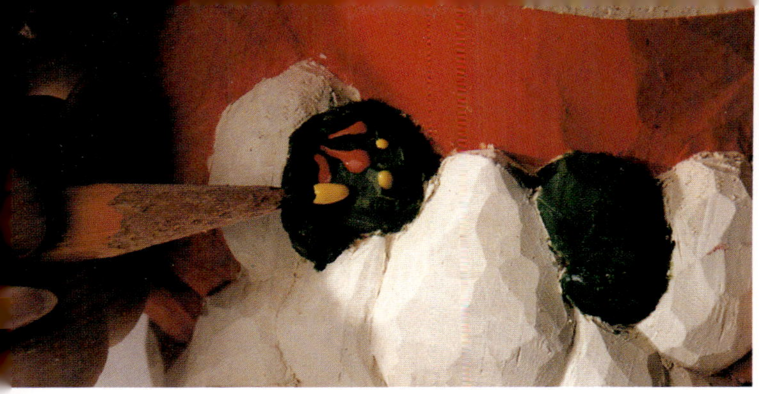

Finally add three yellow dots, one at the end of each of the red lines.

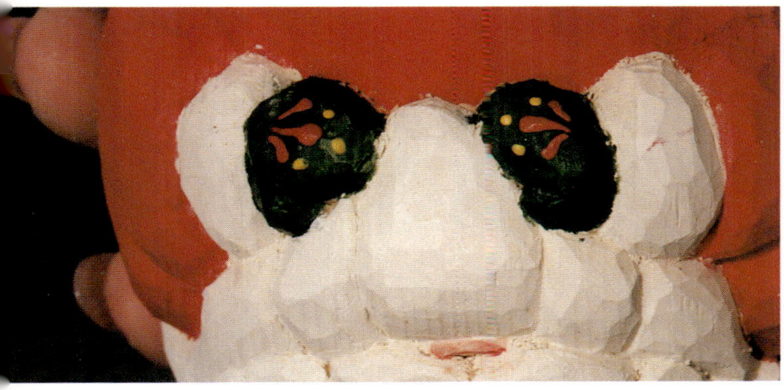

The glove pattern.

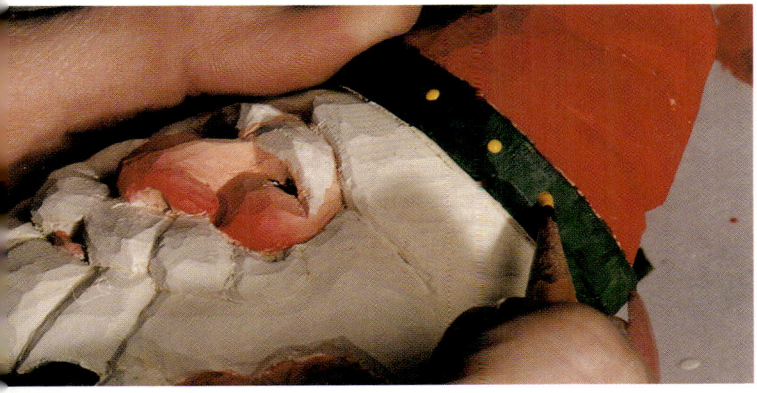

The hat band is trimmed with a nice colored pattern. Begin by laying dots of yellow about 1/2" apart.

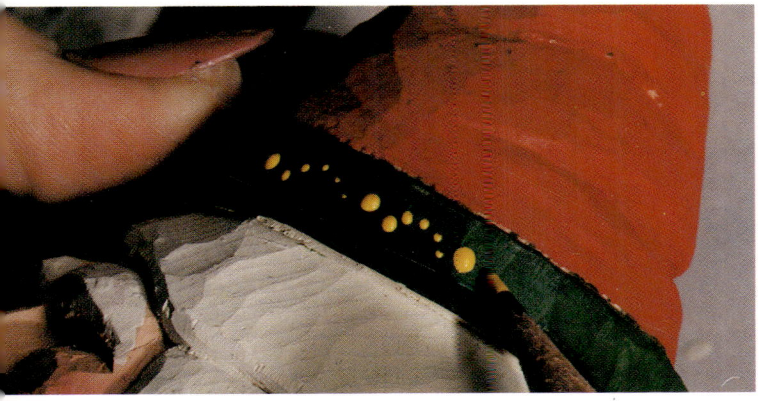

Between the large dots of yellow there is an arc of five smaller dots, of decreasing size.

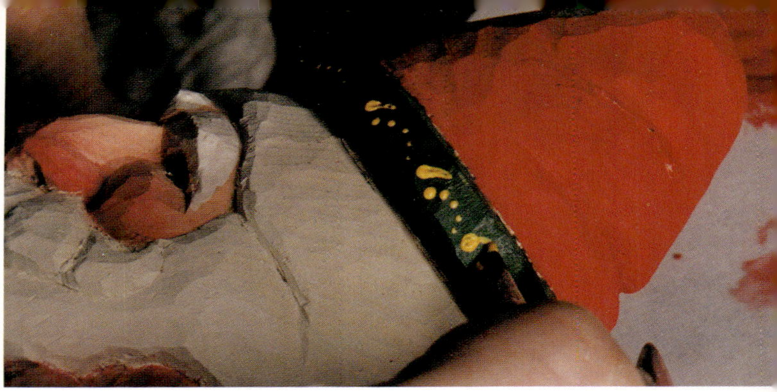

Drag the heavy dot to make a little flare.

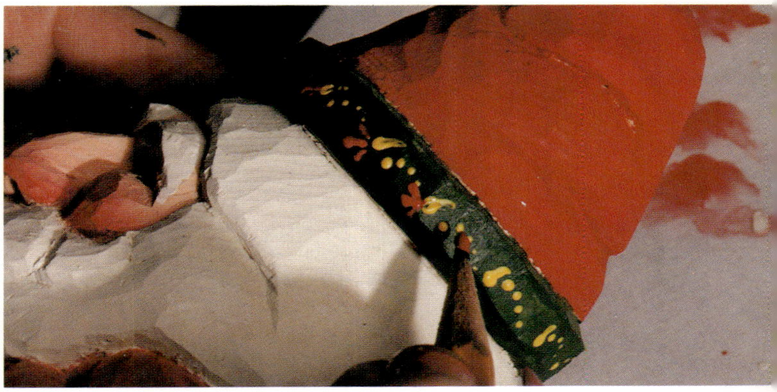

Finally create a pattern of red at the opposite end of the larger yellow dot. These three lines are done by making red dots and dragging them toward the yellow dot.

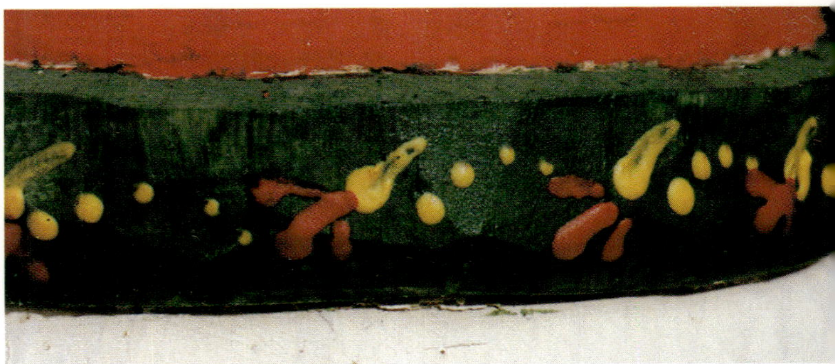

The hat trim complete. Allow the paint to dry.

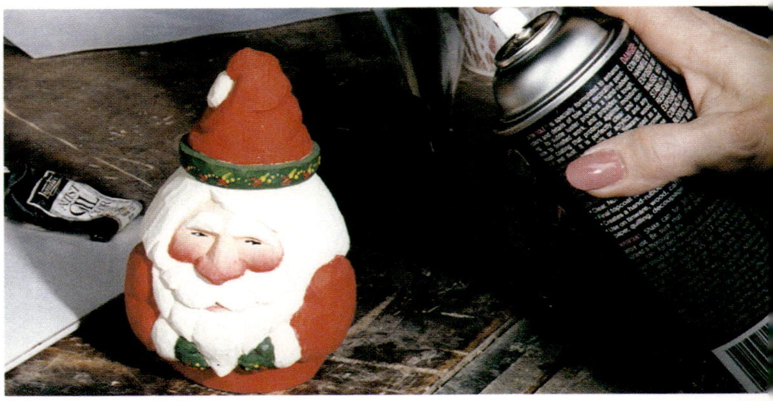

Spray with a clear satin finish. You will need three good coats. Otherwise the oil will go right into the paint and turn everything brown.

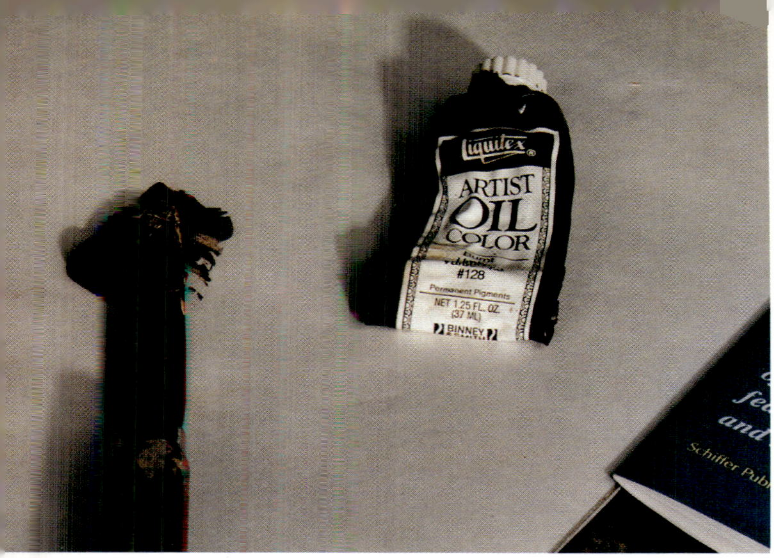

To make the antiquing mixture use burnt umber oil paint...

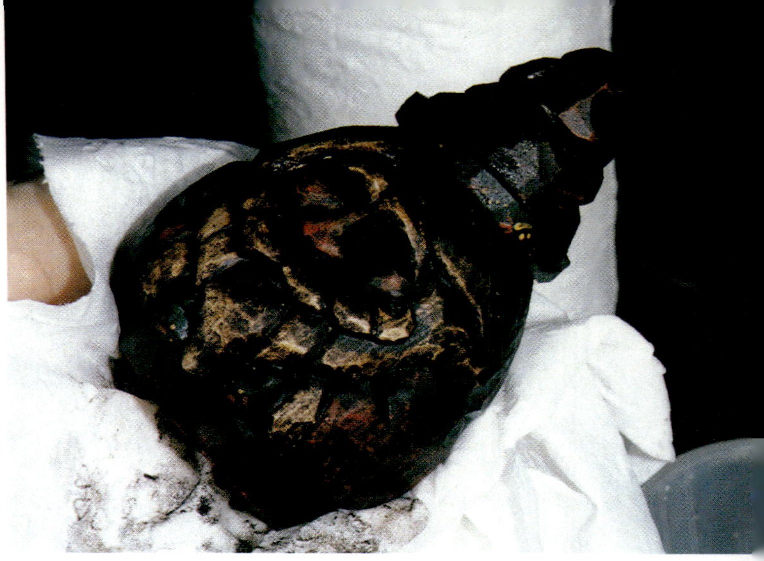

Ready for a rub down.

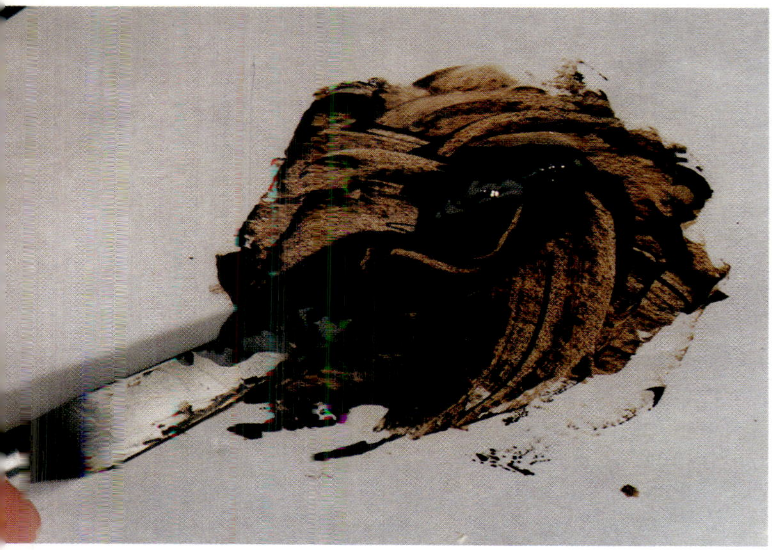

and thinner until it is the consistency of melted chocolate chips.

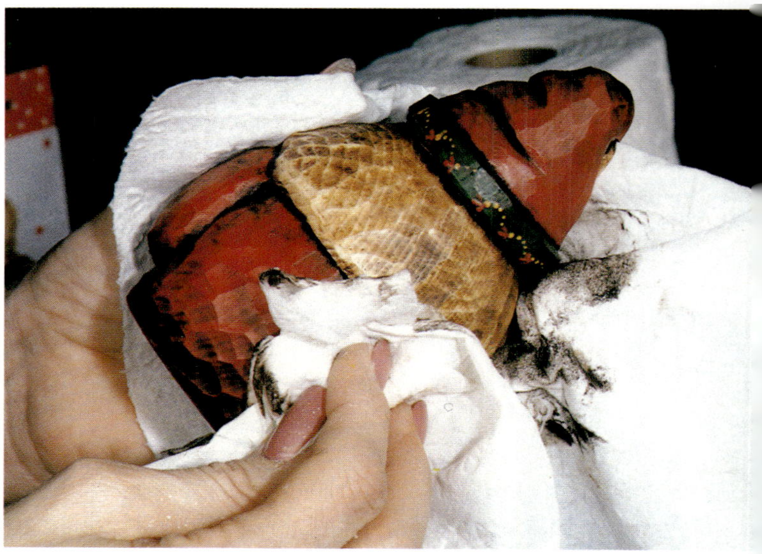

Wipe off the antiquing. The more you wipe the lighter it gets, so you can go to any degree of antiquing that you desire.

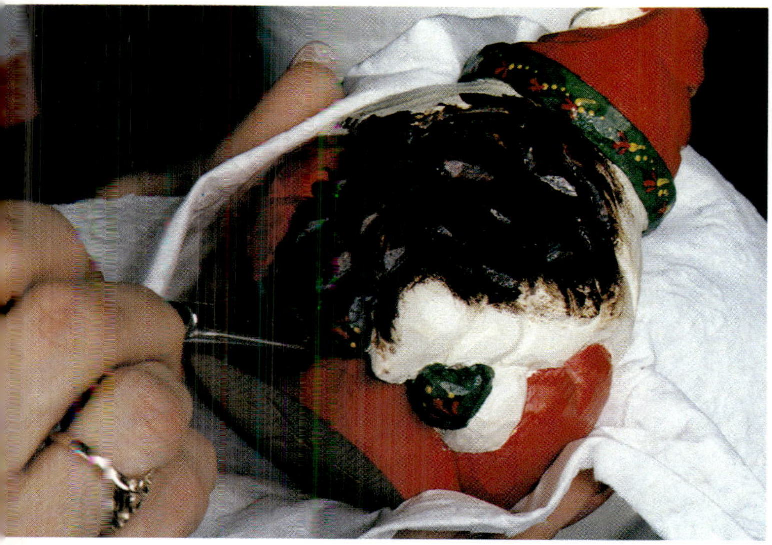

When the varnish is completely dry cover the carving with the antiquing mixture.

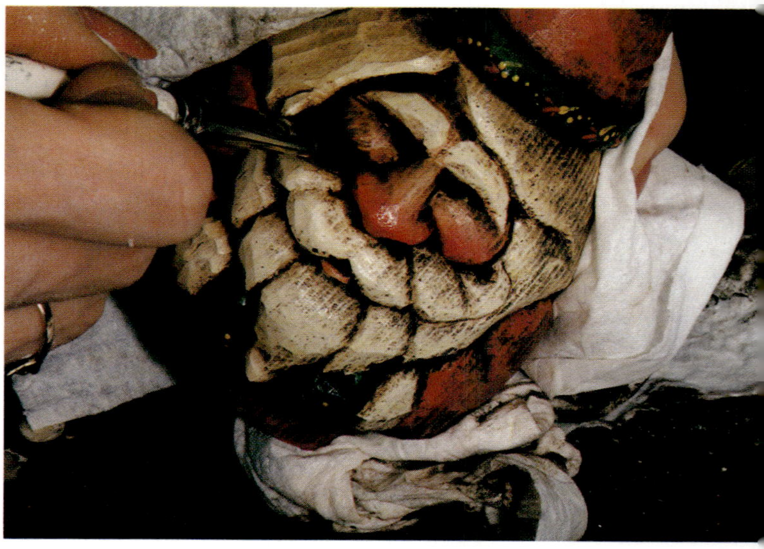

A dry clean brush can be used to take some of the antiquing out of the crevices so it isn't so harsh.

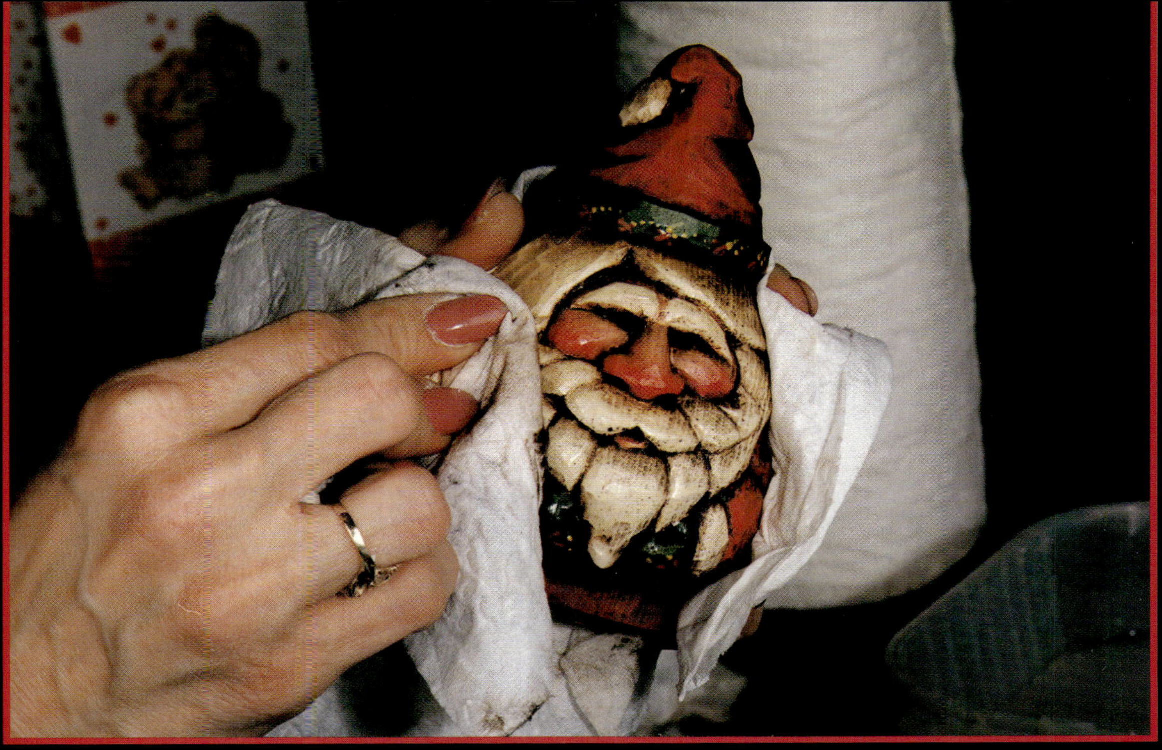

Rewipe after using the brush.

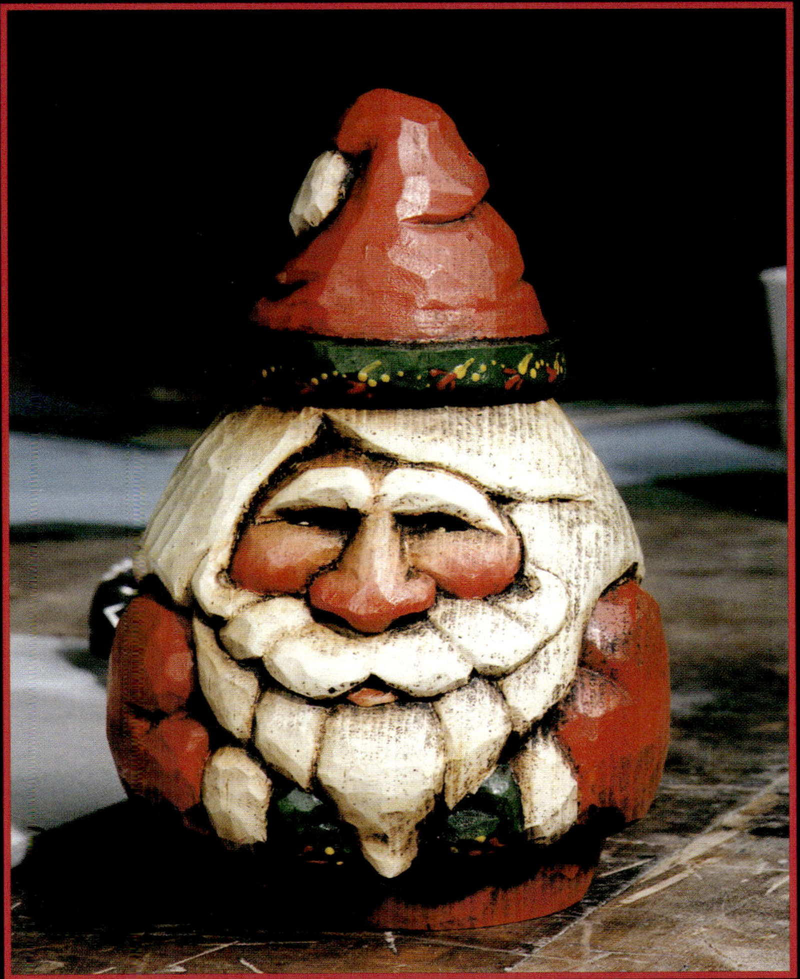

Ready for a final varnishing. Remember, the papers you used with the oil paint can spontaneously combust so be careful to dispose of the them properly

Gallery of Figures

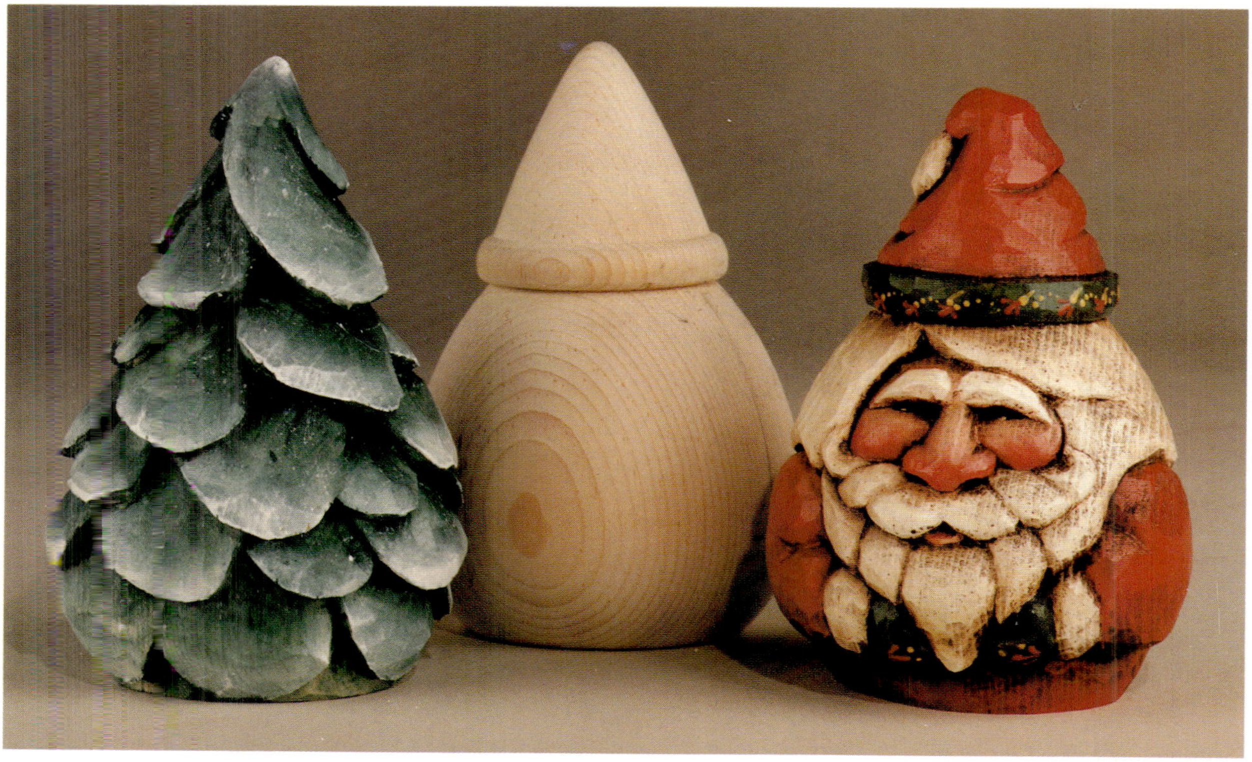

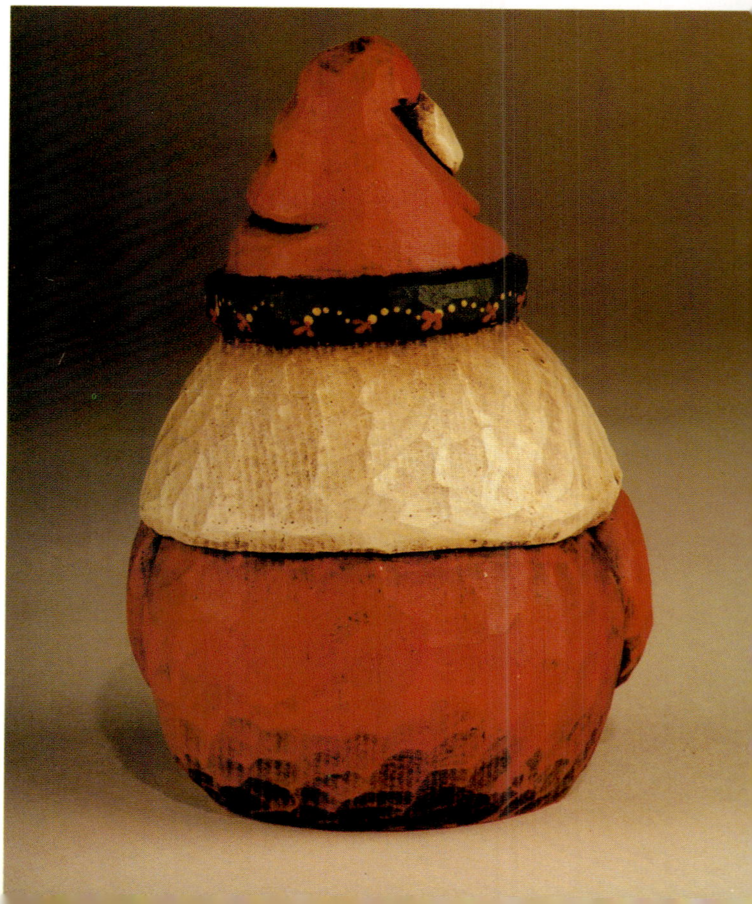

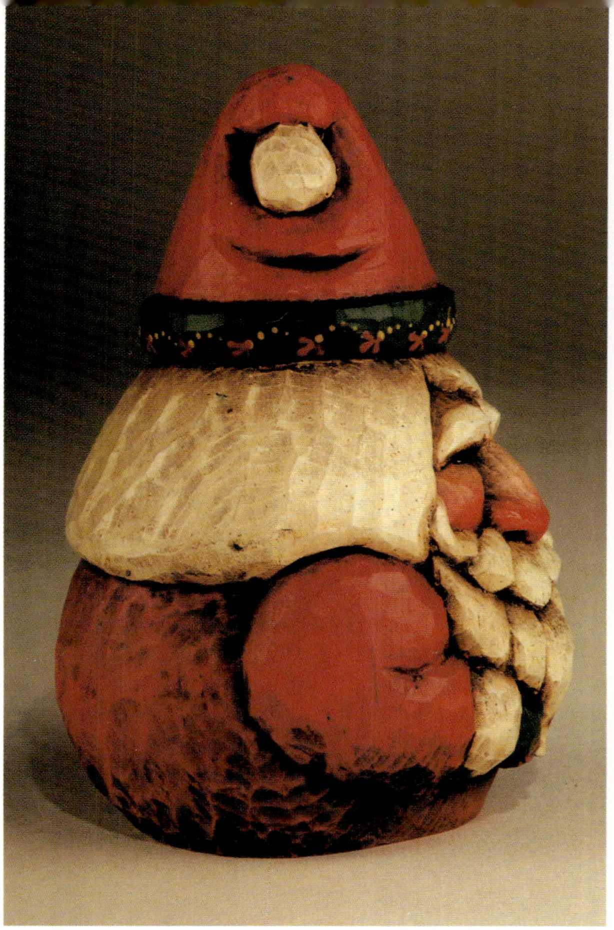
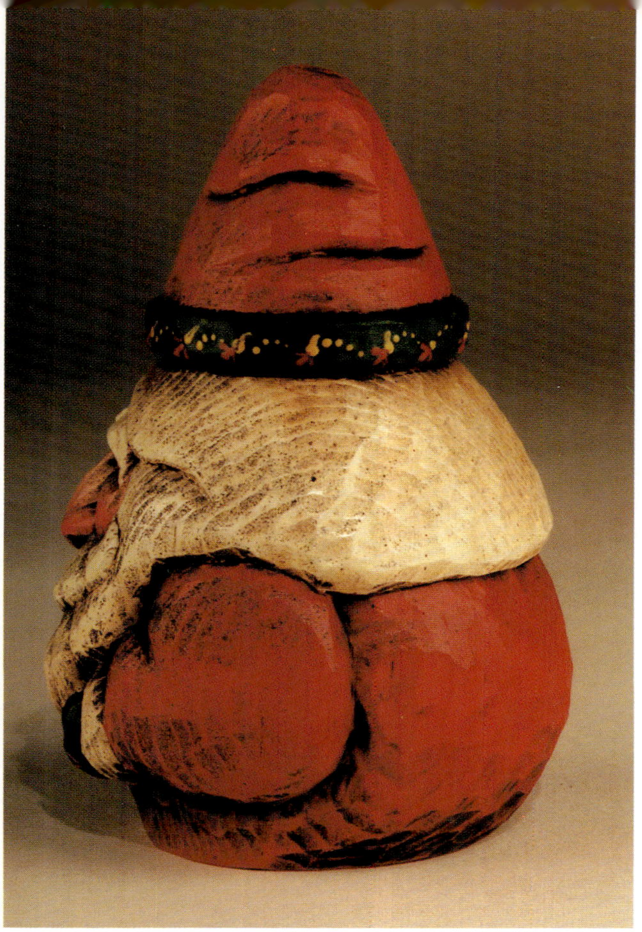
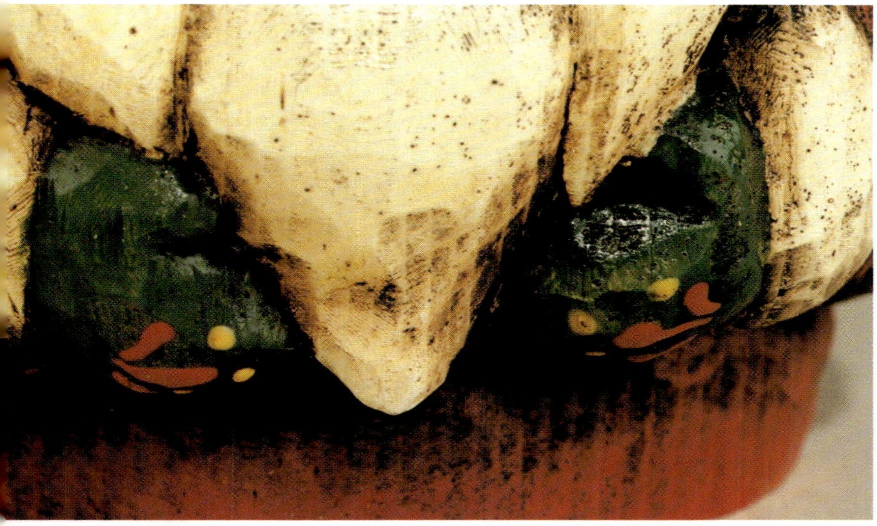
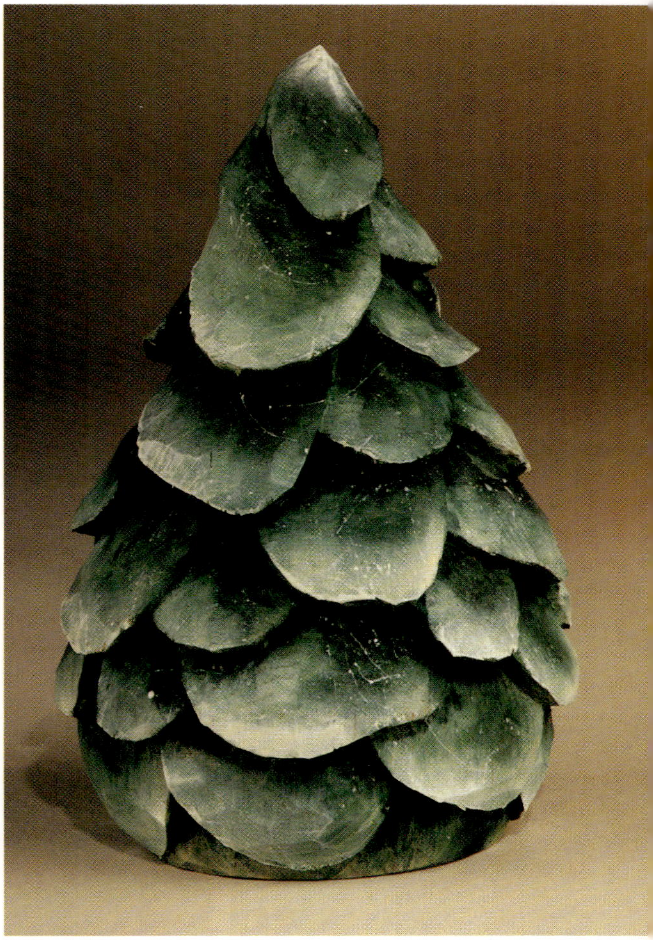
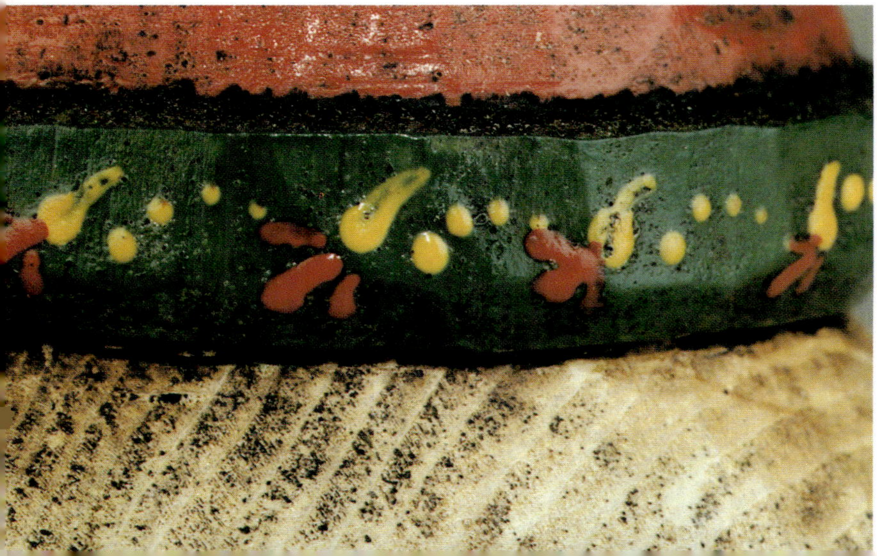

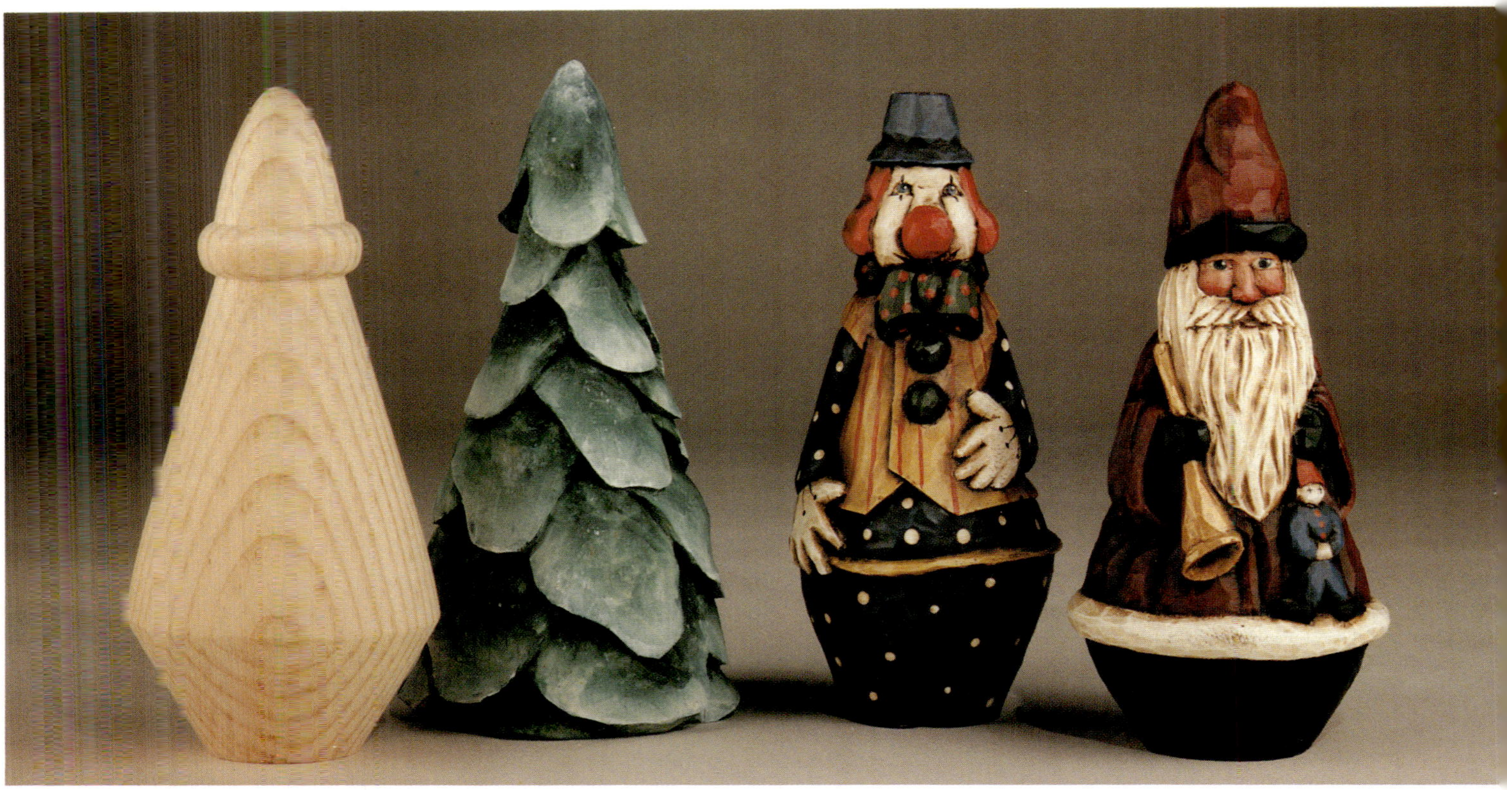

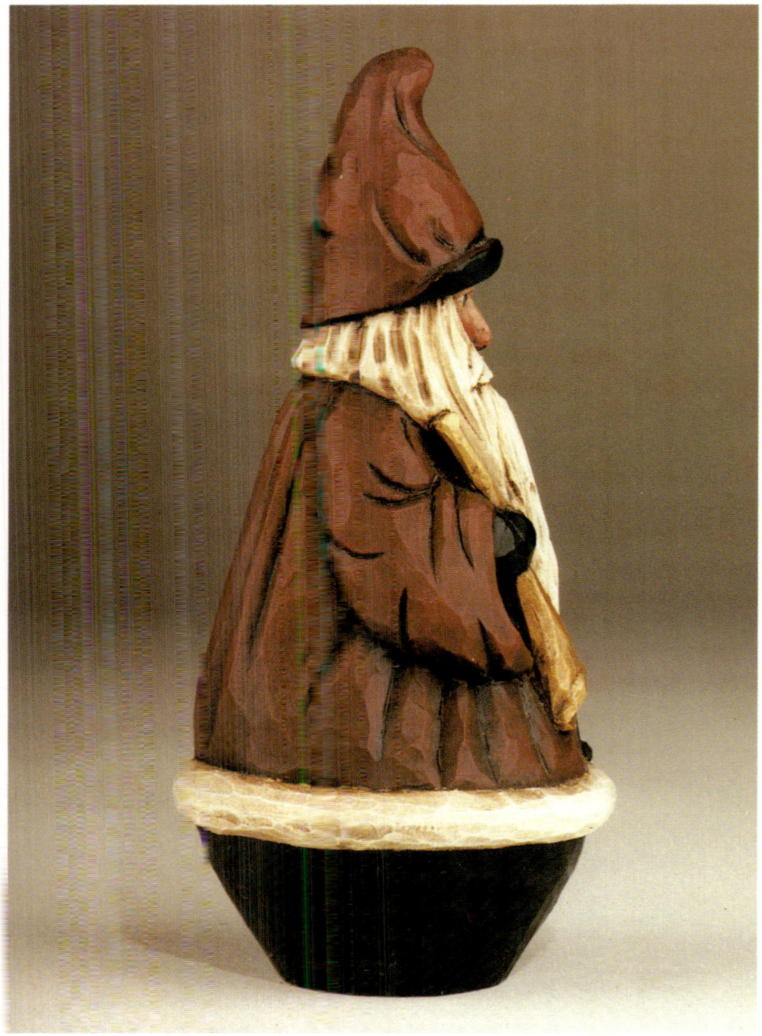

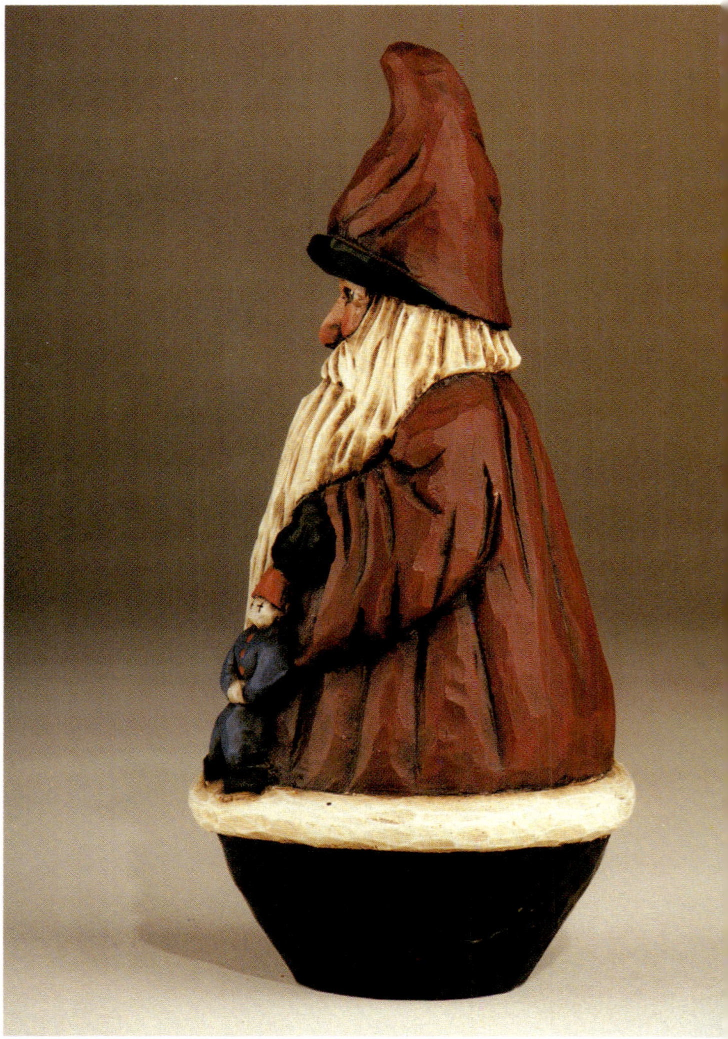

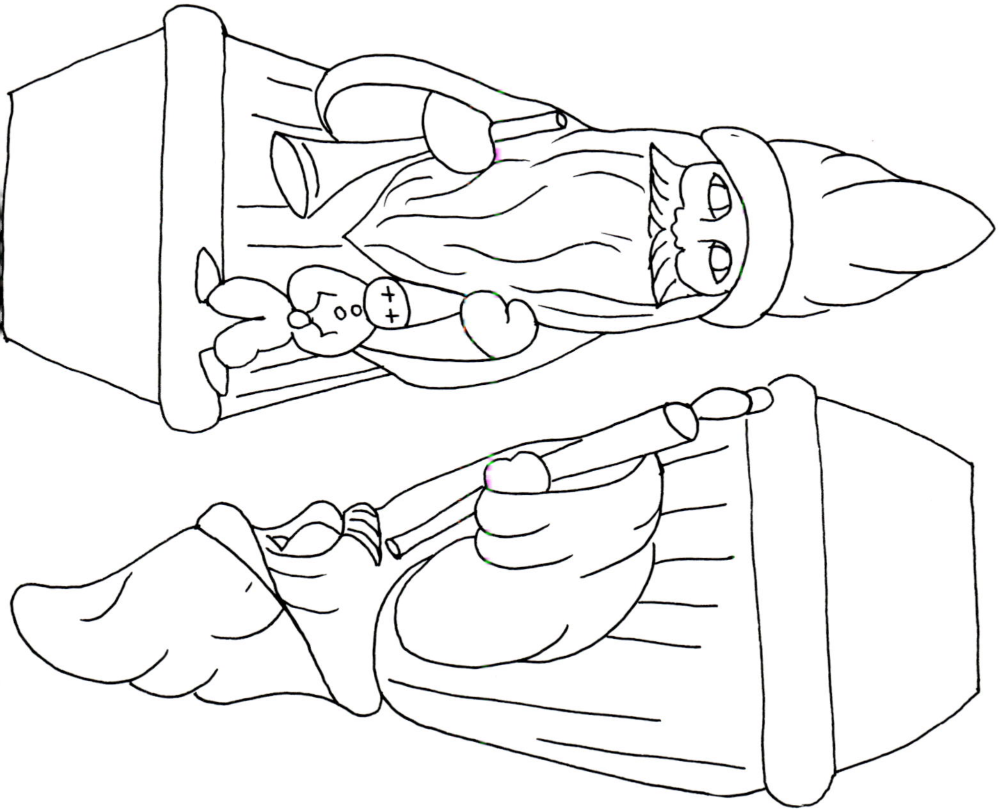

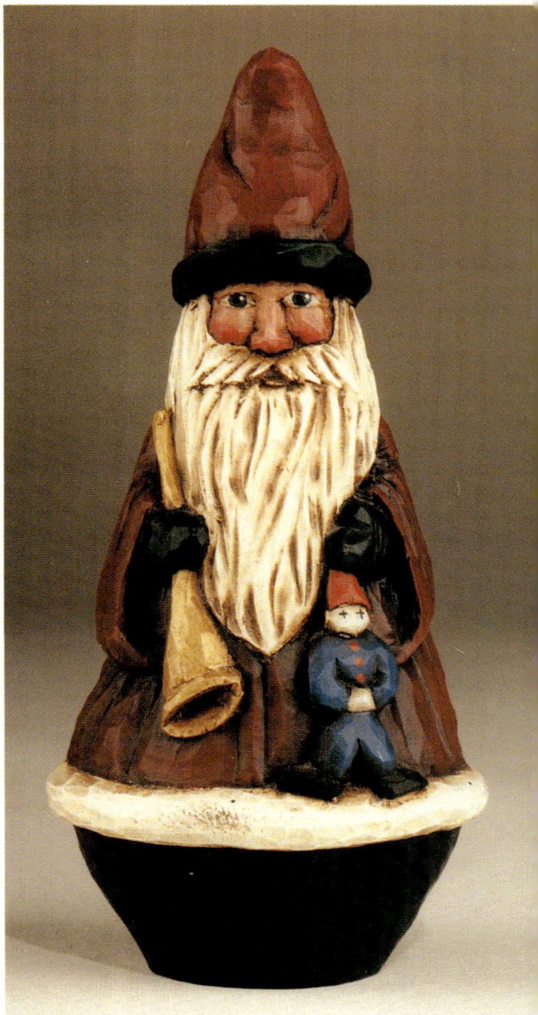

Patterns have been reduced to 70%.

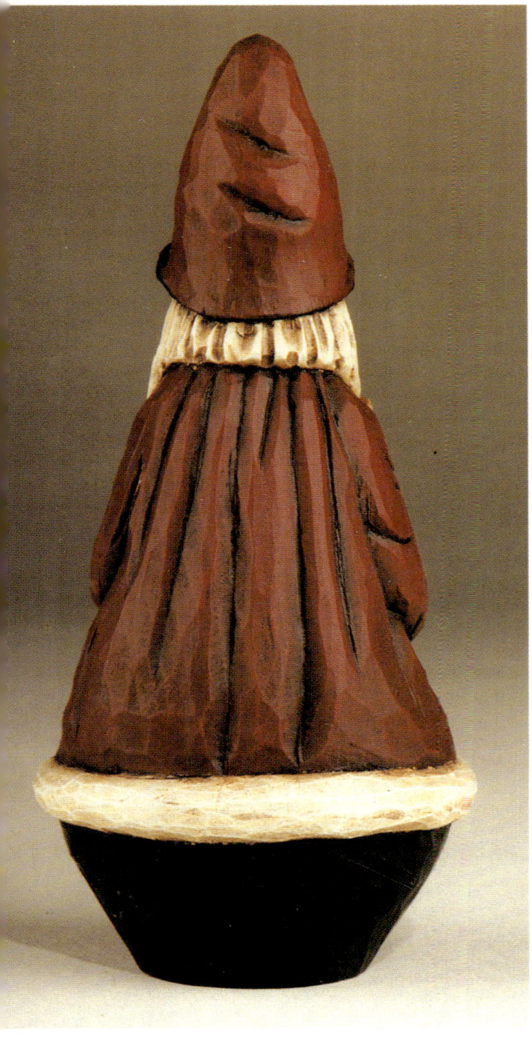

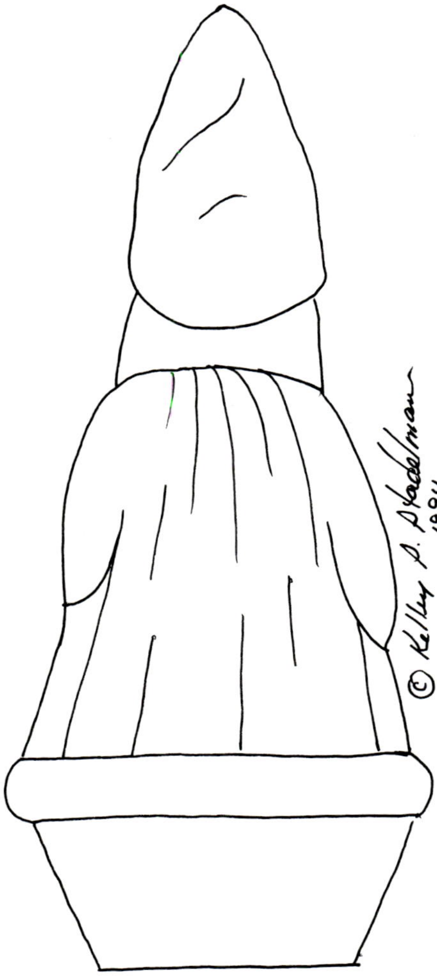

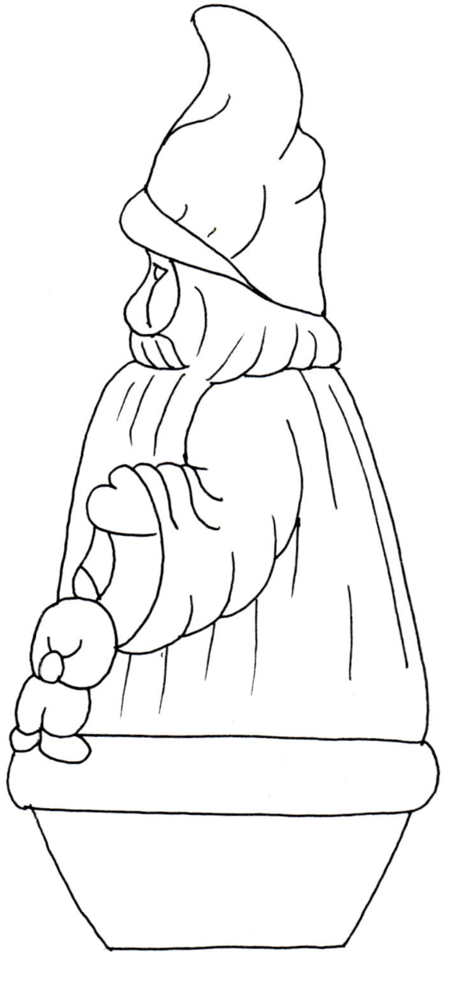

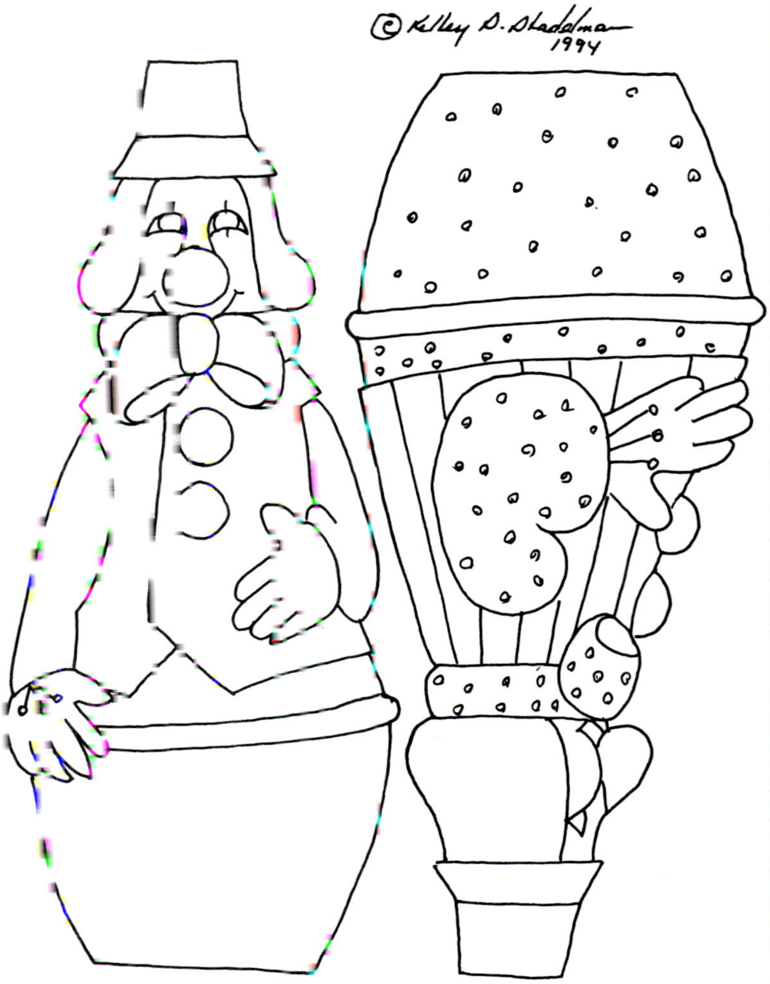

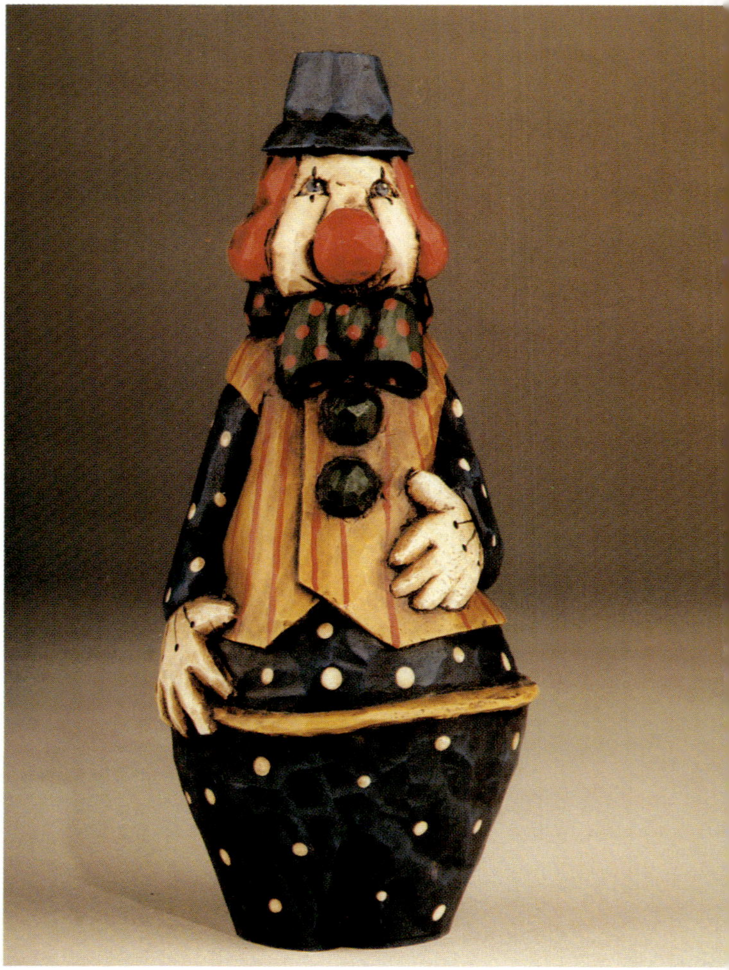

Patterns have been reduced to 70%.

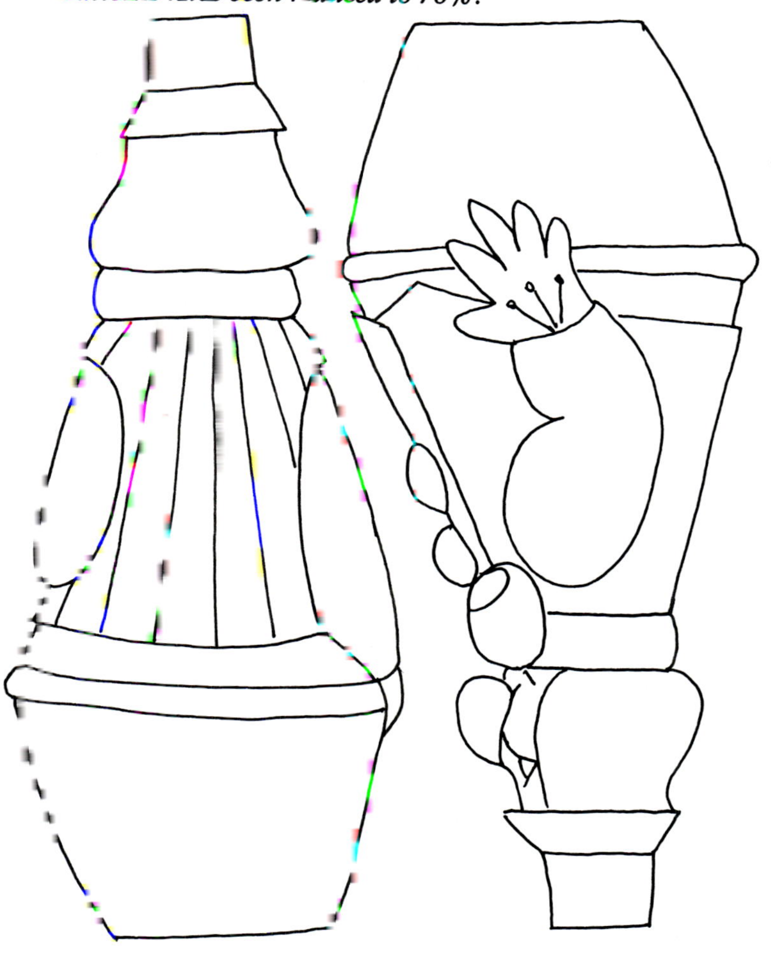

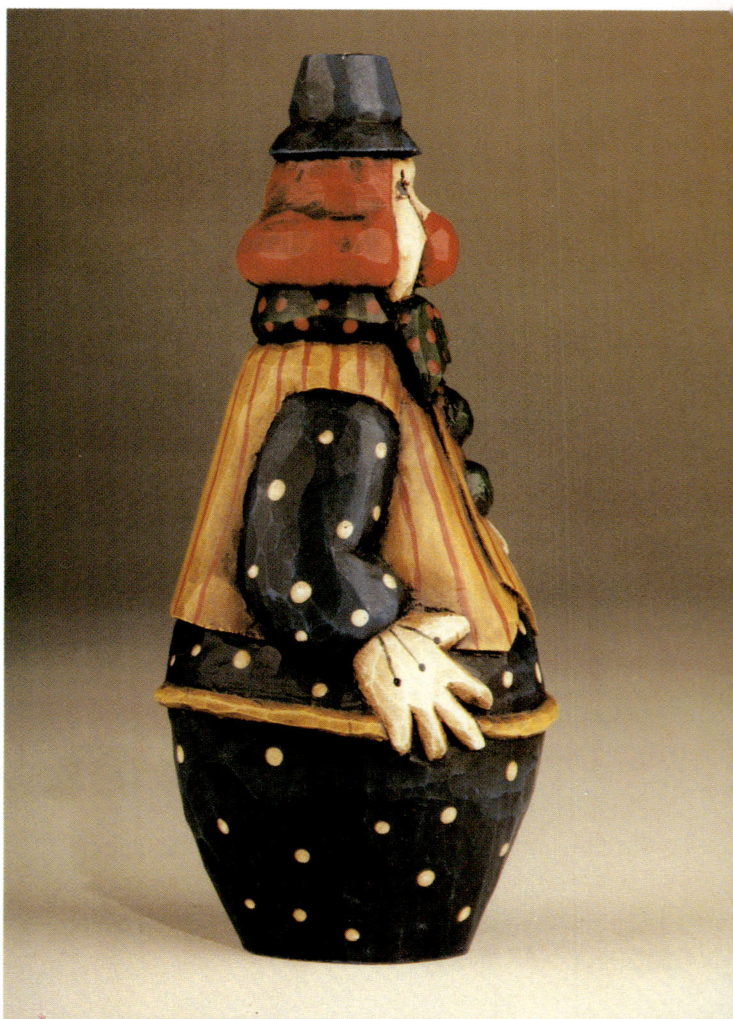

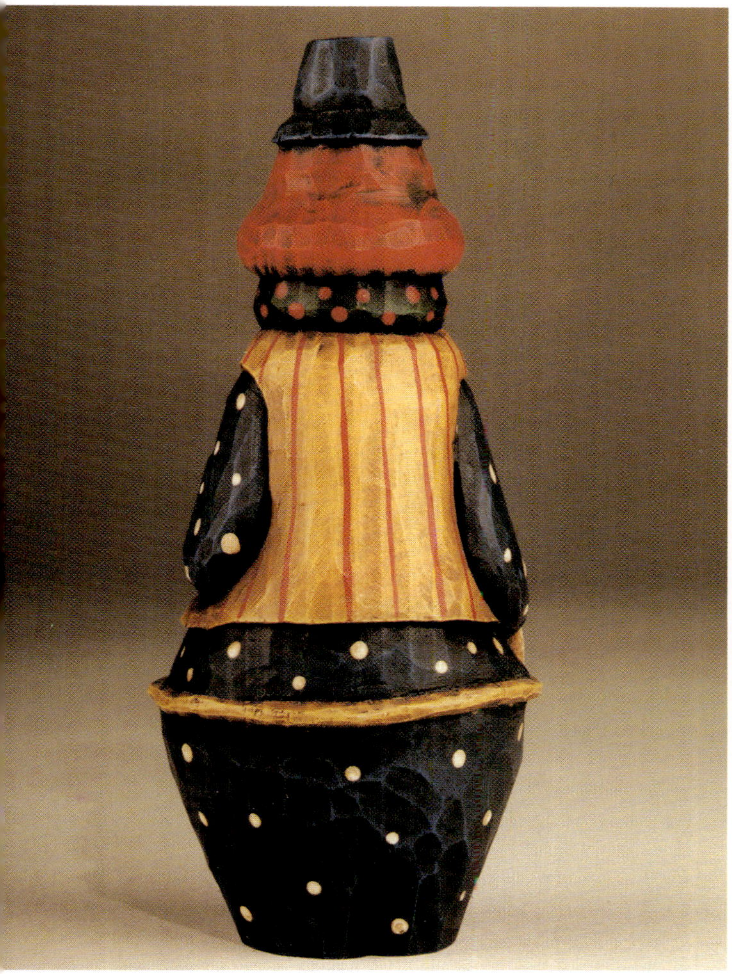
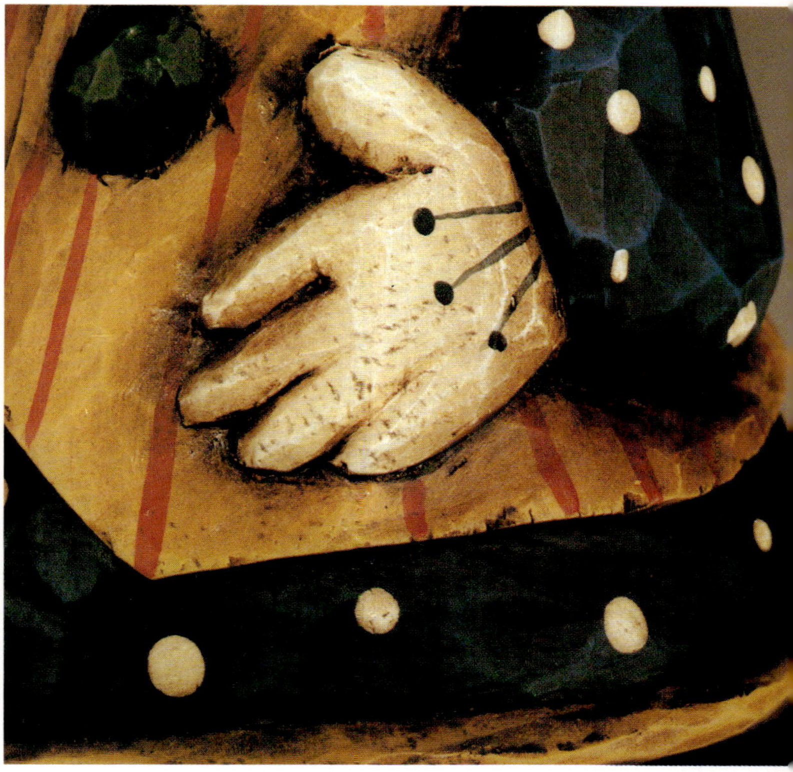
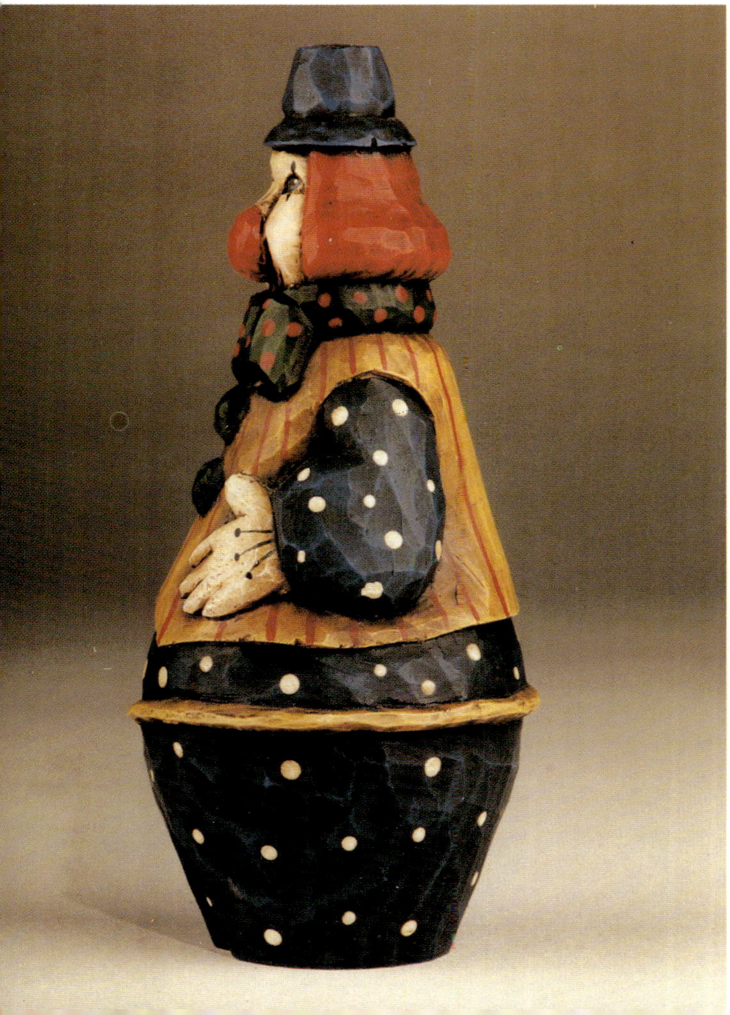
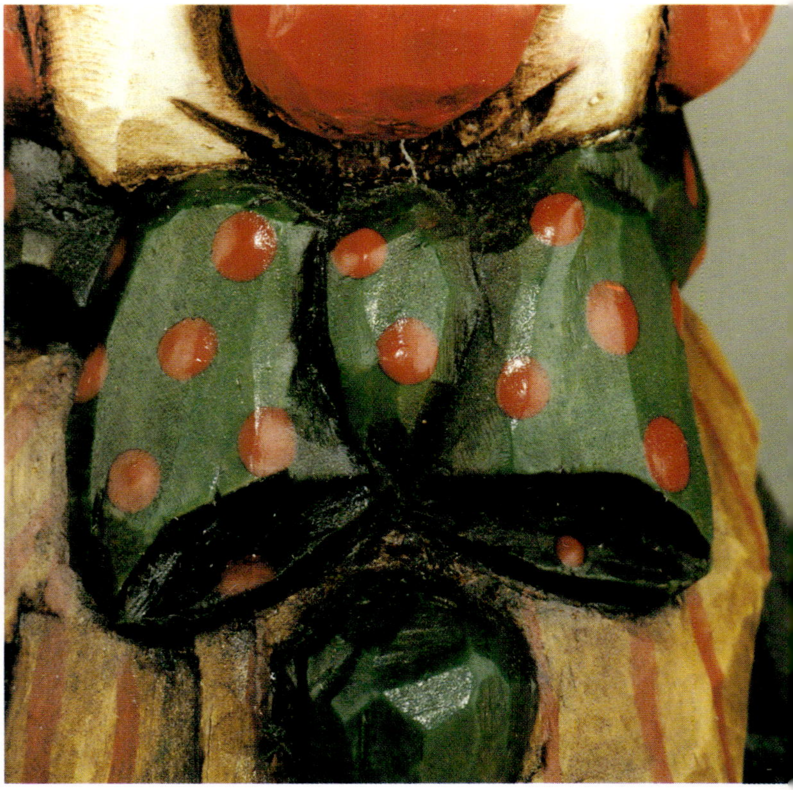

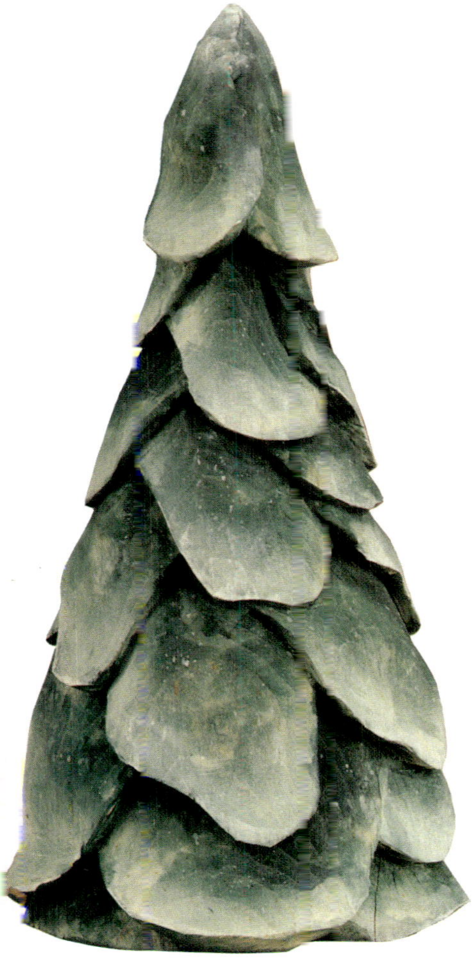

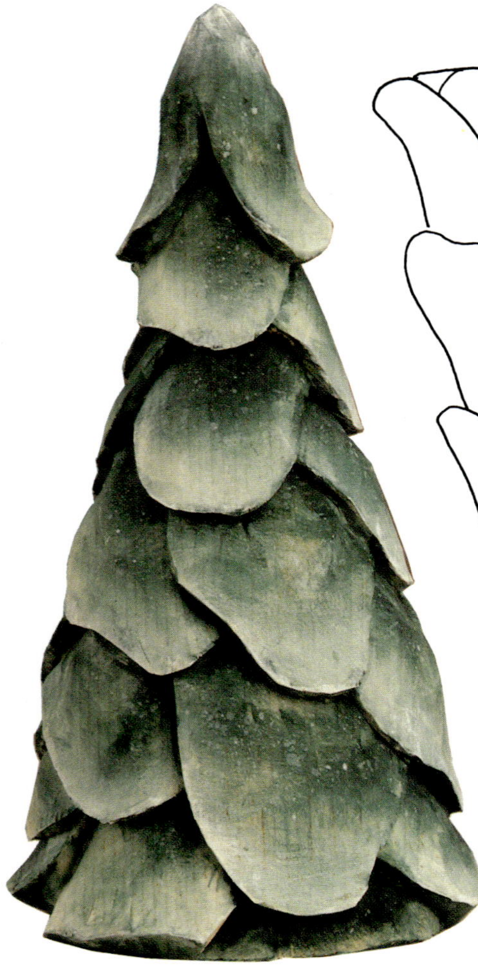

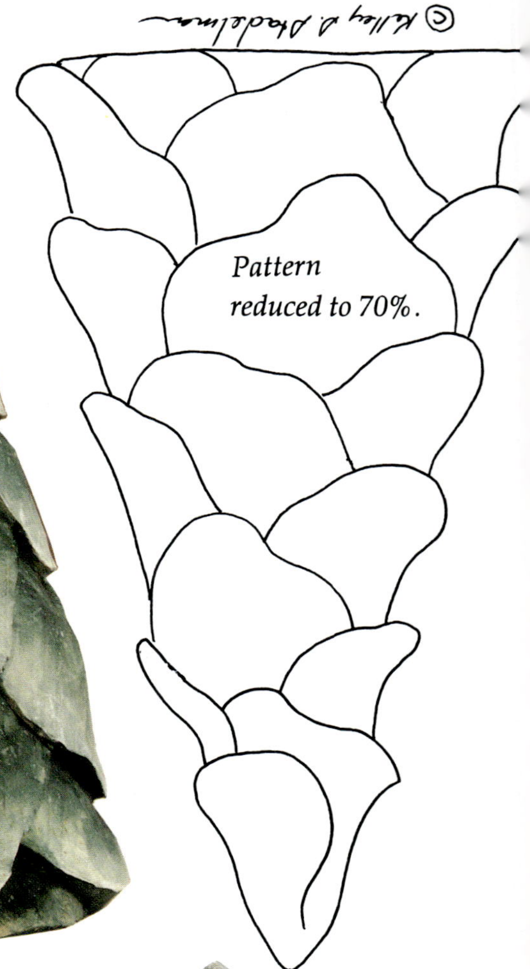
Pattern
reduced to 70%.

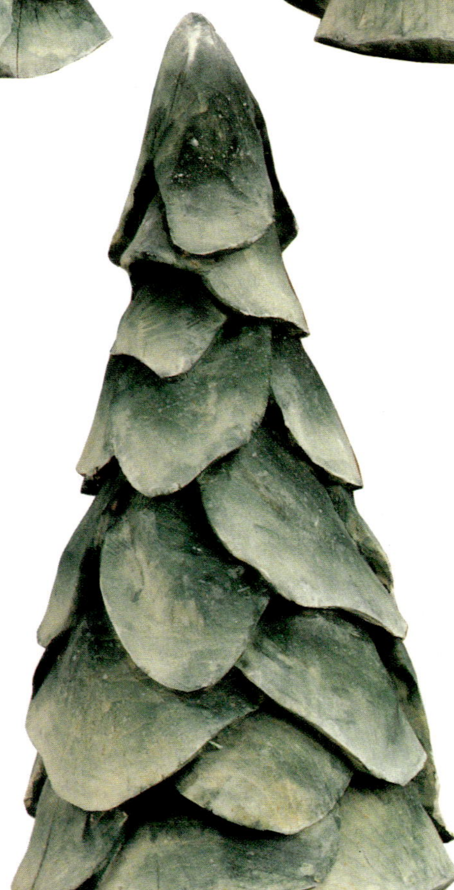

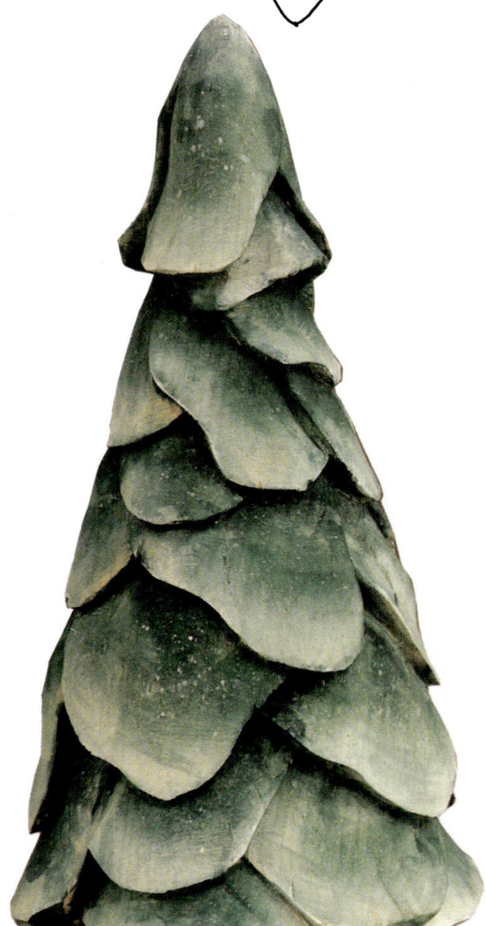

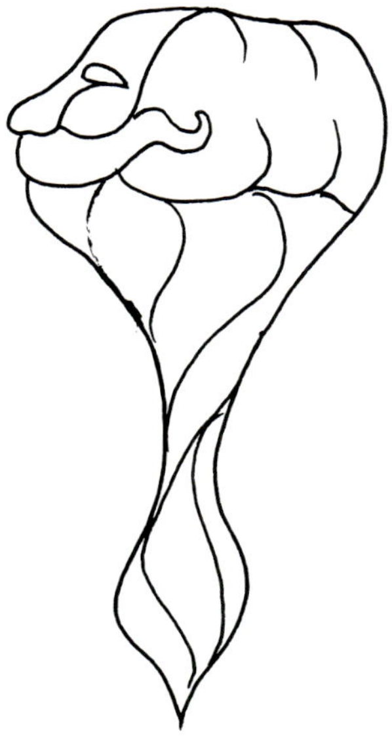

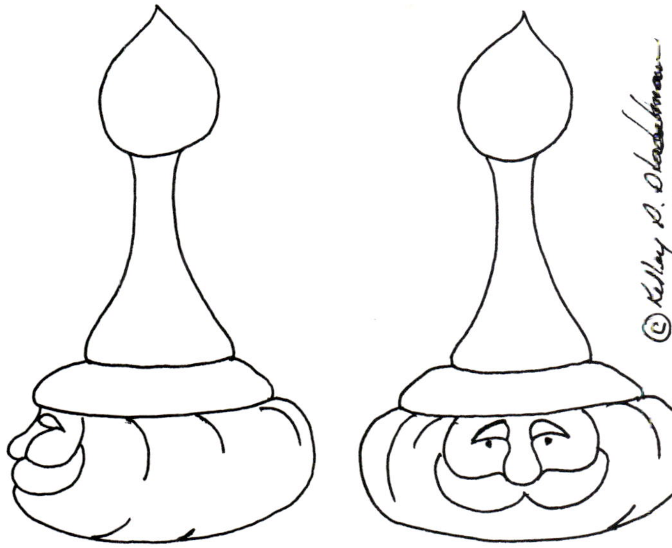

Patterns have been reduced to 75%.

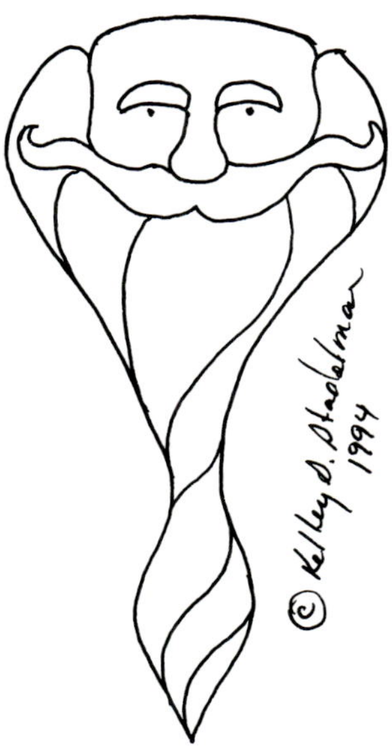

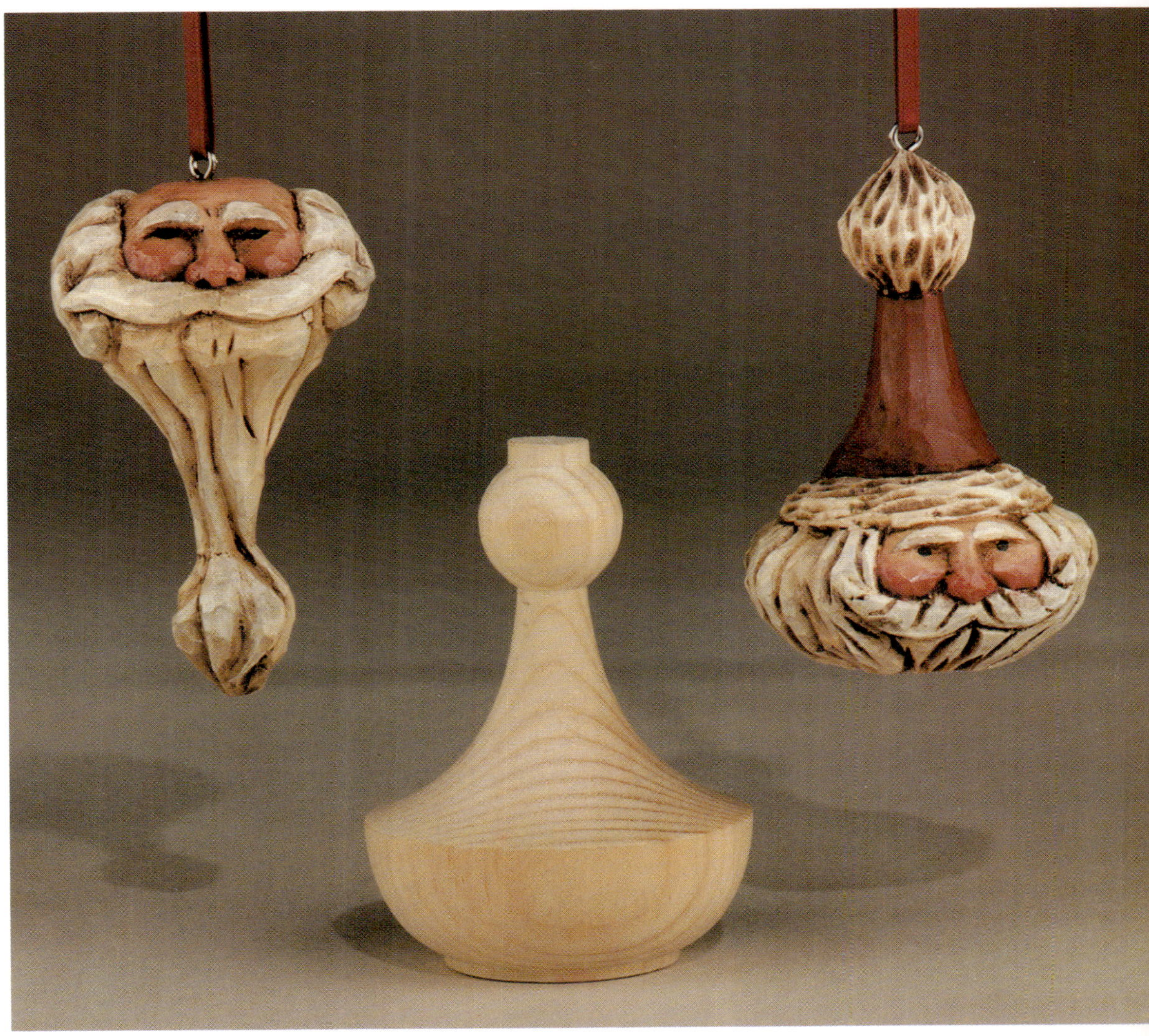

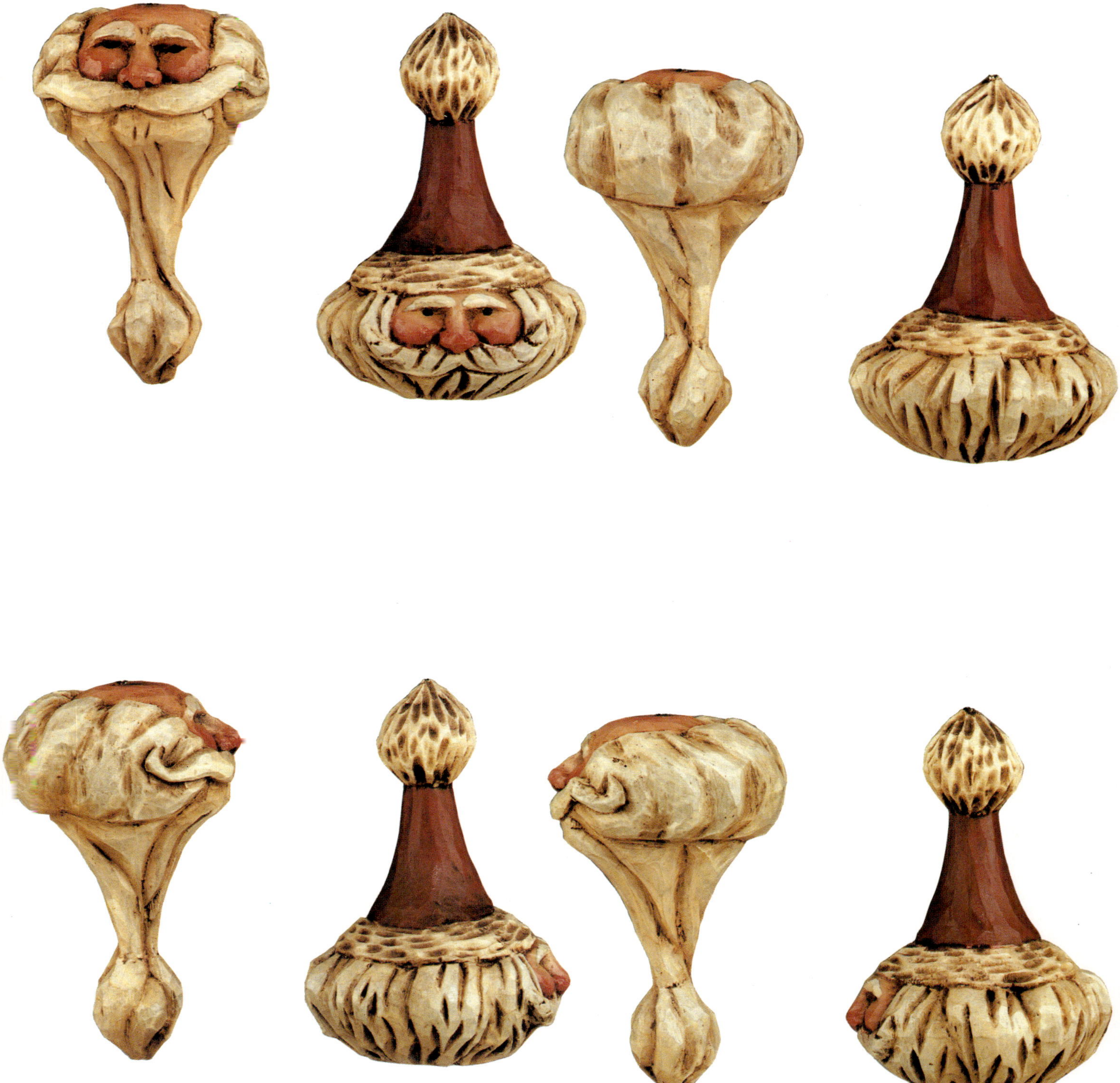

Patterns have been reduced to 66%.

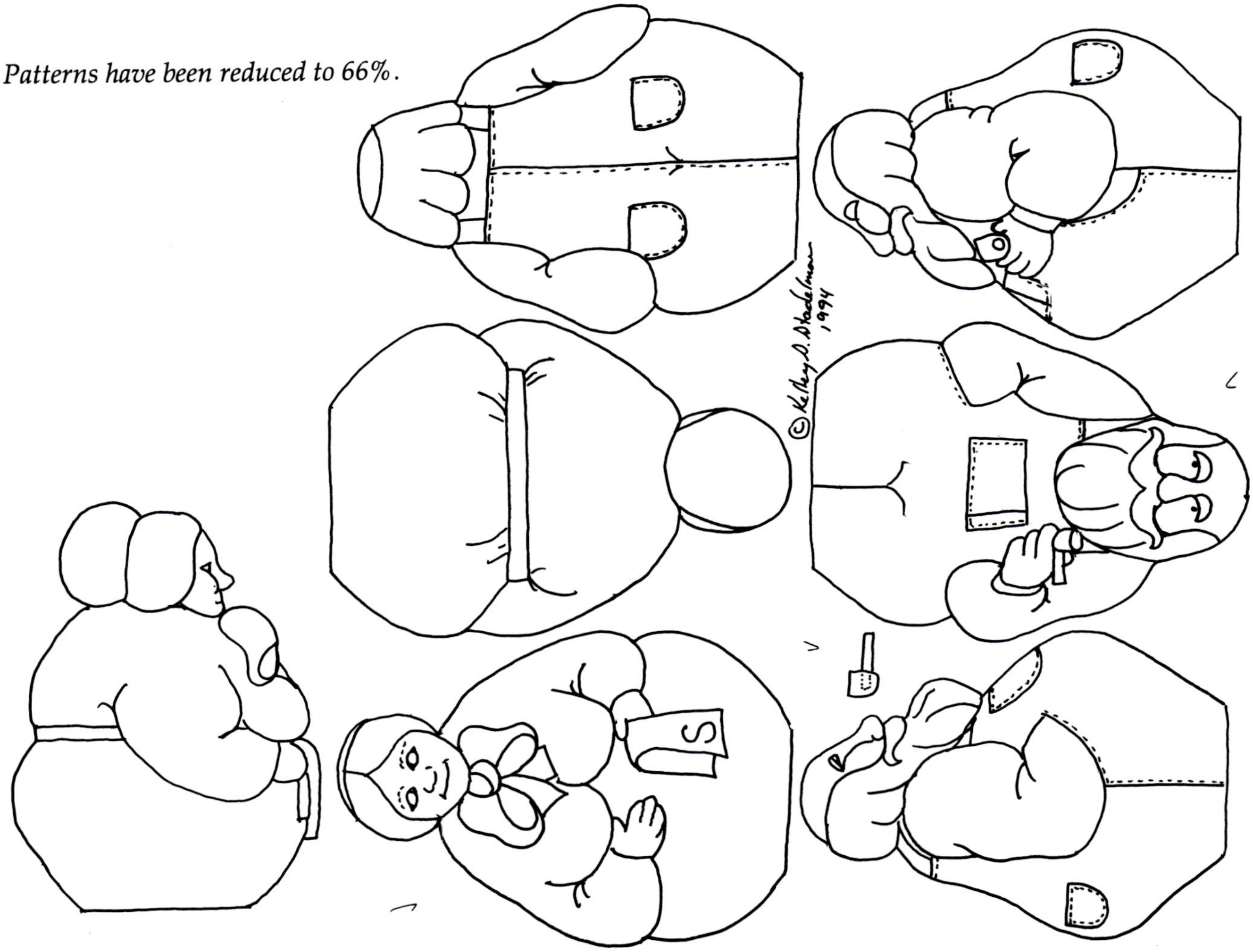

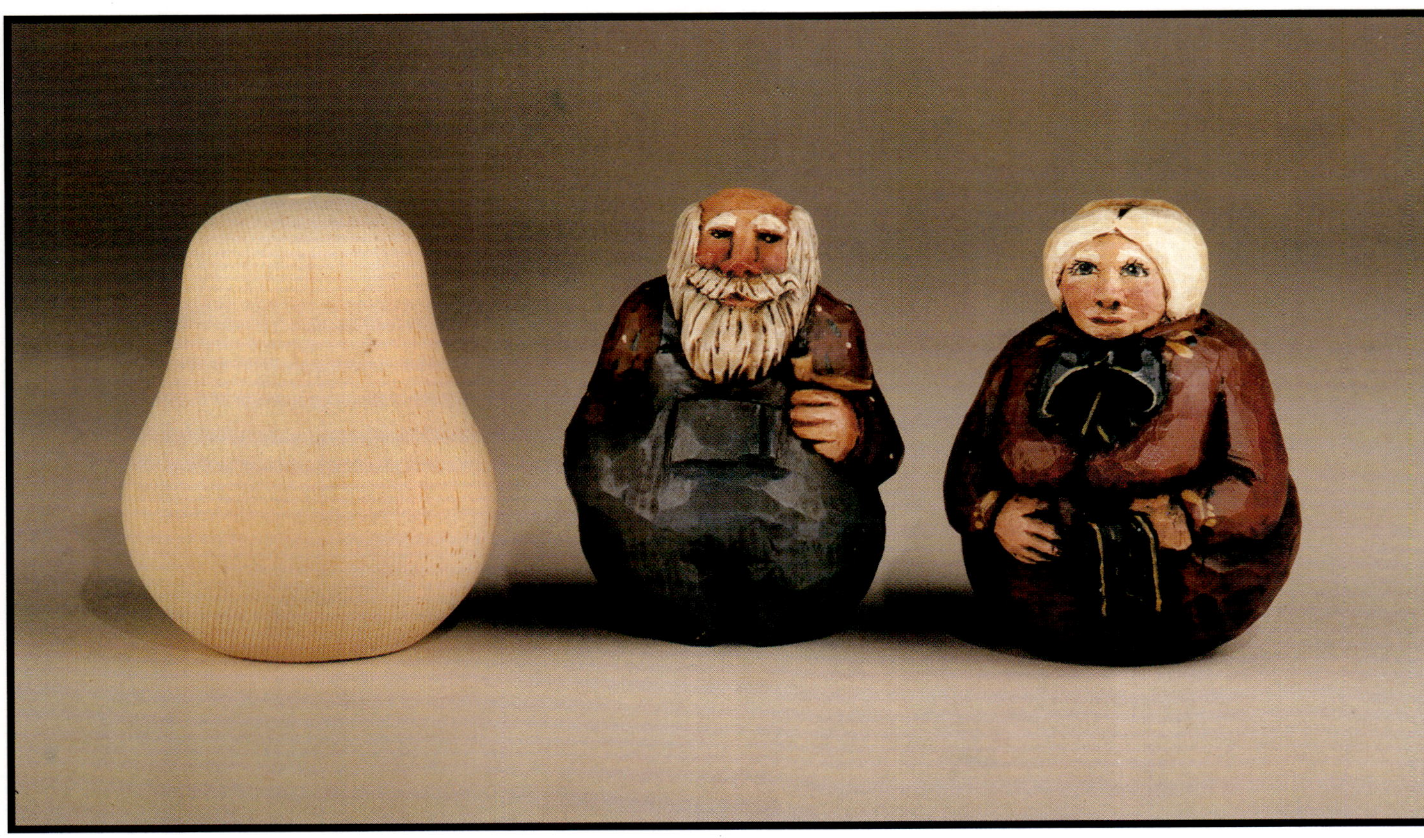

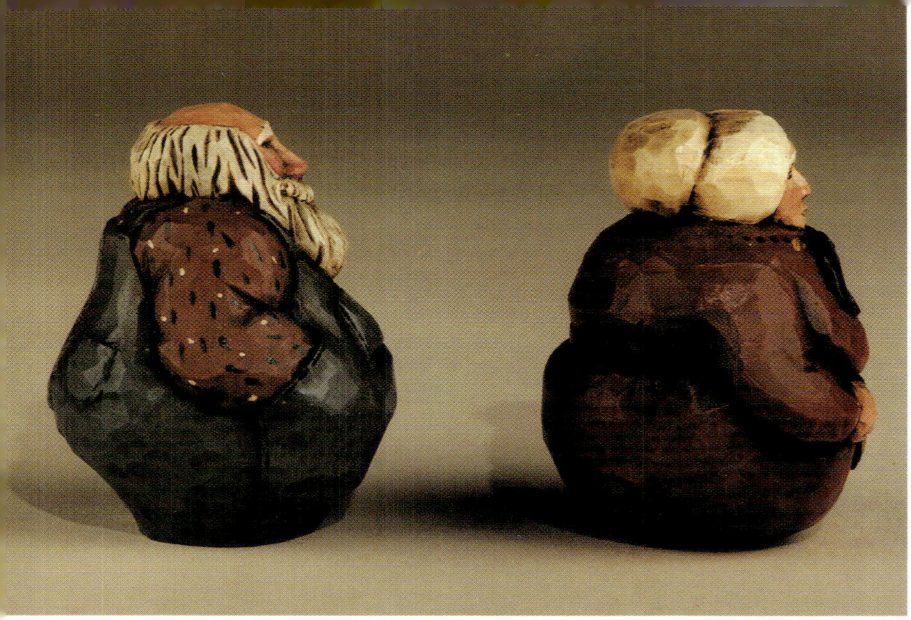

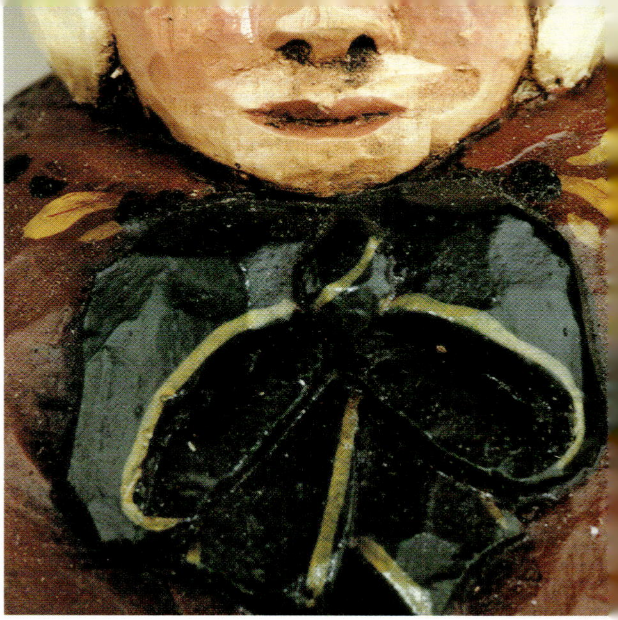

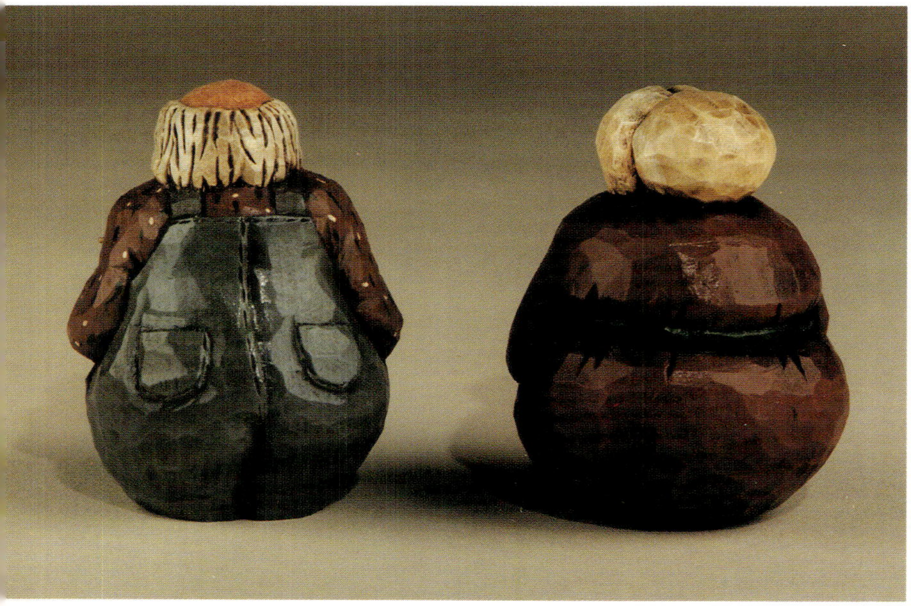

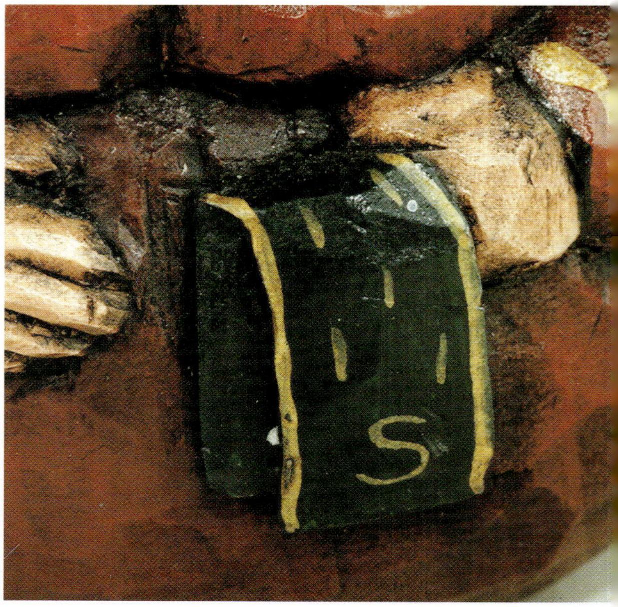
S

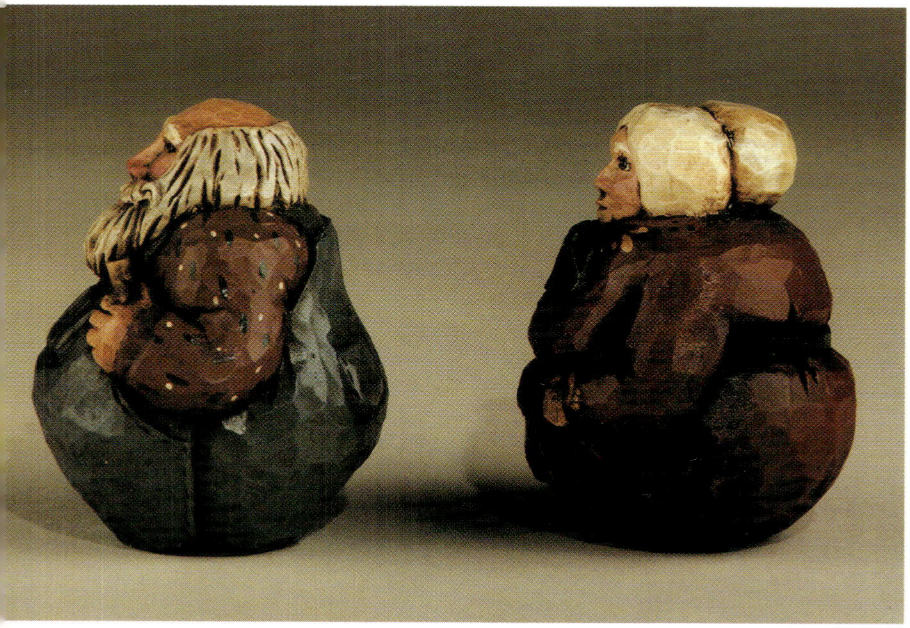

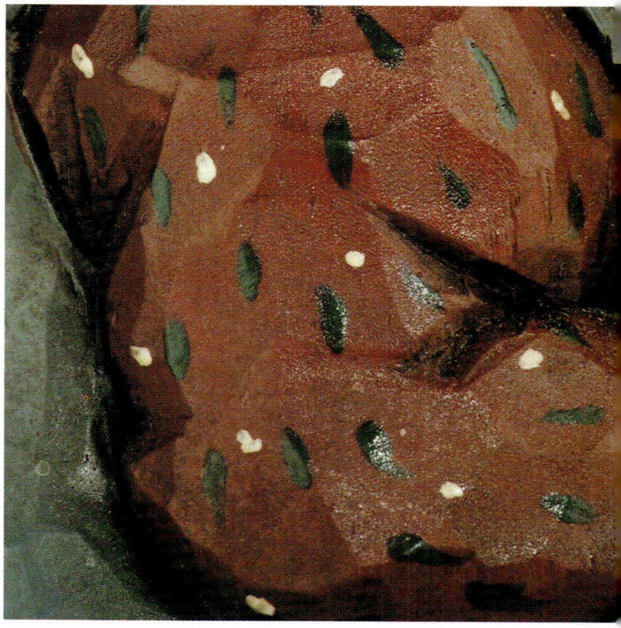

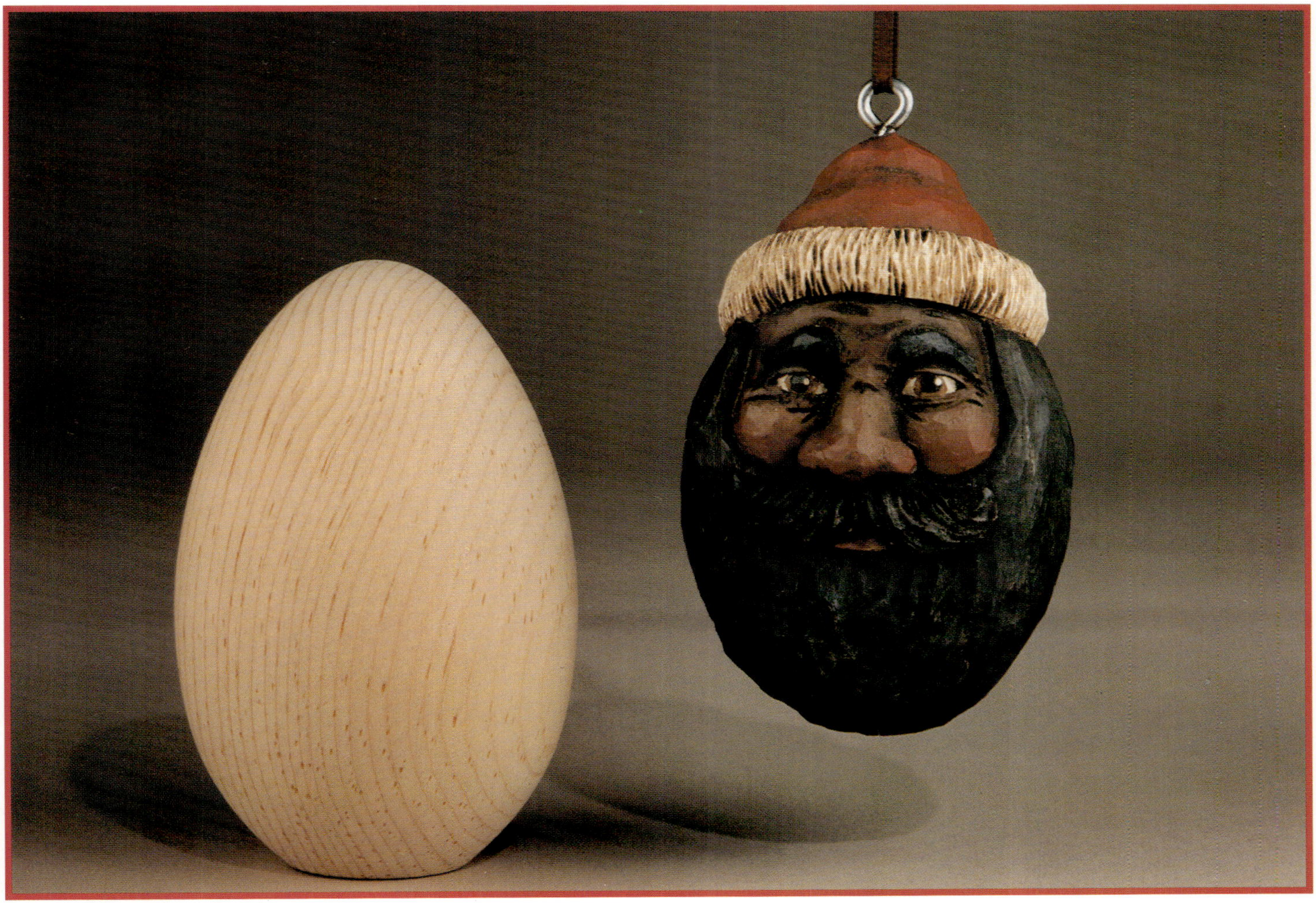

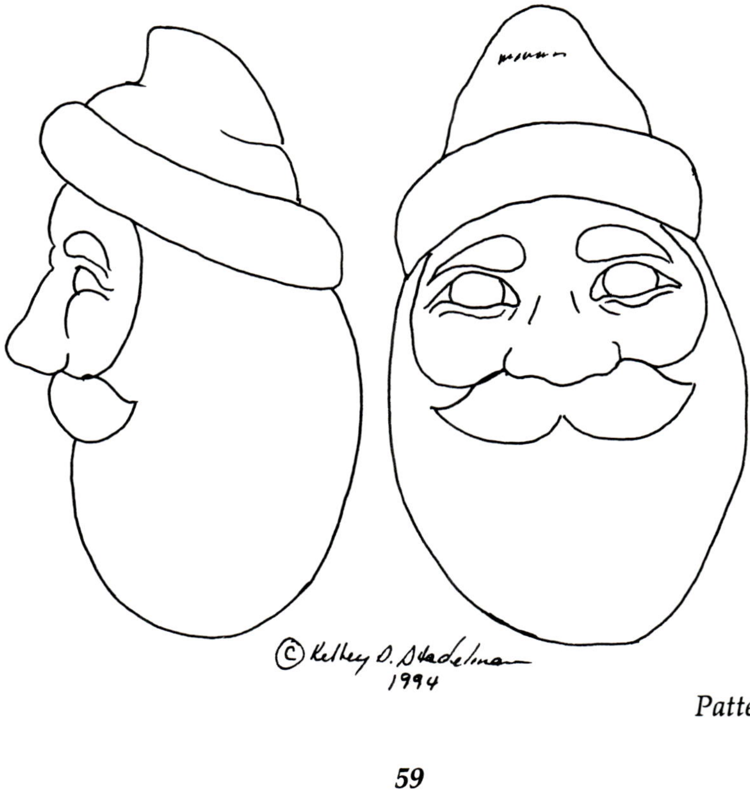

Patterns have been reduced to 75%.

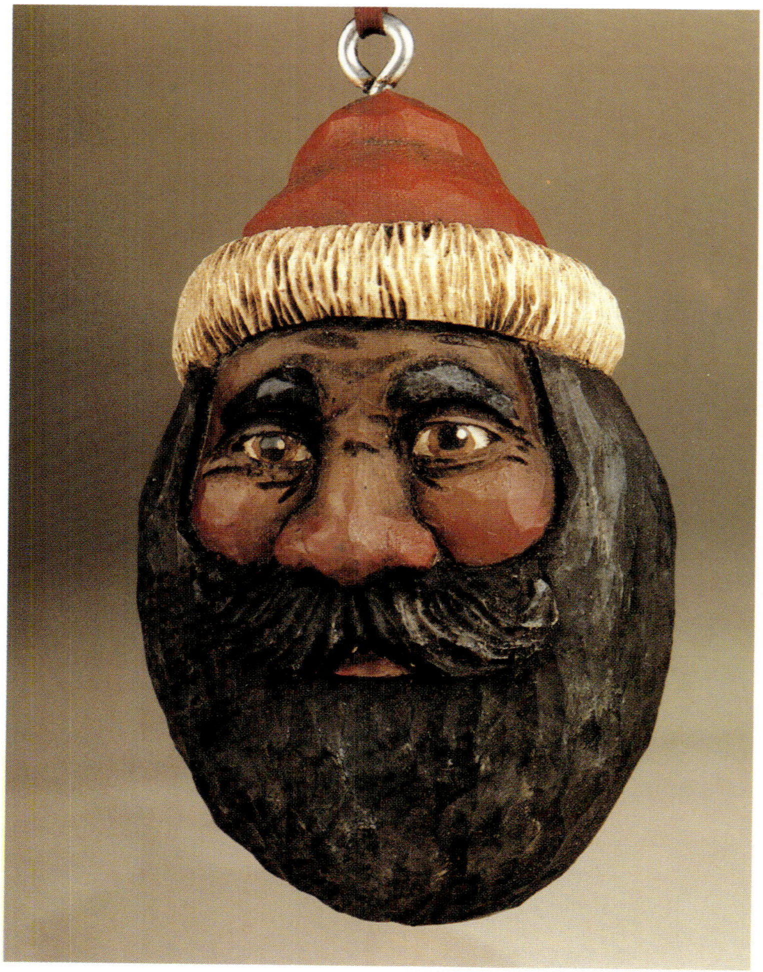
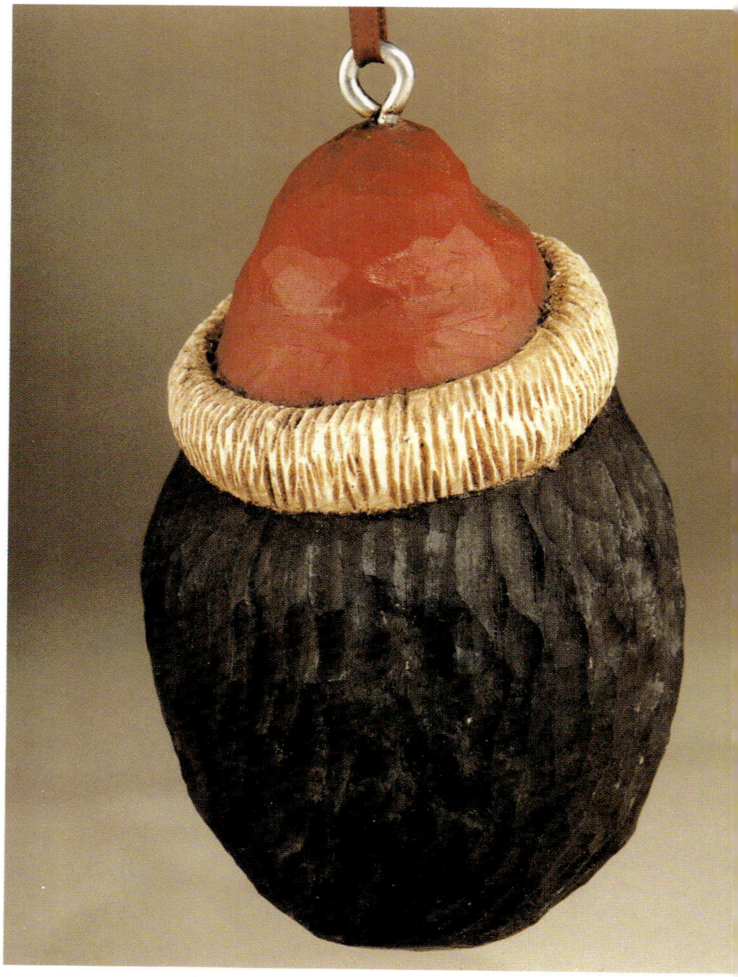
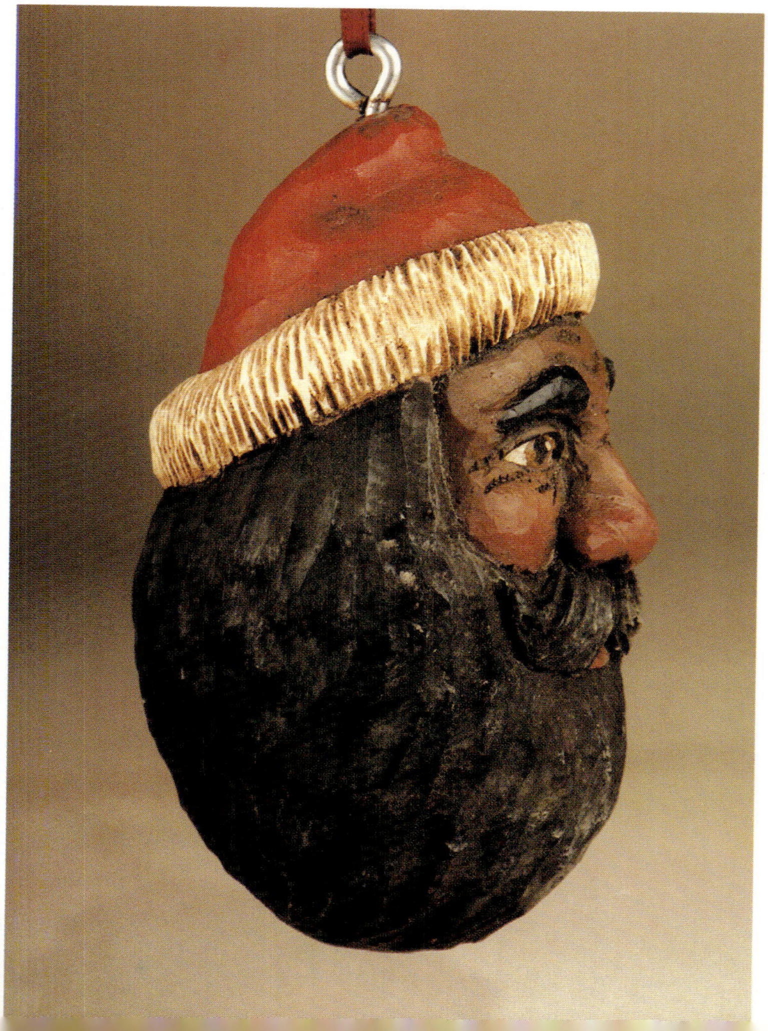
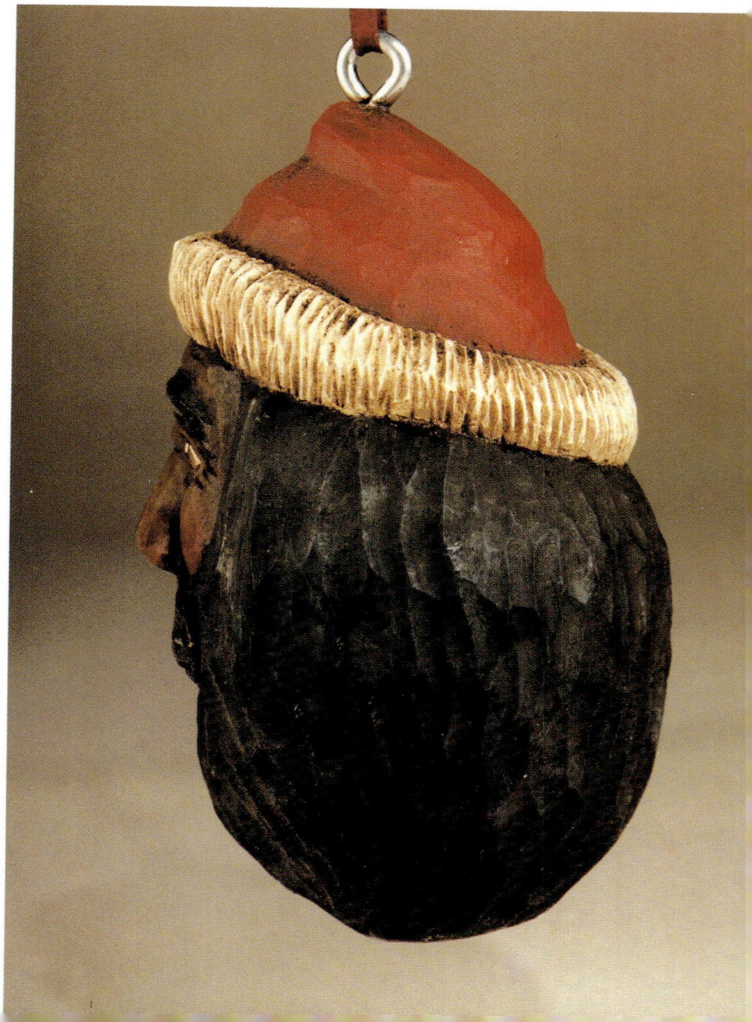

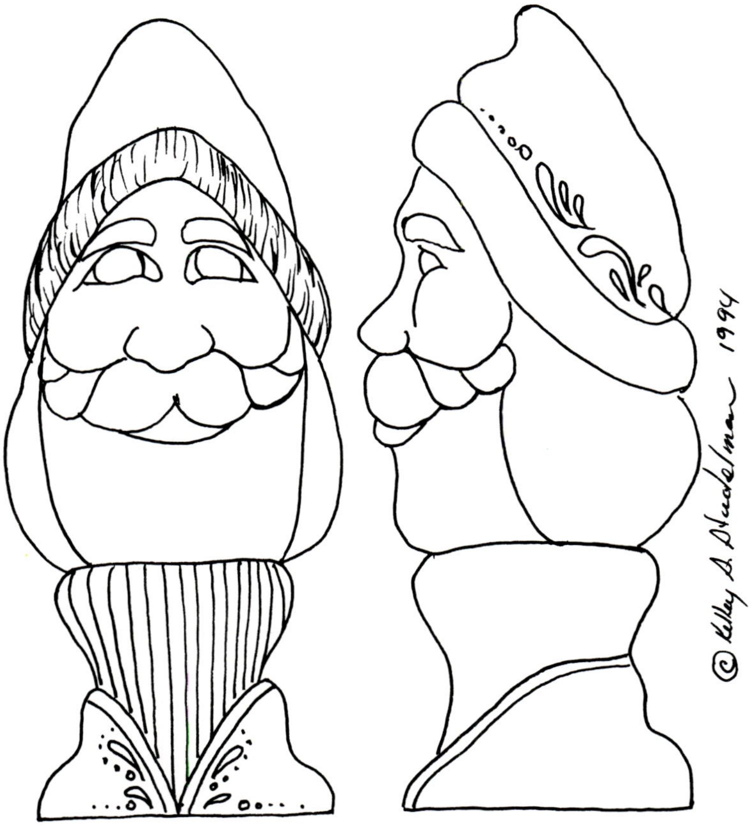

Patterns have been reduced to 75%.

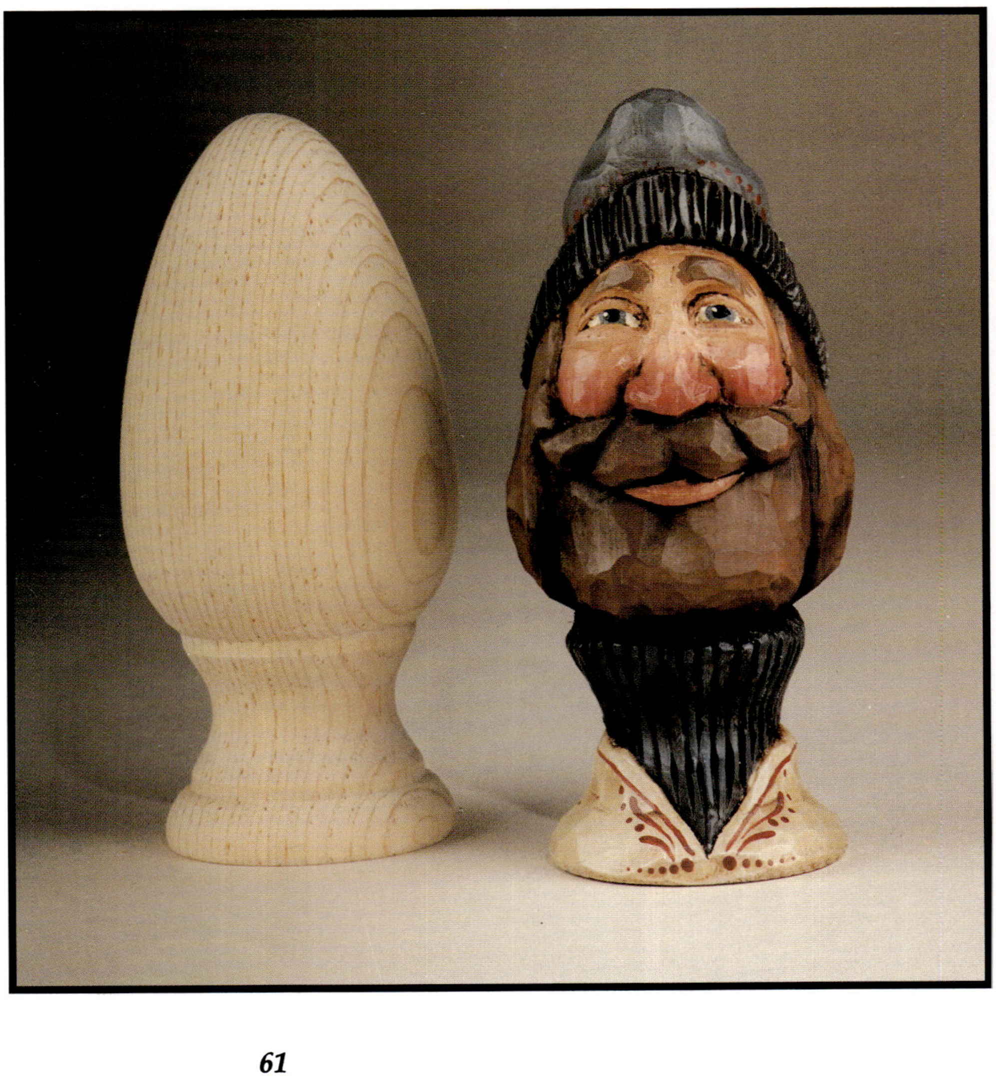

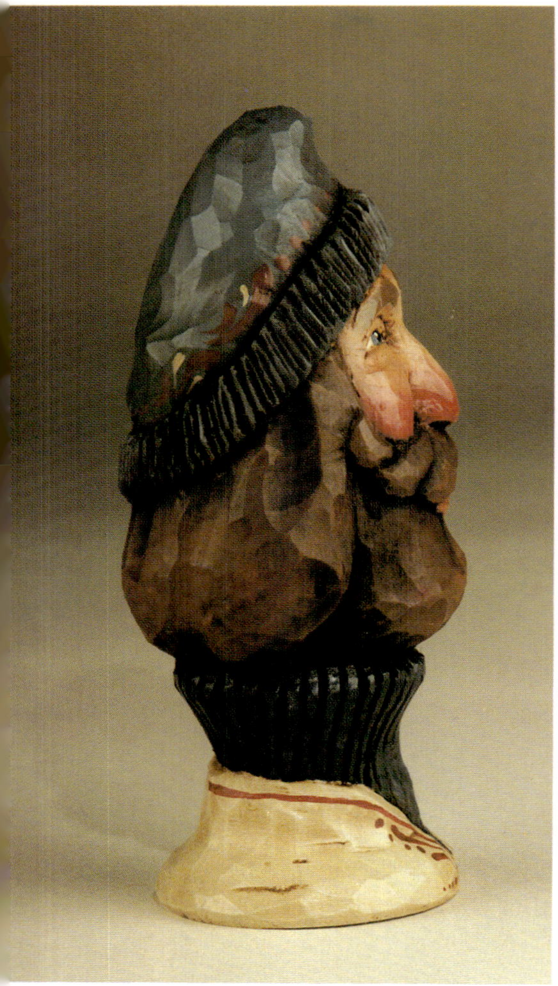
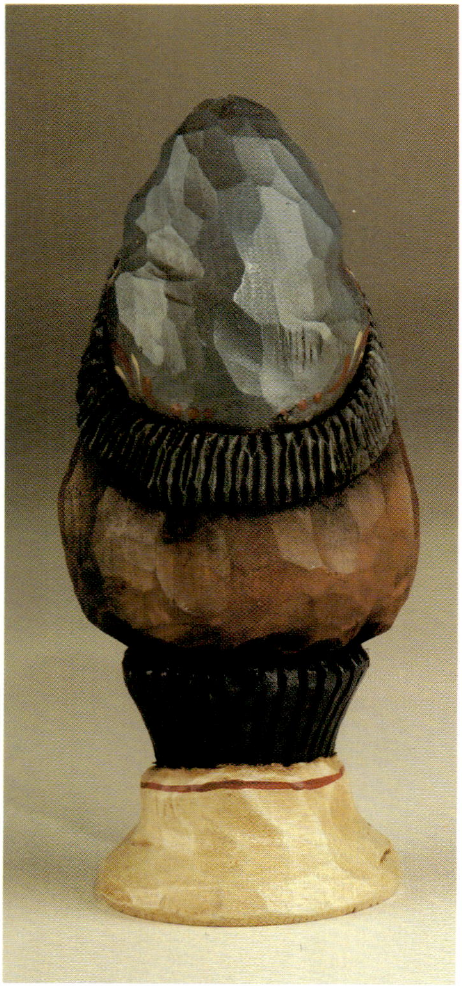
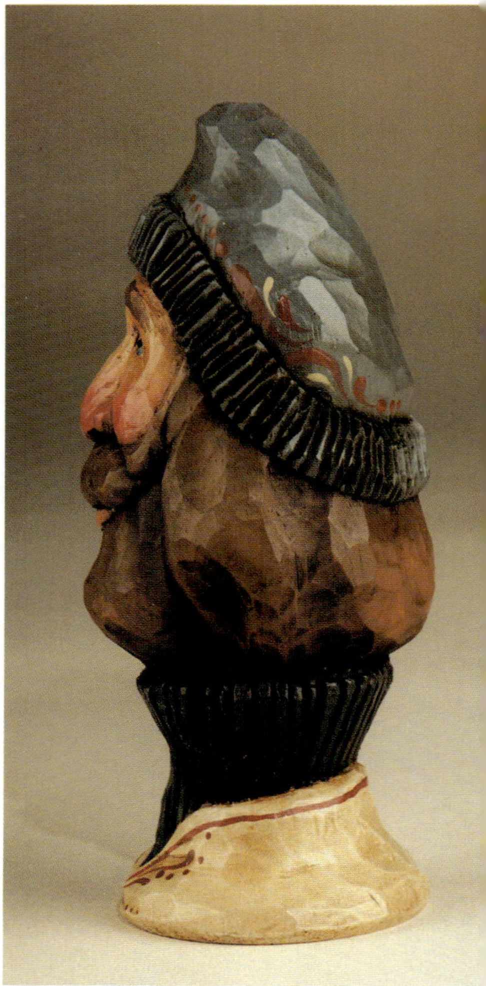
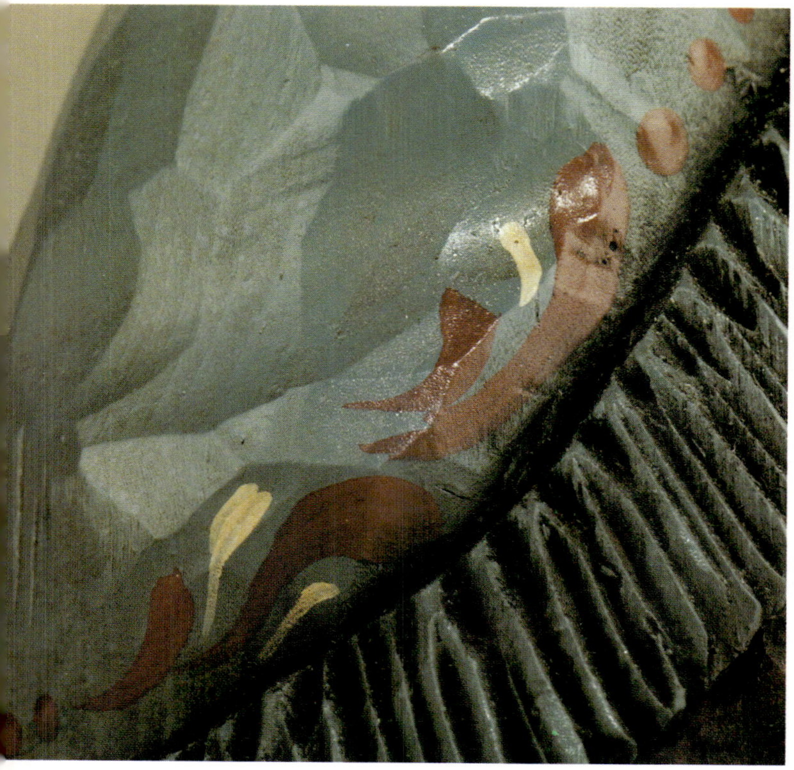
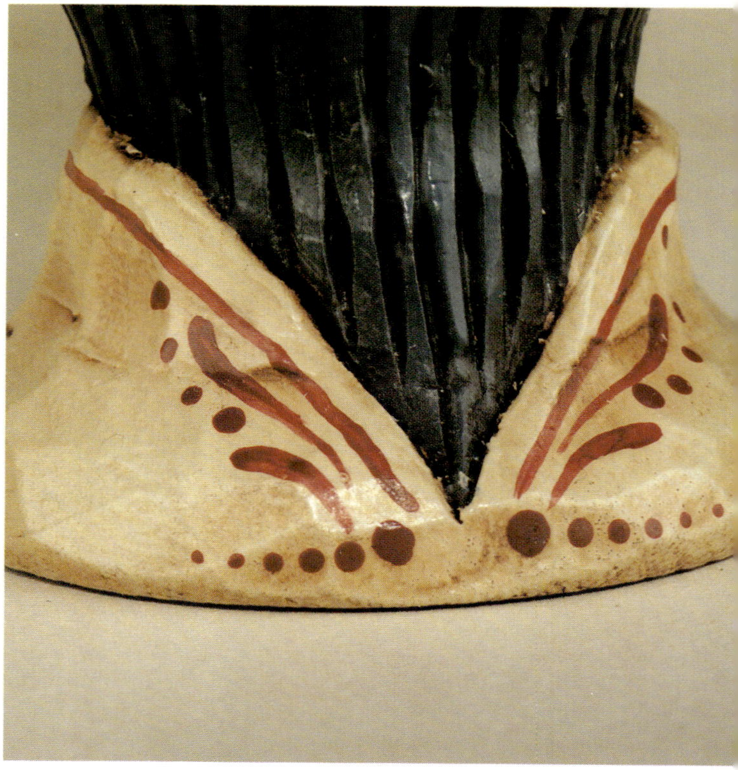

Patterns have been reduced to 91%

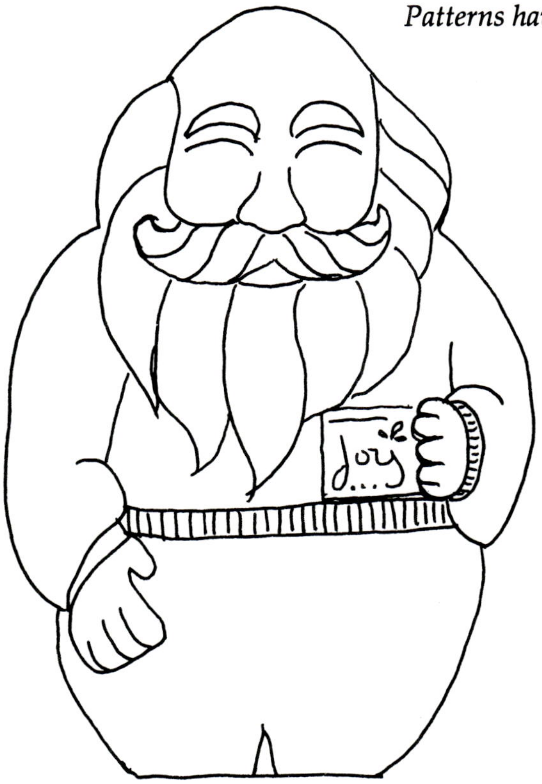

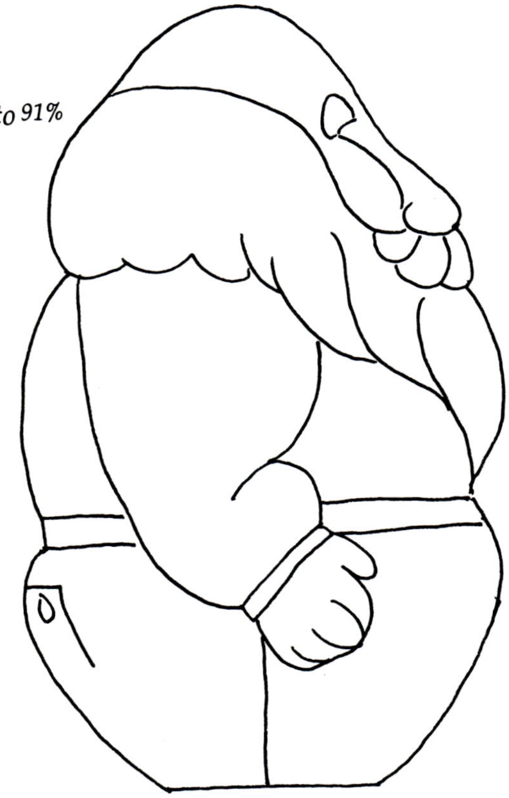

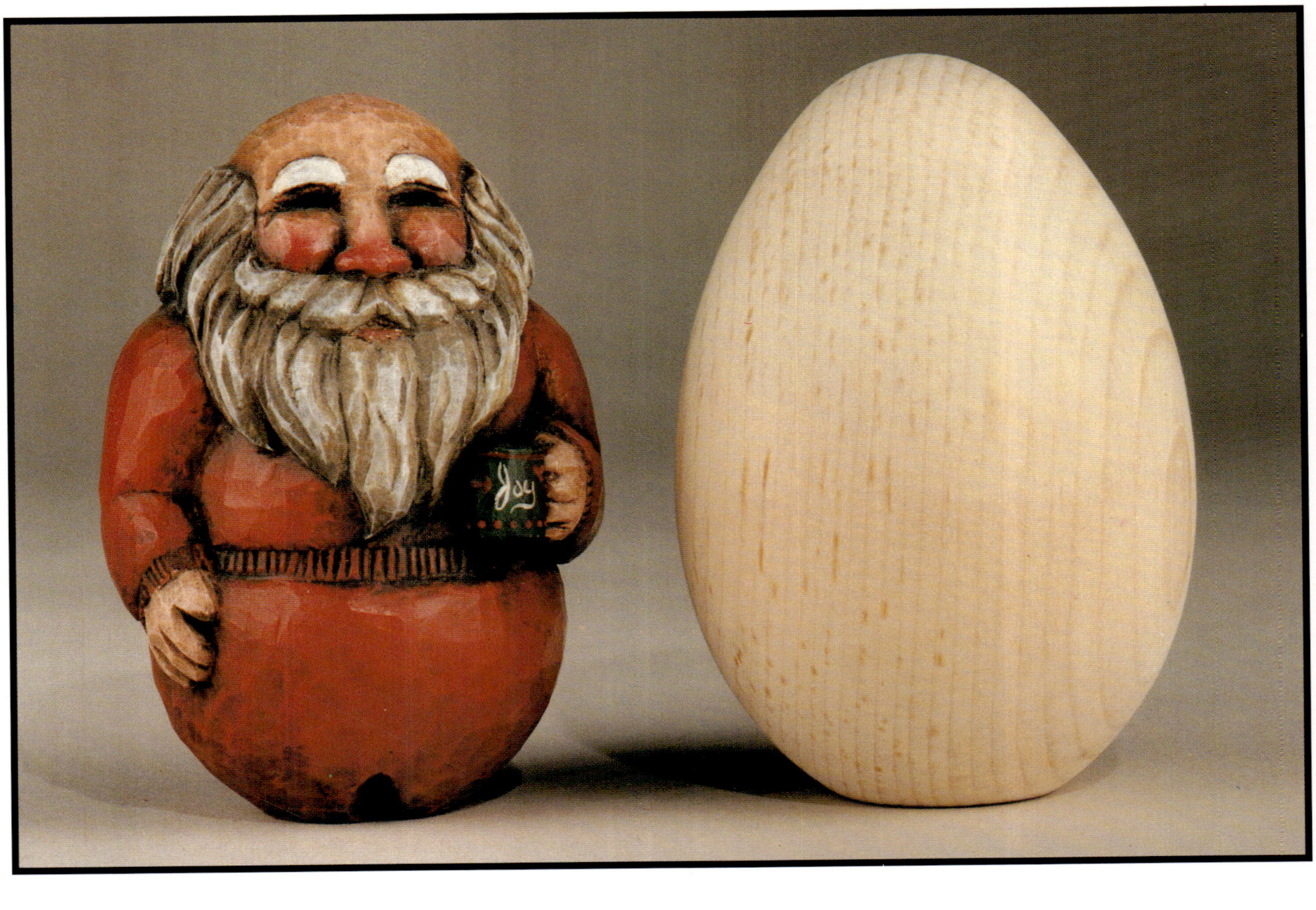

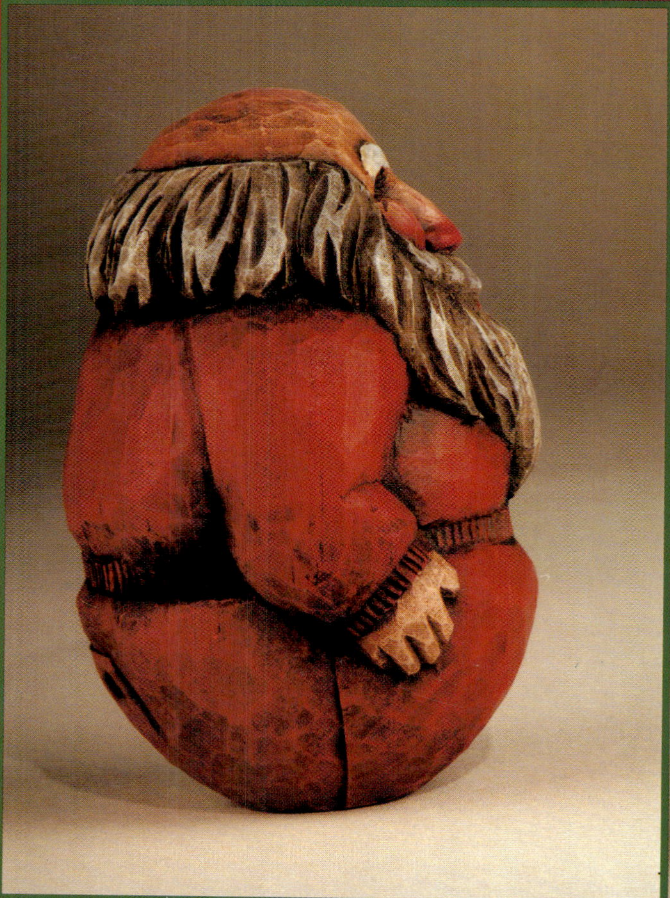

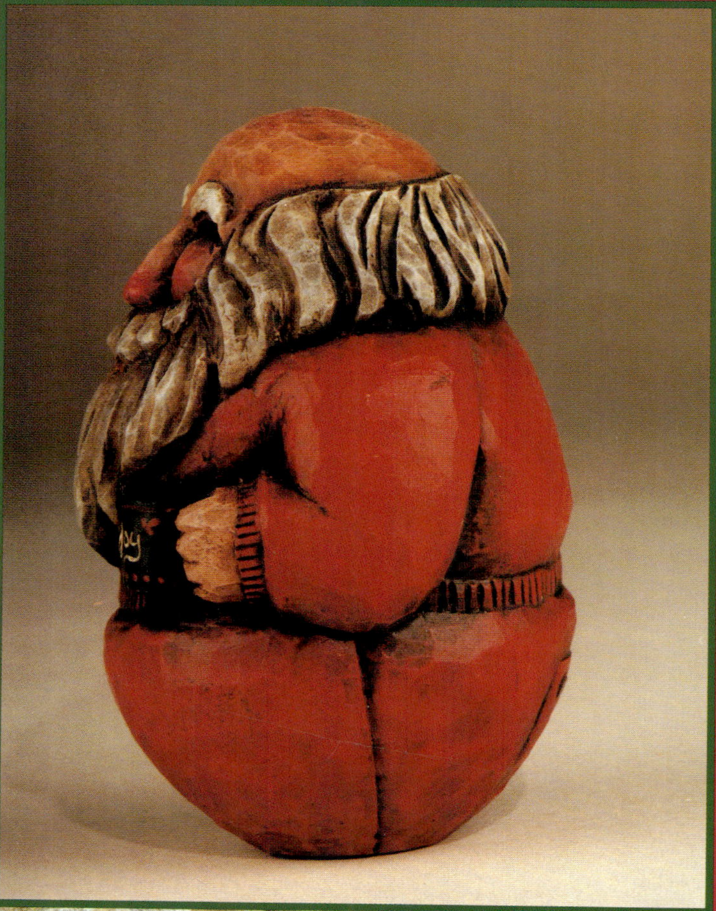

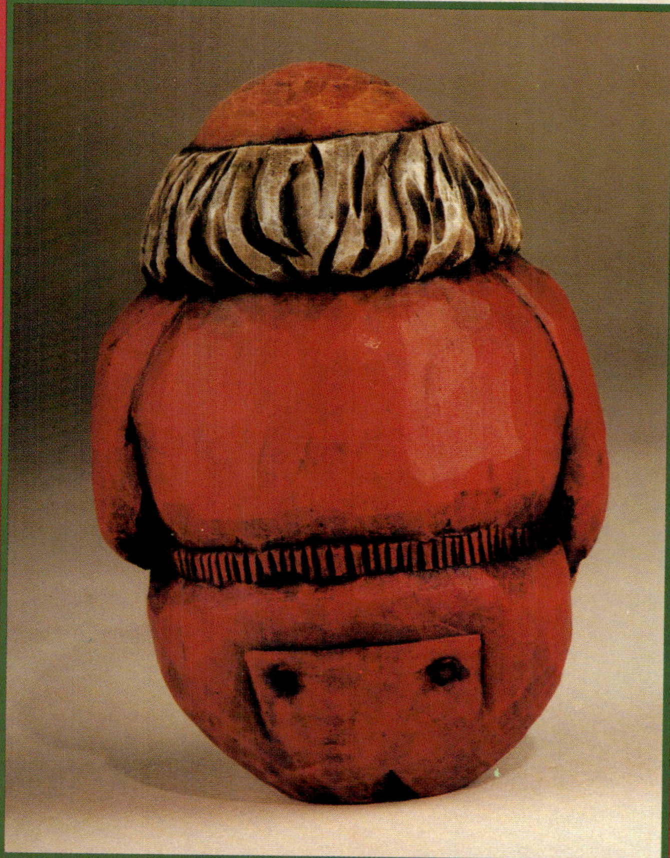

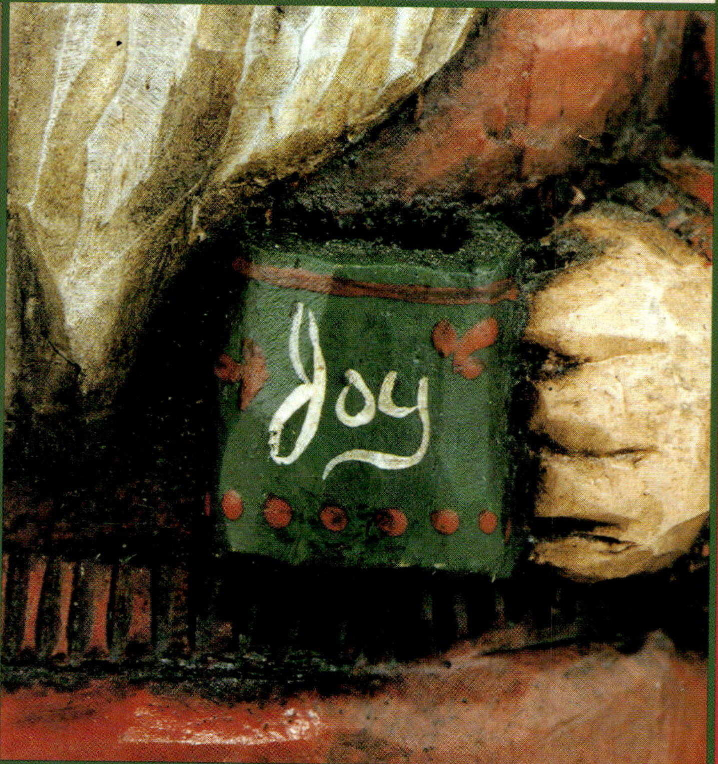
Joy